his

... is an authorized facsimile made from the master copy of the original book. Further unauthorized copying is prohibited.

Books on Demand is a publishing service of UMI. The program offers xerographic reprints of more than 136,000 books that are no longer in print.

The primary focus of Books on Demand is academic and professional resource materials originally published by university presses, academic societies, and trade book publishers worldwide.

UMI
BOOKS ON DEMAND™

UMI
A Bell & Howell Company
300 North Zeeb Road ❦ PO Box 1346
Ann Arbor, Michigan 48106-1346
800-521-0600 ❦ 313-761-4700

Printed in 1997 by xerographic process on acid-free paper

Organization Dissonance and Change

Organization Dissonance and Change

Jan Koolhaas
Graduate School
of Management Delft

1807 1982

JOHN WILEY & SONS
Chichester · New York · Brisbane · Toronto · Singapore

Library of Congress Cataloguing in Publication Data

Koolhaas, Jan.
   Organization dissonance and change.
   Bibliography: p.
   Includes index.
   1. Organization. 2. Organizational change.
   I. Title.
   HD31.K5989 658.4'06 81-16368

ISBN 0 471 10140 0 AACR2

British Library Cataloguing in Publication Data:

Koolhaas, Jan.
   Organization dissonance and change.
   1. Organizational change
   I. Title
   658.4'06   HD58.8

ISBN 0 471 10140 0

Phototypeset by Dobbie Typesetting Service, Plymouth, Devon.
Printed in the United States of America.

Acknowledgements

First of all I want to thank Professor Doorman and Professor Malotaux for reviewing the final drafts in such a short time and for their valuable advice. Then I would like to thank Marijke de Kovel and Will Sommeling-Geurtsen who did all the typing and drew the figures with admirable speed and single-mindedness. What everybody said was impossible, Marijke and Will achieved.

Furthermore I want to thank Debbie Cummings, who apart from correcting my English, was one of the very few people who showed genuine interest in the study itself.

Last but not least, I thank, although not without the greatest hesitation, Maart-Jan Bellaar-Spruyt. Despite his often abominable behaviour, he aroused my initial interest in the sociology of organizations. His endless depreciatory remarks made me all the more determined to persevere, just to spite him.

List of Figures

Figure 2.1 Relation between organization theory and natural sciences . 19

Figure 2.2 The relations between the level of inclusiveness and the level
of complexity of theoretical relations. 27

Figure 3.1 Woodward's categorization of production systems 35

Figure 3.2 Thompson's environmental variables 44

Figure 3.3 Perrow's technology variables 48

Figure 3.4 Perrow's raw material variable. 48

Figure 4.1 The analytical orientations and aspects of organization 64

Figure 4.2 The individual as a member of an organization and as a
citizen; the organization as a subsystem of a society 66

Figure 4.3 The three dimensions of complexity. 71

Figure 4.4 The three dimensions of dissonance. 73

Figure 4.5 Structure of the aspects of an organization and its subsets . . 79

Figure 4.6 Dissonances at the level of the individual 80

Figure 4.7 Dissonances at intra and interdepartmental level 81

Figure 4.8 The three orientations of organizational dissonance 82

Figure 4.9 Complexity of the model of the domain that is used to solve
task related problems. 84

Figure 4.10 Planning systems described as specific forms of
transformation in the two modes of planning in the
lighting fixture department 86

Figure 4.11 Cognitive structure................................... 93

Figure 4.12 The dissonance between transformation and cognitive
structure 100

Figure 4.13 Task structure...................................... 105

Figure 4.14 Dissonances between transformation and task structure.... 110

Figure 4.15 Dissonances between personal norms and values and the
control structure..................................... 119

Figure 4.16 Dissonances between task structure and control structure... 123

Figure 4.17 Interdepartmental task structural dissonances 131

Figure 5.1 Two dimensions of sociological theory 138

Figure 5.2 Partial classification of operational control system 152

Figure 5.3 Plan of sales domain (Köster and Hetzel) 154

Figure 5.4 Hickson's strategic contingencies theory of intra-
organizational power................................ 157

Figure 5.5 Intraorganizational power based on the availability of
information and models 160

Figure 5.6 The opposing trends in the development of society as a
whole and organizations 168

Figure 6.1 The relation between the supply of and the demand for
different types of labour in the twentieth century......... 180

Figure 6.2 The development of the individual's cognitive structure
through education 183

Figure 6.3 Development of the nature of work due to the improvement
of the knowledge of products and production processes 183

Figure 6.4 Growing dissonance between the ability of the individual
worker and the demands set by the organization. Alienation
of the worker because of the content of his task 184

Figure 6.5 Interdepartmental dissonances....................... 191

Figure 6.6   Intradepartmental inter-group dissonances.   193

Figure 6.7   Intradepartmental dissonance in the engineering
              department   193

Figure 6.8   Intradepartmental dissonance in the development
              department   194

Figure 6.9   The individual as a member of different groups and
              therefore as a transmitter of inter-group dissonance   199

Contents

List of Figures vii

Introduction. xiii

Chapter 1: Interdepartmental Conflicts 1
Mr Thrasher's Dilemma 1
The Automated Information Rationale 12

Chapter 2: In Search of Typologies and Theories 16
Theoretical Typologies. 16
Theories 20
Theoretical Requirements 25

Chapter 3: Theories of Organization, a Critical Survey 29
A Historical Perspective 29
Natural and Unnatural Sciences 31
Woodward 34
The Aston Group 37
Thompson 40
Perrow. 45
Lawrence and Lorsch 50
Others 52
Summary 55

Chapter 4: Towards a Theory of Organizational Dissonance 56
Introduction 56
The Dimensions of Complexity 70
The Structure of the Dissonance Theory 79
Technology: the knowledge of how to get things done 82
Cognitive Structure. 88
Cognitive Structure–Technology Dissonance. 98
Task Structure 109
Transformation–Task Structure Dissonance 112
Role and Control Structure 112
Norms and Values 114

Control Structure 117
Normative Dissonances 118
Task Structure – Control Structure Dissonance 123
From Technological Imperative to Multi-level Equilibrium 129
Interdepartmental Task Structure Dissonance 131
Interdepartmental Control Structure Dissonance 132
The Organization as an Open System 133

Chapter 5: Towards a Theory of Organizational Structure and Change . 137
Introduction 137
'Price' in Theories of Organization 139
Dissonance and Change 141
The Multi-level Interrelation of Organizational Aspects and Change . 147
Designs for Change 151
Intra-organizational Power and Change 155
Technological versus Social Contingencies 160
Designing Organizations, and Consultants 166
Changing Organizations, and Consultants 167

Chapter 6: Interdepartmental Conflict Analysed 169
Introduction 169
An Imaginary Conversation 172

Bibliography 200

Author Index 204

Subject Index 206

Introduction

During the seven years I worked in industrial organizations I was asked a number of times what theoretical categorizations could be made to describe organizations in order to select planning or control systems for them. Such a typological effort proved extremely hazardous, even after studying many earlier attempts. The original demand did however raise the question of why certain types of organizations should use specific kinds of planning or control systems. The answer lay in an implicit assumption that seemed to be made universally within the organization I worked in, but also in most of the literature I studied, that organizations are goal oriented. And that the maximization of the efficiency of the manner in which the goal is achieved is the ultimate objective of organizational behaviour. This assumption did not at all coincide with what I saw in the organizations I worked in. In the accepted theories a social harmony model is assumed whereas in reality people were constantly flying at each other's throats and putting each other down. Career competition does not seem to fit in with a harmony model, and there was plenty of that going on. The clear difference between what was preached and how people acted became the motivation to describe a theory in which this difference could find a place.

The object of this study is to present a theory of organizational dissonance, and linked to this a theory of organizational change. The theory is founded on the theories that were developed in the 1950s and 60s, and which concerned themselves to a large extent with categorizing organizations. The concepts that are used in the dissonance theory have also been used by many of my predecessors. Their interpretation is often different. This necessitates a certain extensiveness in the description of these concepts — an extensiveness that makes the more theoretical chapters in this study less easy reading.

Structure of the Book

In order to introduce the reader into the organizational setting in which the theory can be envisaged, the first chapter of the book describes two cases or situations. These must not be seen as evidence for the 'truth' of the theory but rather as a heuristic aid in understanding what subject matter is involved.

The last chapter returns to one of the original scenes in order to present an analysis of the situation using the concepts and the theory that are developed in Chapter 4 and 5. Here too, this must not be taken as evidence for the truth of the theory but rather as an aid to the reader who is not immediately willing to submerge himself in the bone-dry network of theoretical explanations. An attempt has been made to write these first and last chapters in such a manner that they are accessible to a wide public. After these two rather light-hearted chapters the reader can decide if he is willing to take the plunge and find out what reasoning lies at the basis of the given explanations.

From a philosophical point of view, theorizing is not without its own specific problems. If this were not so, debates on these questions would not divide the scientific community in the way they do. The second chapter gives an indication of the point of view that is employed in this study, in order to supply the reader with a frame of reference in which other theories can also be placed.

A point that has not been extensively treated in that chapter is one which I would like to state here. A theory should be empirically testable by further research. I am very conscious of the fact that this will not be readily possible because the concepts that are employed for describing the theory are not measurable, or rather not yet. The projects by Joan Woodward and others have been characterized by the enormous methodological problems, conflicts and criticism that have been encountered. These methodological problems, still far from being solved, have not held me back from proposing a new theory. The problems concerning the methods of measurement have been sidestepped by presenting a conceptual theory rather than an empirical one. Practical realization through the development of empirical indicators is, in my opinion, still a long way off. Attempts at measuring may well befuddle rather than clarify or prove anything, because in this field of social studies no explicit and acceptable measuring theories exist.

The third chapter presents a short overview of theories that have been influential in this area, and have to a large extent determined the shape of the present theory. An apology may be appropriate here. The situations as encountered in the first case that is presented, where there is a tremendous emotional tension between persons and between departments, cannot be described, and certainly not explained, by the existing structural theories. This led to a degree of exasperation with the existing theories, and to some sharpness in the criticism that is presented. However, all of the authors concerned are widely accepted in their field of work and I imagine they must have built up considerable resistance to criticism. Without criticism in this form, theories will probably develop along the lines of progressive refinement of existing theories. In this study the objective was to go right back to the theoretical foundations and see if alternatives could be developed.

In the fourth chapter the theory itself is presented. Because it is to a large extent descriptive, much attention has to be paid to the specification of the terms employed. This may make it difficult reading at times. By means of ample illustrations based on the case studies from the first chapter, the tedium should be kept to a minimum. The theory is presented as a way of facilitating the understanding of what goes on in organizations, and for looking for possible changes in organizations, or the objectives of change processes, and not for prescribing these processes.

The fifth chapter treats this dynamic aspect of organization structure. It shows that there are more alternatives to chose from than one would initially think when confronted with most structural approaches. If the criteria on which choices are based are reduced to one only, the minimization of technical coordination costs, then we find ourselves confronted with the technological imperative. If, however, we also take into account the nature of the labour-force and the society from which it has to be recruited and translate worker dissatisfaction into comparable cost factors, then other alternatives become viable.

Process and Structure

The fashion of distinguishing between process- and structure-oriented theories of organization has lasted for some time and can be compared to the distinction Dahrendorf (1959, page 161) makes between conflict and harmony models or between the integration and the coercion theory of society. The integration theory of society conceives the social structure in terms of a functionally integrated system held in equilibrium by certain patterned and recurrent processes. The coercion theory views social structures as a form of organization held together by force and constraint and reaching continuously beyond itself in the sense of producing within itself the forces that maintain it in an unending process of change. The integration theory as displayed by the work of Parsons or other structural functionalists is founded on a number of assumptions of the following type.

1 Every society is a relatively persistent and stable structure of elements.
2 Every society is a well-integrated structure of elements.
3 Every element in society has a function, i.e., renders a contribution to its maintenance as a system.
4 Every functioning social structure is based on a consensus of values amongst its members.

In various forms, these elements of (1) stability, (2) integration, (3) functional coordination and (4) consensus, recur in all structural functional approaches.

The coercion theory can also be reduced to a number of basic tenets, although here too they oversimplify and overstate the case.

1 Social change is ubiquitous.
2 Every society displays at every point dissent and conflict: social conflict is ubiquitous.
3 Every element in society renders a contribution to its disintegration and change.

4 Every society is based on coercion of some of its members by others.

The integration theory conceals conflicts, whereas the coercion theory emphasizes them in order to mobilize the forces of change towards a state of less conflict. The structural approach and the process approach to organizations can be compared to the above-mentioned schools of theories. They are mutually dependent even if much of the literature on organizations would have us think otherwise. Likewise, in economics we speak of balanced or unbalanced growth. This only makes sense if we have first defined the equilibrium between the factors that are either balanced or unbalanced (see Machlup 1963, pp.43–72). In static and dynamic mechanics similar distinctions are made, but there a theoretical framework exists that shows how they are mutually related.

In this study the emphasis will be on the structural aspects of organizations, which to a large extent have been deduced from problem-solving and decision-making processes that take place in organizations. The social processes are much more difficult to analyse, not only because they are possibly more complex but rather because they are less visible than the processes related to the technical functioning of the organizations.

When a structural theory is employed for the analysis and guidance of possible changes in organizations, knowledge and insight into these processes is certainly necessary. However, the structural constraints define which processes are possible or appropriate and in which directions the changes will be most suitable.

Structural theories are often identified with static theories and the process approach with dynamics. As Samuelson (1947, p.311) remarks: 'We damn another man's theory by terming it static, and advertise our own by calling it dynamic.' There seems little reason for this distinction.

The connotation of conflict often has unpleasant emotional associations. In the case of organizations, certainly within a harmony ideal, it is seen as disfunctional or detrimental to the operating of the organization and should be exorcised. This is not necessarily the case. Kahn *et al.* (1964, 54) state,

'In arguing that the consequences of conflict and ambiguity are by and large unfavourable, it is not necessary to adopt the view that conflict is harmful. To regard conflict simply as a disruption of an otherwise harmonious way of life is to overlook the fact that conflict often provides the basis for individual achievement and social progress. The same can be said for ambiguity, for while ambiguity implies disorderliness that is antithetical to the very idea of organization, it also permits a kind of flexibility that can facilitate adaptation to changing circumstances'.

Instead of using the term conflict, dissonance has been chosen. This does not necessarily have the same emotional associations except possibly for the very musical readers. Furthermore it leaves the possibility for saving 'conflict' for overt clashes between parties.

It must be emphasized that dissonance is not necessarily to be identified with the concept of cognitive dissonance as it is used by Leon Festinger (1957). Dissonance has a wider meaning.

If a coercive relationship between elements is to exist, there must be a structural basis for this. The strategic contingencies theory of intra-organizational power by Hickson *et al*. (1971) supplies part of this basis and will be further elucidated in Chapter 5. This theory presents only one medium for the transmission of power. It may well be hypothesized that there are many other media. However they fall outside the scope of this study.

Different Chapters for Different Publics

The structure of the book is aimed at reaching a number of different publics. The professional managers interested in recognizing their own problems and seeking viable solutions may best be motivated by Chapters 1 and 6 to read Chapters 4 and 5. Organization consultants may be more interested in Chapters 4 and 5 and see Chapters 1 and 6 as a rather frivolous addition. Hopefully the more scientific readers will use Chapters 2 and 3 to judge the pretensions of the theory presented and critically read Chapters 4 and 5 to see if they can meet the standards that were set.

As to this last point I think some mitigating circumstances should be brought forward. The demands which a theory should meet have been formulated rather sharply and I doubt whether they can be met. It seems improbable that *all* the variables that are important to describe and explain structural conflicts in organizations can be specified in such a manner that they can meet the demands that were formulated. The subject of the study is too wide to meet these demands all along the line. Its publication is a step in a certain direction, and is aimed at further development by those specialists concerned with those specific subjects of organizational activities which we usually call scientific disciplines, and to further develop a mode of multi-disciplinary analysis.

Chapter 1

Interdepartmental Conflicts

Two descriptions will be given of problems as I have encountered them in a large organization. As problems, they are very complex, as a large number of people and different groups were involved. However, similar problems are, in my opinion, widespread and can be categorized under the heading of inter-departmental conflict. As I hope to show in Chapter 4, the conflicts are not only interdepartmental, but also intradepartmental, and between organiz-ations *in toto* and their environment. Hopefully, the theory that is to be presented will also contribute to solutions of these organizational problems apart from aiding their analysis.

MR THRASHER'S DILEMMA

Case 1

The image of large organizations which presents them as producing highly complex technical products in incredible numbers and runing like well-oiled machines can only find acceptance with those who have never worked in such a large organization. The coordination of activities of groups of individuals, although of good will, proves to be an extremely thankless task — a task I once unknowingly took upon myself.

The first introduction was a visit to a cathode ray tube factory. My superior and I had an appointment with Mr Thrasher, the vice-president of the division responsible for the development and production of such electronic components. To reach his office, which was situated on a gallery along the factory hall, we walked up grimy concrete stairs past a number of blue fireproof doors. At the top we passed through such a door into the heat and din of the factory. Below the gallery were tremendous ovens into which the television tubes disappeared on pump units. Along the ceiling ran unending chainbelts carrying cradles on which the tubes were transported through the factory. Everywhere men lifted the tubes from the cradles onto machines that were often rotating, and back again. I only caught a glimpse of the factory before we entered the secretary's office, but was immediately struck by the heavy work that was done. We had to wait for a moment while she warned her boss, and after a couple of minutes a portly gentleman in a badly fitting suit came out of the room, nodded at us and entered an office on the opposite side of the secretary's room. We were ushered in.

If the veneer panelling had ever had any warmth of colour, it had gone. It was the same yellow-grey as the whole factory complex. This was accentuated by the pale autumn light slanting in obliquely. The view from the high window was no more exciting than the interior decoration. Across the narrow courtyard, packed with parked cars, loomed the laboratory building, even higher than the factory. From here you could watch the people behind their desks or busy behind their tables in the ever present blueness of fluorescent tube-light, and only guess at what they were doing.

The vice-president got up from behind his desk on which stood a vase of white and yellow chrysanthemums, the only point of colour in the room. He smiled benevolently at us through his gold-rimmed glasses, greeted us in a friendly fatherly manner, and bade us take our places at the long conference table, which was of the same yellow-grey colour as the panelling. The secretary came in and brought us coffee in porcelain cups, a clear mark of hierarchical position because at all lower levels coffee was served in plastic cups.

My superior and Mr Thrasher had both been with the firm for more than thirty years and started by exchanging small talk and inside information. This gave me time to look around. Aerial photographs of various factory sites and a colour portrait of the chairman of the board hung along the wall. The floor was of grey-green linoleum, and under the large desk and chair there was a yellowish rug. The room was filled with the humming of the factory, soon forgotten. The vice-president wore official uniform; grey suit, quite well fitting for a change, white shirt and a light tie. Most remarkable was a gold tooth which glittered when he smiled.

When they were finished with their coffee, my superior introduced me, explaining what I had studied and what my job had been in the last year. Mr Thrasher nodded every now and then, showing that he was still with us. Then he told us he was glad we had come to listen to his problem and he hoped we would help him solve it: He set off to clarify what the problem was.

The television tube factory produced colour tubes both for use within the company and for selling to competitors. They had a number of factories all over Europe making essentially the same product, with essentially the same production problems. In the mother factory, new types were introduced and when the initial production problems had been solved, the other factories took over the production. The consequence of this was that the factory was always beset by difficulties which had to be solved by the development department. The development department, across the courtyard connected by an air bridge, was responsible for developing new types of tubes. They had intensive relations with the laboratories for basic research where they could find special-ized knowledge in certain fields of chemistry and physics when necessary. These relations, however, were often strained and basic research was also done in the development laboratories. The development program had been very success-ful in the past, resulting in a very strong position for the company on the European market. However, with the American market nearing the point of saturation and the Japanese competition stepping up, they realized that it was necessary to pay more attention to the organization of the development of new products. One of the problems they encountered here was the difficulty in acquiring instruments and machines, necessary in the laboratory, from their own engineering department that designed these instruments and machines, and the workshops and the machine factory that made them. What they were looking for was a system that would facilitate the planning of, and the coordination between the different departments. If they wanted to stay ahead of the competition, they realized they would have to cut down their development time by intensifying coordinative activities. Did we think we could help them with this?

My superior, who had much more insight into the problems typical to this kind of organization, was very sceptical about possible solutions. I, being young and somewhat rash, found it interesting and said so. We left Mr Thrasher and told him that we would think about it. We made an appointment for a fortnight later.

On the way to the railway station we spoke about it because I would not be seeing my superior, being stationed at another factory quite a distance away. He thought it was an unsolvable problem, certainly under the local circumstances, and said we had best react negatively. To me it seemed quite interesting, all the more because the product technology could prove to be an important influence on the organization.

Two weeks later, at the next appointment, Mr Thrasher again illustrated how important and interesting the problems were, and asked if we were willing to aid him with their solution. My superior said he had grave doubts about feasible solutions and feared that it would prove to be a waste of time. A short and rather fierce discussion ensued in which it became clear that Mr Thrasher thought that this was rather an unhelpful stance because he would be left with an important problem unsolved. He addressed himself immediately to me and asked me directly whether I would like to work for him and join his department. This was a difficult question to answer, and I said I needed time to think about it. I would notify him within a week. As there were no other interesting assignments foreseeable in the near future I decided to take the plunge. I could start immediately.

My position in the organization was an ambivalent one. I was assigned to both the head of the engineering department, Mr Ripple, and the head of the development department, Mr Barton. In all I was to stay there for two years, until the time when Mr Thrasher was pensioned off.

Now for the problem that was set; the coordination of mechanization, development and production programs. In order to get some grip on the subject I thought it was best to come to terms with each department first, and started off with the engineering department.

I was given a room adjoining that of Mr Ripple, the head of the department, and thus could acquire a good view of the activities that took place in the department as a whole. Mr Ripple was a small, extremely active man in his early forties. There were few people in the business that had his knowledge of the design and construction of all the machines employed in the production-process, but also of many of the technical aspects of the production problems. He had stood at the cradle of the introduction of the TV production immediately after the war and had seen it grow to one of the most profitable product lines of the company. His grasp of technical details was astonishing. The blackboard on the wall of his room was covered with enviably neat drawings in chalk of machine parts; enviable for their neatness and their sureness of line and shading, they were a pleasure for the eye and combined the clarity of a craftsman and the skill of an artist. Not only did he head the design department with about 40 designers and draughtsmen, but also a production workshop and the whole repair and maintenance team for the factory, a large electrical and electronic workshop, and a test workshop where it was possible to make experimental machines and instruments. Furthermore he was responsible for the coordination of the production and supply of all production machinery for a number of factories scattered over the globe.

Mr Ripple loved the gritty details of complicated machinery and the intelligent solution of difficult technical problems, and he loved craftsmanship. Many innovations in the production process originated not from economical necessity, but from technical aesthetical motives, sometimes leading to problems with the control department over appropriation of budgets. He enjoyed the meetings with the development department as long as they stuck to the discussion on technical problems related to the difficulties of producing new types of products. Subjects of a more down to earth nature, such as the delivery of machines and instruments, were by his definition not only solvable but already solved as soon as he had said he would see to delivery. A truly remarkable engineer in the most literal sense of the word.

In order to get accepted within the department it proved necessary to join the team on a technical plane and prove that there was at least a clear understanding of their technical problems and their possible solutions. My background in mechanical engineering came in very handy.

An inventory of projects under way showed that the head of the department was not in control of the amount of work that circulated within the department and that there was little or no insight into the financial consequences of this. Furthermore, in the initial stages of a project plans were made, but these were never revised, just forgotten. These projects were usually very expensive affairs running into hundreds of thousands of dollars. From a classical organization theoretical point of view this department was, to say the least, very interesting, because there was a clear hierarchical authority structure, but there was very little delineation of responsibilities between the different subdepartments. The contacts between the engineering department and the development department were officially funnelled through one officer, but when this proved to be difficult, parallel channels were easily found.

It took eight months to get a regular review of the progress of projects organized and to keep the financial status of each project up to date. Once I felt that I understood the problem from the side of the engineering department, it was time to step over to the development department. Here it proved to be much more difficult to come to grips with the problems of the department. Here too I spent a tremendous amount of time mastering the technical problems of the department in order to be able to assess the relative importance of different claims within the department. Only when I had proved that I understood these problems was it possible to get discussions under way on possible solutions to some of the problems that might have planning aspects. A short review of the progress of certain projects was added to the fortnightly meetings. Usually very little was said about the amount of time to be spent by the different subdepartments on the different projects.

More than a year and a half after my arrival I fully understood why my former superior had been so sceptical. Planning systems in development departments within the concern were on the whole planned disasters. The very nature of the work that is done in such departments seems to rebel against the guiding pressure of anything that reeks of planning. Lip service is paid to guidelines from above, and only when the pressure is really stepped up is there any possibility of an apt reaction.

It became clear to me that there were a number of important issues in the development department. The first was that there were a number of projects running parallel that kept switching on the priority scale. The second was that the same people that had to develop new products had to solve the production problems that arose in the factory and concerned their specialty. The third was that due to the lack of dependability of their own demand and also to the lack of dependability of the engineering department there was a tremendous friction in the supply and demand of instrumentation and parts.

The consequence of the first problem was a lack of coordination between different groups within the department. The second issue had a much more drastic effect; because of the fire-fighting that had to be done for the factory a number of important people had no idea of what they would be doing the next day because of incessant interruptions. The third problem was often used as scapegoat for the lack of internal consistency within the development department.

The switching of priorities had a dual origin. The first was that those developments that showed a marked progress in a short time got a higher priority, or *success breeds priority*. The second was that the commercial department reacting on market information also had great influence on the pressure on certain developments. This became very clear when a meeting was called by Mr Thrasher, bringing together the commercial department and all the heads of the departments concerned with product development.

The meeting was to start at 1.30 p.m. I was a few minutes early as I wanted to find out how the discussion would start. When I came in Mr Barton, the head of the development department, was already there. Mr Thrasher sat behind his desk leafing through his mail. Mr Barton stood in front of the window, his hands behind his back, looking out onto his own department building. He hardly took any notice of my arrival but went on with his monologue on the progress of two of his main projects. He found a willing ear with Mr Thrasher, who had spent many years as product developer in a related field and was thus thoroughly at home in the type of problems concerned. 'The solution we are looking for to solve the problems of a poor colour separation is very nearly within reach. If we could put some more capacity into taking this last hurdle, I am quite sure that we could clinch it within three months. But at the moment much of our time is taken by fire-fighting for the factory. With the introduction of the modification to the FX type, they seem to have many more problems with the exposure machines and the lenses. For this they often need our help. This makes it very difficult for us to plan our activities, which is extremely detrimental to our progress. We have to keep on measuring and testing and tuning the instruments in the factory so that the quality of the tubes remains within limits. All the time spent in the factory is lost for the online tube project. That is completely unacceptable.' His full round vowels betrayed that he was a foreigner, which might also explain his precise, perhaps dry formulation of his point of view and his perennial seriousness.

Mr Thrasher looked up at him, gold-rimmed glasses, silver-grey slicked-down hair, his hands on the edge of his desk, looking like the benign grandfather he was. He lightly tapped the desk with the tips of his fingers before speaking.

'It is an awkward position you are in and we must do something about this problem of planning the different capacities necessary to your department. That is why we have Koolhaas here.' With this he acknowledged my presence in his own characteristic manner, and also showed that he understood the problem and that he had delegated the solution to somebody else. 'When the modification has been implemented all along the line you will certainly have more capacity available.'

'I am sure the factory will then supply us with new and even more urgent problems. You know that the last year and a half we have had constant trouble with the quality of the screens; the modifications that are now being implemented will only make this more problematic. We have been against this early introduction. It is only because the commercial department exerted pressure and forecast that we would lose clients that we have taken this unsatisfactory step.'

Mr Ripple came in just as Mr Barton was finishing his sentence. It was clear that only from this snatch of information he had understood what it was about. After the 20 years they had spent together in their related jobs, half a word was enough. Mr Ripple walked to the conference table, laid down his large black note book with the numbered pages and aligned his black and gold fountain pen along the edge. I knew he thought meetings like this a waste of time — time that should be spent keeping abreast of the technical problems of his department. Mr Thrasher nodded his greetings and addressed Mr Barton.

'You must not be so pessimistic. It is very important that the brighter tube comes into production soon, I know both the United States and Japan are going to put comparable tubes on the market too. We don't want to lose our leading position.'

'That is fine, but if you don't want to lose our leading position you must give us the facilities to make this possible, you must protect us from the incessant demands of the production department, and you must not let our pilot plant downstairs make tubes for the commercial department. It is impossible for my people to do their work when they have no idea what will be waiting for them when they reach their room, and when they cannot get their test-tubes made.'

'I think it is quite reasonable that because of the introduction of the new modifications the yield of the factory has declined and that in order to be able to meet the demand the pilot plant temporarily has to make tubes for the commercial department. After all that is where the money comes from.'

It was clear that Mr Barton was vexed. His speech had become even more clipped and he turned away from the window and sat down at the conference table, diagonally across from Mr Ripple. 'I can hardly remember the time when we were not incessantly pestered by the factory to solve their petty problems. It is about time we got down to doing more important work without being interrupted, and with the facilities that have been promised.'

'We have 20 men working for you, full time', Mr Ripple answered. 'They are never allowed to finish the work they are doing, because you always have some modifications which they have to incorporate into their design. Or they have to do something quite different because your priorities have changed. I don't think you have much reason to complain in comparison to our other clients.'

Mr Thrasher interrupted, sensing that the present confrontation would serve no purpose whatsoever. 'I think we should try to review our programs for the next six months and see if we can stabilize them. My secretary will make an appointment with the three of you.' He went on, 'We are trying to devise a planning system that should facilitate the communication and coordination between your departments. Maybe some extra attention should be given to this attempt. Koolhaas suggested the resumption of these meetings between the four of us, to evaluate the progress of the different projects and what effects can be expected for related projects. The last one was four months ago. We must see if we can give a new impetus to our coordinative efforts.'

It is not bad to get support for your ideas, but it is a pity when it comes from the wrong party. Mr Ripple and Mr Barton had interlocking problems which only they and not Mr Thrasher could solve. It was predictable that the next meeting would again meet resistance from their side because either or both of them would be pressured into making concessions which they did not want to or could not meet.

'During the last meeting you mentioned the stationary assembly machine,' Mr Thrasher said to Mr Ripple. 'When is it going to come into production?'

'It is being tested in the prototype workshop and apart from a few minor problems it is working well. I will give you a demonstration if you like. It is interesting to see how much simpler this machine is than the present rotating machine. And also what can be done with air pressure logic devices. This is the first time that we have fitted a machine without electronic switching gear.'

'We shall see if we have time after the meeting.' There was no hope that this would be so because these meetings always lasted much too long and the workshop closed early.

'When are the machines going to be produced? Will that place heavy demands on the machine factory?' Mr Thrasher went on.

'We haven't planned them yet, as they do not seem to have a high priority with our factory. When they do go into production, the demand will not be great, a couple of thousand hours, depending on the size of the series. Why?'

'I was speaking to Mr Roe and he complained of the fluctuations in our ordering and about the constant changing of our priorities.'

'They always complain. They complain when they think they do not have enough work, and when they have too much. They complain when they have the right amount of work but of the wrong kind. I would not pay too much attention to these complaints,' Mr Ripple retorted.

'Still we could try to level out our orders.'

'Of course we could. I have a pile of orders waiting for them. I have issued them twice already but have had to recall them because, as you know, the underlying decisions keep on getting reviewed and retracted. As I prefer to remain good friends with the machine factory, I only give them orders once they are definite.'

Two men in well-cut suits and slightly more colourful ties came in, each carrying an attaché case. Their personal appearance could certainly not be called gaudy, but it was in marked contrast to the other men in the room. Apart from me, they greeted everybody jovially. I introduced myself and Mr Thrasher explained my presence by telling them that I was to devise a planning system which could help solve the coordination problems between the different departments.

Mr Tilbury and Mr Southend were respectively the head of the commercial department and his second in command, who specialized in television tubes. They had called the meeting in order to revise the development program in reaction to what they thought were important changes in the market. Mr Tilbury explained that he had just returned from a trip abroad which had brought him into contact with their most important customers, and he gave the impression that the future prospects were dark. The competitors were about to spring a new product on the market. This product which was also being developed in our own laboratories but it had been given a low priority because, in the opinion of both the commercial and the development department, there were other more promising prospects. The low priority status combined with the urgent problems of the production department had brought this development to a virtual standstill with only a few independent subprojects continuing. The specialists occupied with these subprojects were not in direct demand elsewhere.

Mr Tilbury concluded, 'We must immediately set up a plan to bring this product on the market as soon as possible. And I propose that a liaison officer should be appointed to keep my department in the picture and to adapt the program to developments in the market.'

Mr Barton replied, 'The last time we met you agreed to giving the matrix project a high priority and the in-line a low priority. You cannot expect us to keep changing this around.'

'At our last meeting I did not have the information I have now. If we miss this chance I am afraid we will lose a large part of the market —a part we will not easily get back when we eventually can market the matrix tube. Our customers will have made contracts with our competitors,' Mr Tilbury reiterated.

Mr Barton said aggressively, 'You must realize that this will mean an important change in our activities. It will mean that the matrix tube development will be delayed.'

'I think you exaggerate. The work on the matrix tube can go on, but there must be a shift in emphasis. The in-line tube has the highest priority, but that does not mean to say that the matrix tube is not important any more. If we want to stay leading in this field we must have an alternative development at the ready.'

Mr Barton complained, 'That is all very well, but I have only a limited number of people capable of solving the necessary problems and they are very much hampered by the lack of assistance they get in testing their ideas because of the lack of capacity and difficult coordination with the engineering department.'

Mr Ripple interrupted,' 'Designing and making machines takes time which you do not give us. Nowhere will you find more capable people than in my department. But when you keep changing your ideas, as is about to happen now, we get no chance to deliver the goods. Only two months ago we dropped work on the design of the jigs for the in-line tube because you needed the modified screen clamp. If we change over again many hundreds of hours will be lost because the existing design will certainly have to be adjusted.'

Mr Thrasher tapped the rim of the table with his outstretched fingers. 'Gentlemen, if we lose our customers we would not even get the chance to develop other products or machines. I think we must solve the problem on hand and then see how the others fit in.'

Mr Barton did his best to hold his ground but realized that the odds were against him when he said, 'But you realize that the in-line means no real improvement in the visual quality of the tube. The viewer cannot distinguish between the two. I doubt if we should react to these hectic impulses from the market. The decision we took two months ago was based on solid arguments, which I do not hear refuted now.'

Mr Thrasher replied, 'On the one hand you are quite right Mr Barton, but on the other hand, the customer is not our customer but the customer of our customer, if you see what I mean. The set-maker at this point does not seem sensitive to the arguments presented two months ago.'

The door opened and Mr Anderson, the factory manager came in, portly and busy.

'Sorry I am late, but the problems with the introduction of the FX modifications needed my attention. I am afraid it will be some time yet before we can be in full production. I wish the products and the production machinery were better tested before production started. Now we shall be making large losses the next few months and it is a very open question whether we can meet our orders.'

Everybody was silent for a moment. The problems of the production department always weigh heavily because, after all, that is where the money is earned. He went on:

'I hope you are not dreaming up new ideas for modifications. That is the last thing we need. It is about time we had some peace and quiet on the factory floor.'

'You must not worry too much,' Mr Thrasher said reassuringly. 'Of course developments will keep occurring but we shall phase them as carefully as possible.'

Mr Tilbury and Mr Southend conversed together while Mr Thrasher was speaking and looked up when he had finished.

'May I summarize our point of view? It is very clear that our customers expect an in-line tube to be developed by us at very short notice. If we do not succeed in this we will lose many of them to our competitors. Because of this we propose that the in-line tube is given the highest priority. That does not mean to say that the other developments should come to a standstill.'

Mr Tilbury stopped a moment and directed himself to Mr Barton.

'In order to achieve this we propose that Mr Southend is to be our liaison with the development department and that a plan will be made to coordinate different activities necessary for speedy introduction. In regular meetings between Mr Barton, Mr Southend and possibly Mr Koolhaas, progress can be assessed and possible action can be taken when delays occur.'

Everybody was silent for a moment. Although the incessant humming and whirring of the factory penetrated the thin partition, one could imagine the sound of a time bomb ticking under the meeting—a bomb disrupting the existing division of responsibility by means of the attempt of the commercial department to get a more direct influence on the product development.

Mr Barton drummed on the table in a restless rhythm with the fingers of his left hand, pursed his lips and directed himself to Mr Thrasher. 'I think we are fully aware of the necessity to come on the market with a new product. But before we take a decision on which specific choice we are to make I would prefer to see more thoroughly prepared arguments on the merits of the different alternatives. I could imagine that the set-maker too can be sensitive to the argument of a quality jump in our product.'

'We have not time to bicker about alternative choices.' Mr Tilbury interrupted. 'We have discussed all these alternatives with our customers and this is evidently the best.'

Mr Thrasher lifted his hand: 'Gentlemen, gentlemen, please let's try not to be too impulsive. If I understand the commercial department rightly, they have weighed the different developments, together with our customers, and they have come to the conclusion that this will lead to the best results. In the first place because the in-line, apart from a few details, is nearly ready to start being test-produced, whereas the matrix tube is still in a somewhat more problematic phase of development. In the second place because the in-line is more in keeping with the expected new products of our competitors, we stand a better chance of keeping our customers. Furthermore I think it will be a good idea if the contacts between the two departments are organized on a more regular basis, but it does not seem necessary to institute a new kind of control over the activities of the development and the engineering departments.'

'I must stress the utmost importance of the consequences of our action. At this moment we are still in a very profitable line of business.' Mr Tilbury halted for a moment to emphasize his point. 'We must be very careful to remain in a leading position. Due to changing market situations this will become increasingly difficult. Whereas in the past we could depend on our technical lead, we will now have to listen much more attentively to signals from the market. This demands a new approach to the setting of targets and priorities for the development of new types. We think this will also demand new regular contacts on a high level between us and the development department.'

Mr Thrasher nodded his approval but was evidently not willing to shape these future contacts in a definite way yet. 'I quite agree, but we also must not jump to conclusions. I suggest we make an appointment for the next meeting. Between now and then we can discuss the method of coordination that is necessary and discuss it when different alternatives have been weighed.'

'That is fine,' Mr Tilbury immediately answered, 'but we insist on a more formalized plan for the progress of the in-line tube — a plan that can be discussed the next time we meet. It is not good enough to discuss how we are going to coordinate; at the same time we must also see to it that urgent matters do not get delayed.'

'Mr Barton, do you think you can present a plan for the development of the in-line tube?' Mr Thrasher asked.

'I can present as many plans as you want, but first I have to know what facilities will be available and how long we will have to wait for parts and instruments.'

'Maybe Mr Koolhaas can help in formulating these facilities and necessary arrangements with the engineering department, and also with the technical aspect of presenting such a plan in a clear manner.'

The tension in the meeting subsided gradually as a few other minor subjects were spoken about. By the time it was over it was too late to go and see the stationary assembly machine.

Much time was spent in devising planning systems which might help the coordination of activities in the development department. They were of little or no avail. Even extensive budgeting operations did not have the necessary effects because the results were too difficult to check.

Now six years later I have taken the trouble of finding out if much has changed. That is not the case. The same kind of problems still exist. The only difference for me is that I think I can now give a much clearer picture of what the problems really are than I could then. Because of this clearer picture it also seems likely that more appropriate solutions can be sought than sophisticated planning systems. The solutions are not new. It would be strange if they were, when so much attention has been paid to similar problems elsewhere. However the motivation and the description is different. What is even more important, the number of organizational variables that are taken into account is much higher. This makes simple solutions less likely. Because the influence of these variables may be contradictory, simple solutions may well be inappropriate. For this clearer picture and the possible indication of solutions, you will have · to bear with me a while, so that I can first present the concepts that are necessary to describe the situation. Before I do so I want to present another example which led my attention to the theoretical approach that is to be presented.

THE AUTOMATED INFORMATION RATIONALE

Case 2

Some years after the first illustration I came across a problem that is quite as interesting. From a technical point of view it had the makings of a tremendous success. It proved to be otherwise.

Operations research has developed into a toolkit of great sophistication. Whereas it was originally an approach to defining what the relevant problems were that led to certain detrimental results, it is now an accumulation of quantitative techniques of great refinement. These techniques have been greatly aided by the introduction of the computer. The case I am about to describe concerns the application of the above mentioned techniques to a large organization. It concerns the building of and the attempt at introducing a specific computerized information system for the control of a goods flow network.

The project was initiated in a research department concerned with the automation of information systems. It was based on the theoretical notion of the possibilities of optimizing the effectiveness of decisions based on quantitative information concerning customer demands and the necessary capacities of a production organization. It was started by a survey in the future client organization by a number of specialists. The survey was descriptive rather than oriented towards problems or their possible solutions. The goods flow and information and planning flows in the trajectory from the purchasing department up to the sales department were inventoried and analysed. Theirs was not the first survey or attempt at innovation within the organization. Previous experiences had already conditioned the reactions towards the initial survey.

In the next phase the research department proposed to follow up the initial survey with a study towards an improved goods flow management system, based on the information of the initial survey. The essence of the proposed system was to create a short cut by taking the information stream from the sales department directly to the purchasing and production departments. This was to be effected by a restructuring of the goods and information flow aided by an automated information system that could also take many of the routine decisions. The advantages of such a system were clearly formulated and seemed economically very interesting; an improvement in return on capital of between 20 and 40% was forecast. And possibly no less important, a great improvement in both the stability and flexibility of the production system as a whole was predicted.

Although the management of the division in which the survey had taken place had some doubts about the correctness of the forecasts, they were interested in the possibilities that were presented and authorized a further, more detailed study. The project had to be given a more organized form in order to be able to handle the large amount of information that was necessary in the design phase. Members of the client system and of related staff departments were recruited to participate with the specialists from the information department in the preliminaries for the design. Because the total control system was so complicated a division was made into subproblem areas which were allocated to different working groups—six in all. Together with these working groups, a steering group was instituted. This steering group should coordinate the activities of the working groups, and resolve possible conflicts between them.

The specialists of the information department already had a quite clear picture of the solution to the goods flow control problem. This foreknowledge resulted in little attention being paid to the orientation of the other members of the team, or formulating the nature of the problem. Open discussions on possible alternative solutions hardly took place. Advantages and disadvantages were elaborated no further. The activities mainly consisted of collecting information and fitting this into the existing preconception of an information system and constructing a more detailed control system. These activities were planned rigorously and little delay occurred in this phase of the project.

The specific nature of the conflicts between the different groups will not be presented. It may, however, be said that there was little or no rapport between the operations research specialists of the automation department and the other members of the teams, including future clients. Certainly a great difference in understanding, language and objectives fed the conflicts.

The conflicts became more clear when a seventh group was formed to design a simulation model for the whole production control system. This model was deemed necessary in order to test the system before it was implemented. Originally it had been the intention that one of the first six groups would design the model. The steering group, however, decided to form a new group because the problem proved to be a large one. Except for one member, this seventh group consisted of specialists from the automation department. Their meetings could be attended by the members of the other groups, but this hardly ever happened. The simulation model was extremely important for the evaluation of the design for the control system.

The different working groups laid down their findings in reports. From these, a total design of the control system was developed. This conceptual control system was evaluated and improved step by step, according to a number of criteria of an economic and cybernetic nature. Increasing precision of the results led to further development of the simulation model, and increasingly sophisticated methods of analysis.

All these activities took place within the team of specialists from the information department. The only contact with the client system was with experts from the bookkeeping and records departments. The steering group still existed, but no longer met regularly.

Possible organizational consequences such as the interrelations between the control system and the different tasks or roles as they existed in the client organizations were neglected. Problems concerning the implementation of the system and the acceptance of the consequences were not discussed. This is all finally resulted in the presentation of a final report describing the design of the system and an explanation of the economic forecasts. It was a purely technical-economical approach with little or no relation to the organizational context in which it was to be placed.

Because the future clients had participated in certain subaspects of the development of the system and had invested both time and effort in it, and also because it had already cost a lot of money and had been approved by the upper management levels, it was difficult for the client system to refuse implementation of the system. But decisions on the implementation were delayed because the client organization was large and complex, demanding much coordination before being able to come to a decision. The reason for the delay was that the total control system was very complex and not yet worked out in all its details and it was therefore very difficult to envisage all the organizational consequences. Furthermore at certain points the implementation of the system would be incompatible with the existing policies of the organization. Taking certain routine decisions by the computer instead of by members of the organization also proved to be tremendously problematical. Thus the decision to implement the system kept on being delayed. Before coming to a final decision, a number of uncertainties had to be cleared up. A new committee was instituted which began to survey the total control system, made an inventory of the problems and finally reached a limited decision. New questions about the consequences of implementation were formulated and another committee was instituted. These delaying tactics were repeated a number of times. During this process the hierarchic level of the members of the committees became lower and lower, and the manpower capacity in hours went up.

What were the final conclusions? The primary conclusion was that due to the integral nature of the control system it did not fit the existing organization structure. Because the system took no account whatsoever of the location of the consequences of its decisions, it necessitated important changes in departmental goal structures. This was deemed inacceptable and the integral system was turned down.

However, it was recognized that the system incorporated many attractive ideas which might enhance the efficiency of the organization when implemented individually. A new survey was started, to find out which parts of the system could be implemented independently and where.

The committee that studied the consequences of partial implementation came to the conclusion that partial implementation would result in practically the same economic benefits as the integral system would have done. Finally, this resulted, after still more study and testing, in implementing only a few parts of the total system.

Why is this so interesting as an illustration of those phenomena in organizations that are going to be explained in this study? In the first place because one might have expected the information department to learn about the resistance of their client systems to integral control systems. This was not the case. Secondly because it gives us insight into the dichotomous nature of organizations.

Within the information department, this and other failures generated the question of whether a theory could be devised which would predict which categories of information systems would be acceptable to which categories of organizations. This demanded an organizational typology in terms of relations with different types of information systems. The problem of organizational typologies led to the dimensional analysis as will be presented in this study.

Chapter 2

In Search of Typologies and Theories

This chapter makes explicit the philosophical point of view that is adhered to concerning the nature of theories and the demands that one may set. The relation between the nature of theories (and the terms used therein) and the domain of the theory is one of the main points of discussion in the philosophy of the social sciences. An indication is given of a possible means of integrating the theoretical demands and the domain demands by using a general organization theory that is independent of what is organized.

THEORETICAL TYPOLOGIES

There are nearly as many typologies of organizations as there are authors. This led Burns (1967, p.119) to note,

> '. . . the history of sociology, from Montesqieu through Spencer, Marx and upto Weber himself is littered with the debris of ruined typologies that serve only as the battleground for that academic street-fighting that so often passes for theoretical discussion.'

This has not made me decide to refrain from adding a one more to the list. However, it has made me realize that it is necessary to define what the requirements are for a worthwhile typology. The essence of typological effort lies in determining the *crucial* variables for differentiating the phenomena under investigation. Whether or not they are crucial depends on the theoretical context in which they are to be used. This leads to a more general discussion on what the requirements are for satisfactory theories of organizations. Before this is undertaken a distinction has to be introduced between different areas of activity in the field of organization or management science. Attempts at classification of the approaches to the study of this field, as for instance made by Koontz and O.Donnell (1968) have themselves little or no recognizable ordering principle, for they provide no notions whatsoever for a theory of either management or management research.

I propose a distinction in theoretical status based *not* on the area of study but rather on the *form of representation* of the acquired knowledge or insight into problems related to this field. The distinction is as follows.

Management theories are not really theories at all, in the sense in which the

16

word is to be used in this study. Usually they are pronouncements on how organizations are to be managed effectively or efficiently. They are to be considered as prescriptive statements rather than descriptive and/or explanatory. Implicitly they are based partly on theories. Such theories are predominant in this field of study and seem to allow the 'theorist' more leeway in the use of concepts and do not set too high demands on the internal consistency of their arguments or reasoning. They are often closely linked to experience in consultory or advisory practice.

Organization Theory versus Theory of Organizations

The distinction between these two types of theories is derived from Rapoport and Hovarth (1968, p.74-75). 'We see organization theory as dealing with general and abstract organization principles; it applies to any system exhibiting organized complexity.' As such, organization theory can be seen as being related to mathematical physics or, even more generally, to mathematics, designed to deal with organized systems. It is a highly formalized theory which is universally applicable to organized systems and is as such independent of its content. Organization theory becomes interpretable in terms of reality when the variables in the theory are applied to recognizable phenomena, as is done in physics or biology.

The theory of organizations, on the other hand, purports to be a social science. It puts real human social organizations at the centre of interest. It may study the social structure of organizations and so can be viewed as a branch of sociology. It may study the behaviour of individuals or groups as members of organizations and can as such be viewed as a part of social psychology. It may study power relations and principles of control in organizations and as such can be viewed as political science. It is the systematic arrangement of knowledge on the specific subjects that are of interest to the phenomenon of human social organizations.

The two types of theory have been developed independently. Theories of organization have emerged profusely from observation in the field of human social activity, whereas organization theory has been slowly hatched in the ivory towers of Academia and nursed into a precarious existence. The proposition is to combine the two approaches, to show that they should be closely related because their integration should have a synergetic effect.

The origin of *organization theory* should be sought in both the development of mathematics, as such, and the development of thermodynamics. Where thermodynamics was originally the theorizing of thermal processes and engines it has developed, especially in the last three decades, into a general organization theory — a theory creating a framework that describes the probability of certain structures and processes. Such structures and processes can be embodied by interpreting them as models of phenomena recognized in reality.

Social Science Theory

It may be contended that the social sciences do not allow the application of organization theory because of the specific characteristics of its subject. This contention is voiced for instance by Strasser (1970, p.17) when he states that in 'Natural science'—in the widest sense of the word—man is seen as a part of the cosmos, a part that does not essentially differ from the whole, whereas in human science we are concerned with the specifically human aspects. And this leads to the anthropological dilemma: 'How can man as a human being make man as a human being the subject of empirical research?' This begs the question of how can man as a thinking part of the cosmos make that of which he is but a part the subject of his empirical research?

Placing the human being outside nature assumes a distinct discontinuity in the nature of the cosmos: man . . . a long gap . . . and then the rest. I, for one, am not inclined to make this distinction. Although I do see that there are a number of important problems that stand in our way towards a more clear understanding of our own situation. These are:

1. The field of study is so complex in the sense that is to be described in this study (see p.68) that is the elements under study are so widely interrelated that the relations are extremely difficult to describe exhaustively.

2. The social theorist, and his theories, are themselves part of the field study. In this sense science no longer merely investigates the world; it also creates the world which it investigates, as opposed to the natural scientist who investigates the world that has created him. This argument can be split up into two categories:

   (a) the first is the 'general Heisenberg' principle, which is rather a problem of experimentation than of theorizing. It can be stated as follows. When experimenting with the system about which we are trying to obtain knowledge, we create a new system. Boulding (1969 p.3) gives a fine example of this. ' . . . a man who inquires through the door of the bedroom where his friend is sick, "How are you?" where upon his friend replies "Fine", and the effort kills him.'

   (b) The second is that the existence of theories changes reality even before any form of experimentation has taken place. Depending on the nature of the theories they are self-fulfilling or self-destroying prophecies. This is the case with, for instance, the social economic theories of Marx, econometric models and possibly Freud's psychology. The (partial) acceptance of such theories influences the behaviour of certain (groups of) actors in such a manner that the constructed model will (not) fit the new situation.

These last two categories become identical in the extreme case of viewing theories as mental experiments.

Organization Theory and Complexity

It may be propounded that the more complex the phenomena under study, the greater the necessity to clarify the means of representing knowledge. This can be done by describing the constraints on the method of representation. Laxity in conceptualization and theorizing is detrimental to both the discussion of the results of research and the development of more acceptable theories. There are no clear constraints in organization theory on its ability to handle complex phenomena. On the contrary, complexity itself as a phenomenon is one of the main subjects of organization theory. It can be said that there is a range of increasing complexity from physics, via for instance chemistry, bio-chemistry, biology, socio-biology, to human social organizations, somewhat in the

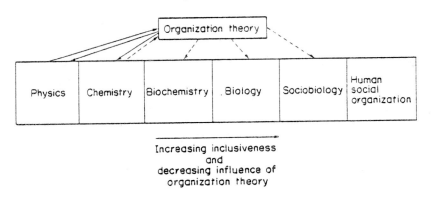

Figure 2.1   Relation between organization theory and natural sciences

manner presented by Carnap (1938). The complexity increases necessarily because the class of phenomena described each time includes the preceding class when proceeding along the chain. There is a hierarchical organization of material where in each hierarchy step new properties of the system come to light. This is somewhat similar to *The Doctrine of Emergence*. (Nagel 1961, pp.366–80) which is sometimes formulated as a thesis about the hierarchical organization of things and processes, and the consequent occurrence of properties at 'higher' levels of organization which are not predictable from properties found at 'lower' levels. If it is difficult to predict the characteristics of water (H_2O) from the characteristics of its constituent elements, it seems quite probable that it will be even more difficult to predict the characteristics of an organization from the characteristics of its members. This is all the more so because it is even difficult to characterize the individual members in a satisfactory manner. In this hierarchy it must be remembered that if one is to give a consistent theoretical description, statements made about the preceding class may not be neglected or refuted in the next class.

Along this line of increasing complexity we see a decrease in the influence of organization theory as a structuring force in the field of theory development.

In my opinion it is a glaring omission from theories of organizations. This has led to concept definition based solely on processes that are easily accessible to experience. The concepts precede the theories that are constructed from patterns recognized in the field of study by applying statistical or other analytical techniques of varying degrees of sophistication (see p.33). It is a rather ludicrous suggestion that, given phenomena of such admitted complexity, much progress can be made in understanding the connectedness of these phenomena by going to work in such a haphazard fashion. The use of organization theory as a tool for constructing a theory of organizations is an attempt to systematize the approach to such complex phenomena as human social organizations without unduly limiting the scope of the field of study. The development in organization theory towards principles of self-organization (Ashby 1962) and towards the analysis of self-organization in non-equilibrium systems (Nicolis and Prigogine, 1977) opens interesting perspectives. Because this approach is not only concerned with structure as such, but also with the dynamics of structure, due to internal and external processes that influence it, they present us with a picture of the possible mechanisms of evolution or development. Beer (1960, p.13) contended some time ago that 'an existing system of human relationships in a large and complex society is to be regarded as self-organizing, as ordered already . . .' Approaching organizations as self-organizing can lead to theories which explain why and how organizations develop various characteristics such as multi-level hierarchy or decentralized authority. But in such an approach characteristics or variables of organizations cannot be taken for granted; they must first be investigated in the light of the theory in which they are used. Norms for the expediency of theoretical concepts are to be derived from organization theory instead of from the widespread use of the terms of the theory in present or past publications in this field. The choice of concepts or basic terms of a theory determines the relation of the theory with its domain. It is strange that this area of methodology is sparsely represented in the literature. Machlup's (1963) *Essays on Economic Semantics* is one of the few instances where a comparison is made between the meaning of concepts, as used by different authors, and the theories in which they employ them.

THEORIES

But why theories at all? Why not just friendly humourous conversations and random remarks? Or why not anecdotal novels describing recurring phenomena in a number of subtle different ways? That would be fine if science as a social activity did not have certain aims, which can be crudely stated as follows.

Men try to extend their knowledge of (science) and their control over (technology) their environment to reach a larger portion of reality. This presupposes communication and mutual understanding. In order to achieve this they have to record their experiences in such a manner that they themselves can in some way recall them and also pass them on to others. In this sense theories can be seen as schemes of communication. Criteria for the 'form' of the theories are then their effectiveness and their efficiency. This last criterion is best expressed by the compactness of the theoretical structure and of the language in which they are expressed. This could be called the pragmatic aspect of theoretical activity. Such efficiency is enhanced when all the different states of phenomena, which are part of our experience, can be described with a minimum of concepts. This distinction between possible states presupposes that there are recognizable variables describing those states and which in different combinations define different states of the system. Organization theory provides us with a logical mathematical model which can indicate what types of variables are fruitful. It provides fresh ways of looking at phenomena by presenting different modes of representation (Toulmin 1953, p.43). Because it is only a method of representation and is not necessarily semantically laden, it is neither true nor false. It only gives us a method of finding out in which ways phenomena deviate from presupposed ideals of order, and allows us to use a formal language that is less ambiguous than the causal relations which are usually expressed in the area of theories of organizations.

Reality and Commonsense

The application of organization theory implies some philosophical problems. They are probably no more grave than those due to any other methodological choice. One of these problems is the origin of order in the phenomena under study. This brings me rather abruptly to the introduction of *commonsense reality* which will be rather crude in order to avoid philosophical technicalities. It seems that organization theory makes a commonsense realistic approach advisable because such an approach not only contends there are objects of knowledge that exist, but also that the order that men recognize in nature exists independently of them. If there were no science, the tides would still turn with the same regularity and the seasons would not cease to exist. The *description* of order is the result of a social activity—science. However, according to some realists, it is more than order that exists, at least order in the sense of recurring sequences of events, according to them there *are generative mechanisms* which produce certain recurring sequences of events. For example, biological evolution is not only a recurring pattern in the development of species, it is the result of a mechanism of mutation and extinction of those mutants with the least appropriate responses to, or relations with, their environment. The discovery of generative mechanisms does not end enquiry in this direction, it is but a step in a continuing process leading to deeper structures. In the case of evolution theory, it leads to theories on mutation and on the equilibrium or non-equilibrium in relations of a system with its environment. Such commonsense realism implies that there is something like a *natural order* which is the consequence of these ordering principles or generative mechanisms. Organization theory attempts to describe these principles or mechanisms in the most general sense.

This in turn implies that the use of organization theory as a basis for a study of human social organizations presupposes that these are to be viewed as a manifestation of natural order.

This can be said to be the semantic aspect of a theory. When a theory is claimed to be true it means that the situation in reality coincides with the description that is given by the theory. When it is accepted that there are explanatory theories in the sense of iconic models, then this means that there are also specific mechanisms in reality which can be described in a theory.

The acceptance of the view that human social organizations are a manifestation of natural order does *not* mean that the forms of organizations encountered in reality and resulting in patterns of social relations best characterized by unequal distribution of power, wealth and knowledge, are the only ones and by 'nature' good or right. It means that such organizations are the consequence of generative mechanisms operating under specific circumstances. *If these circumstances can be influenced by choices open to men, then other forms of organizations might ensue which may be deemed more preferable on the basis of ethical or moral values.* It does not lie in the perspective of this study to define which forms of organization are preferable, nor how to achieve them, only to adumbrate the variables and their mutual relations which are necessary to *describe* the possible forms of organizations and the way they come about.

In this sense theories of organization are, more or less, formal statements on what kind of variables are characteristic to the phenomenon of human social organizations. By filling in and interpreting the empty organization theory into an applicable body of knowledge it is possible to fit Parsons' (1951, p.3) objective of an 'exposition and illustration of a conceptual scheme for analysis of social systems (social systems in the context of this study are organizations and their internal conflicts) in terms of an action frame of reference.' Because the form of the theory has been chosen, determining in which ways cross-references can be made in this filing cabinet of knowledge, the concepts that are devised determine the efficiency of the order that can be brought into the knowledge in this field.

The Pragmatism of Formalization

Summing up, it can be stated that the adoption of such a formalized mode is based on the following pragmatical reasons. It provides a precise characterization of the structure of argumentation, an accurate way to formulate definitions, a better analysis of presuppositions, a clearer distinction between argument and interpretation. It can fall back on metatheoretical research.

From a tactical point of view it can be questioned *when* it is most efficient to choose such a formal mode in the process of theorizing on a certain subject. If this is done at the very beginning it helps to choose or define one's concepts or variables; if it is done after long observation one has the advantage of systematic empirical data. In this study the choice is made on the basis of the reinterpretation of theories and their concepts as described in the literature on the subject in an informal manner.

One of the very few examples I have found of an attempt at constructing a formal (axiomatic) theory of organizations is Hage's (1965) study. He was well aware of the problem of defining his variables, especially in reference to the question of whether they were general enough. He employs Nadel's (1957 p.7–17) distinction of formal characteristics and content categories, of which the first have a much greater generality. Hage points out that formal characteristics have two important advantages. 'They can both differentiate between organizations with similar objectives and also indicate similarities between organizations with different objectives and . . . because they are not time specific or culturally bounded they are useful in studying organizational evolution.' Two examples of variables that do *not* allow comparison between organizations with different objectives are Woodward's technology and success variables. The technology variables apply only to industrial production settings and the success variable does not apply to non-profit or government organizations. Woodward never intended her research to apply to anything but industrial organizations. The findings cannot be generalized without translating the industrial definition of her technology variables by means of a general theory of organizations to variables of a more general nature. Perrow's technology variables, on the other hand, have no such restrictions and make both differentiation and comparison possible.

The desire for formalization, as expressed through the use of organization theory as a framework to be filled in, has important consequences for the definition of variables. Such a formal manner of analysis makes use of most of the accepted characteristics of organizations inappropriate. They are not suitable as analytical categories because they are too complex and ill-defined, or rather undefinable. It is therefore necessary to *construct* new concepts based on the chosen framework. These concepts are not necessarily easily recognizable in a vis-à-vis confrontation with our experience, but they can be used as theoretical building blocks. The translations of these theoretical concepts to recognizable phenomena is itself of such a theoretic nature that the proposed theories cannot be empirically tested in a *direct* manner. Testing presumes theories of measurement.

Testing and Measurement Theory

The only thing that can be watched for is that during the translation through the different levels no tautological steps creep into the theoretical framework. Such tautological steps may arise if indicators are devised that show that proposed relations are true by means of letting the content of the indicator be defined by the result sought. Even in physics these translations from theory to experiment are problematical and imply many theoretical assumptions concerning, for instance the behaviour of materials under the influence of the phenomena that are to be studied. In the social sciences where the phenomena are much more complex than in physics (in the sense as it is to be defined in this study — see p.68) the problems are even greater. Thus the translation of these theoretical concepts to empirical indicators is difficult, to say the least. But it is less difficult than the fabrication of relevant concepts to fit the often ill-defined indicators that are used to supply the empirical data which forms the basis of the present theories. In other words, the translation from theory is less difficult than the construction of relevant theories built on concepts that are defined by their experimental indicators, as is most often the case in social sciences. Such argumentation on the recognizability of theoretical concepts led Woodward (1958, p.38) to remark that highly abstract concepts are 'of little value as a predictive tool in the study of industrial behaviour.'

I hope to have shown that only the combination of sound theory and its mutually dependent conceptualization can supply an appropriate basis for the *design of empirical indicators*. That such concepts help us not only to predict industrial behaviour, but more importantly to understand it and possibly even change it in a direction we find more appropriate.

This brings us back to the beginning of this chapter where it was stated that it is necessary to discuss the requirements for a satisfactory theory of organizations. To estimate whether a theoretical structure is satisfactory it may be considered whether such a construction facilitates efficient communication or understanding the phenomena under study. Such communication is enhanced when an indication is given beforehand on how it will be structured and on how big the claims that are to be made, will be. If the framework for communication is acceptable to all parties the chance of attaining consensus on the meaning of concepts or their relations will be larger. The acceptance of theories is, furthermore, highly influenced by their empirical relevance. This relevance is largely the consequence of using theory in practical settings to predict the consequences of attempted change. In a more scientific context theories gain more acceptance when they can be empirically tested. As empirical testing will be difficult until the necessary theories of measurement have also been supplied, another manner of validation is sought. It is therefore proposed that while awaiting theories that will make empirical methods of testing possible, theories be judged by the plausibility of the explanations they supply and by the predictions they make in their domains. This leads us to the conclusion that the *presuppositions* that are necessary for the construction of a theory must *not* first of all be judged by their plausibility or truth but rather by: (a) their simplicity and elegance and (b) the degree to which they lead to credible or empirically testable results when they are combined to a specified logic. When the results are not credible or prove to be untrue, then one should either doubt the presuppositions or the combinatory logic that was used. However when a presupposition is evidently deficient, as for instance the *homo economicus* is in economics, then the theoretical structure built on it will show many more deficiencies.

A theory is no better than its presuppositions.

THEORETICAL REQUIREMENTS

To enhance communication with the reader, directed at furthering the acceptance of this theoretical activity, a number of requirements for a theory of organizations are formulated.

These requirements have *not* been constructed on a purely methodological basis. Rather, they are the consequence of an iterative process of studying existing works on organization structure and technology and are an attempt at formulating pronouncements on the mutual relations between structure and technology. These requirements concern the structure of the theory itself, and its domain. But there are also a few remarks in general, that should be made.

(A) A *general* theory of organizations does away with the need for the widespread distinction between all types of organizations based on many different criteria (see Hall, 1972, pp.39–78). It is often contended that criteria based on the position of the organization in its environment, as concerned with ownership or profit and non-profit, demand different theoretical references. Furthermore many theoretical and empirical works only concern specific types of organizations, such as Woodward's industrial production organization, and use variables that are only applicable to organizations operating in a specific domain.

It is the objective of this study to present a *general* theory of organizations which can partly describe and explain all human social organizations and not only a specific category of them.

(B) Because theorizing is viewed as a means of efficient communication, mathematics is an attractive medium to express oneself in, because of the widespread consensus on its internal consistency as a formal language. This is emphasized further by the link that was laid to organization theory, which is highly mathematical. This link was recommended on the basis of the attractiveness of viewing organizations as complex systems. It draws attention to those branches of science where much work has been done on the description of the possible states of complex systems. An example of this is thermodynamics.

Mathematical formulation facilitates the emphasis on form rather than on content, and it is the form of organizations that is the domain of this theory. It is the ultimate step in the process of formalizing a theory. By this is meant the most explicit formulation of relations between the different concepts that have been defined.

The Structure of the Theory

(a) A theory, in general, must not only provide explanations (for instance confirming the hypothetic deductive model) but it must first of all provide the means to describe those phenomena. In this context the theory must define its object, the domain of the theory. Only very general theories, of a very high abstraction, do not necessarily have to do so, but then it is usually stated that it is a theory that is universally applicable to all classes of phenomena.

(b) Apart from the description of the phenomena, by supplying a consistent set of concepts it should specify the means of explanation. The 'realistic' point of view that was expressed on p.21 entails the use of generative mechanisms. This means that the structure of the theory will be one with different levels — a tiered structure. The relations between these levels form the basis of the explanatory logic. An example of this multi-levelled nature of explanatory theory can be found in the relation between:

— Kepler's theory of elliptic paths of planets and of their constant angular velocity as well as the third law of planetary motion, relating orbital distances to orbital periods; and

— Newton's theory of general gravitation. This can be seen as theorization on two levels. Newton's theory explains the other theories.

(c) The variables constructed to describe the organizational phenomena must be independent of the classical level of hierarchy of authority in the organization, as also of the level of inclusiveness (in the sense of point 2) to which it is applied. The horizontal and the vertical dimensions in Figure 2.2 must be independent in order to be able to distinguish between intra- and inter-level relationships (see Figure 4.8). This implies that specific relationships may be defined at *any* level of an organization.

(d) The elementary dimensions in which the variables are to be expressed must be applicable to the whole system of variables describing the organization at all levels. When a specific relation is defined, it must be dimensionally consistent.

(e) The dimensions must be as elementary as possible. By elementary is meant that no other descriptive concept can be given that is more basic, and more generalistic than that which has been defined. Through combination of these elementary dimensions, the construction of appropriate dimensions of the variables must be possible. The proof that the dimensions *are elementary* cannot be given.

The Structure of the Domain

(a) When we apply the above-mentioned requirements to the empirical objects of this study, the dimensions must be chosen in such a manner that they can describe both the organizational and environmental variables and the possible relations between them. This also facilitates the conjunction of studies concerning the environment and organization structure and those studies concerning technology and structure.

That the same dimension should describe both the organization and its environment should be evident because of the relations and interaction

Organization level	Individual	Group	Sub department	Department	Division	Total organization	Environment
Dimensions							
Variables							
Theories							
System of theories							

Increasing inclusiveness of empirical organizational phenomena

Increasing complexity of theoretical relations

Figure 2.2   The relations between the level of inclusiveness and the level of complexity of theoretical relations

between organizations and their environment. Furthermore it is certainly necessary, if organizations are to be described as self-organizing systems influenced by their environment as was proposed on p.20

(b) Criticism in the literature on organization structure has been widespread where it concerns the definition of the organizational level of analysis. Many researchers have taken the organization as a whole, setting heavy demands on the homogeneity of the organization, or implying that internal differences are not important to the concept of structure. The level of inclusiveness is a necessary distinction if relations between different units within an organization are to be analysed, as is the case in this study.

CONCLUSIONS

There can be no certainty about the completeness of the requirements presented. They must only be seen as a comparative basis for the theory as it is presented and the existing theories in the same field.

Chapter 3

Theories of Organization, a Critical Survey

The two case studies were presented as a heuristic implement and not as evidence or as illustration of the truth value of the theory that is to be presented. The abstract and dull definition of the concepts that are to be used must be given some substance for recognition; they are therefore transposed to the cases where possible.

Most case studies describe situations where the author's prescriptions work. This study gives no prescriptions. Therefore the case study is not a lesson; it is but an example of organized activity. It should be suggestive, urging the reader to find similar situations in his organizational environment where he can employ the concepts described.

Existing theories of organizations can also be applied to these two cases. Similar problems can be recognized in other organizations, in different countries, which suggest that the problems are structural rather than incidental or linked to specific, interrelated personalities. Because of this, a structural approach was chosen. It must be said that at the time the problems presented themselves, from 1970 to 1975, structural approaches were certainly not *en vogue* with those professionals concerned with solving organizational problems. The tremendous production of literature on *Organization development* and on *the processes of management* made those who advocated research in the structural aspects of organization suspect. This was all the more so when it was argued that structural analysis led to statical views of organizational phenomena, whereas what the organizations needed most was controlled change. The objective of this study is to show that a structural approach must be the basis for *understanding* the dynamic possibilities of organizations. Furthermore, it is necessary to emphasize that such an approach can only give a partial description of organizational phenomena. They are so complex with so many distinguishable aspects that a choice must be made. The field from which the choice has been made is sketchily presented below. Because of the wish to formulate a general theory, the concepts that are used to describe organizations will have to be general enough to fit all types of organizations.

A HISTORICAL PERSPECTIVE

Classical theories of organizations or management theory are not really theories in the sense of this study. As stated above, they are usually recipes

29

based on common sense or generally accepted implicit theories. An example of such a theory is that for every type of activity there is one best way. This 'theory' is the basis of *Scientific Management*. It indicates what the basic ingredients are for organizational activities: plan ahead, register and keep records, write down policies, define tasks, specialize, delegate, remain decisive and keep your span of control down to about six people. Because organizations kept growing and becoming more complex these prescriptions become more and more necessary. They are still important ingredients of the present-day organizational toolkit. When and how these tools are to be used and matched remains a point of discussion. The prescriptions worked but led to tight, inflexible organizations. Changing market situations, as well as changing production techniques put these inflexible organizations under increasing strain — all the more so because labour became a much more critical factor. In about 1938, some in the field of organizational studies came to the conclusion that to orient the organizing process solely on the efficiency of work was not good enough. The *human being* in the organization should be accorded an important place; hence the birth of the *human relations* school. Research was done to see what social and psychological influences could effect the productivity of organizations. Conclusive evidence showed the remarkable fact that when more attention was paid to the individual in his working situation he stepped up his efforts. It also showed that there are mechanisms at work in groups which kept the level of activity of each member within limits acceptable to the group as a whole. Except for a short interruption during the Second World War, this line of thought has since then been very actively pursued. It is a line of thought that is not based on a consistent framework of theories but rather on partial insight or knowledge of subaspects of the social system of organizations and the psychology of its members. The present work on management development and the like is a logical consequence of this line of thought. Studies on leadership also play an important part in the human relations school. In the perspective of this study, these findings are certainly valuable, especially when they are seen in the perspective of the time when they were made. They are not a guideline towards a more formalistic theory of organizations. Furthermore, it is debatable if these findings shouldn't be seen, at this moment, in a different perspective than that in which they were conceived — one that sets stronger demands on the theoretical foundations. The work of the Tavistock Institute in England has created an important start in this direction with their socio-technical systems approach, a line of thought that is very basic to this study.

Because of the continuing growth of organizations and the increasing diversity of their activities on different markets, it became clear that the principles of organization were tremendously important and that the bureaucratic organization could have many advantages. Where the organization theorists had been against bureaucracy, it turned out that managers were not. Responsibilities, lines of communication, authority and rules for organizational activities are clear in a well-oiled bureaucracy, and morale can be just as high as anywhere else. This redirected the attention of the theorists to the more formal aspects of organizations, and a large number of them concentrated their work on the structural modalities of organizations. They did this along a number of different lines of thought which are still pursued independently of each other.

On the one side, there is a group of theorists to whom the problem-solving or decision-making aspects of the organization are most important. Representatives of this school are Cyert, March and Simon. Their perspective is truly theoretical, but concentrated on a subaspect of all the organizational activities. They presented exciting new ideas on the bounded ability of individuals to take in information concerning solutions to problems from their environment. They arrived at rules of organization through induction from theories on individual behaviour.

On the other hand, there is a stream of thought that tries to assess the relations between the classical organization principles such as departmental-ization, formalization, span of control and specialization and the kind of production that takes place within the organization. Woodward, Burns and Stalker, Harvey and the Aston group are important representatives. A slightly different version of this is the research on the relation between the above-mentioned organizational variables and the size of the organization. Important here are Blau and Schoenherr. This line of work should generate a theory from quantitative empirical research. The definition of variables and the construction of operational indicators is the central problem to this approach, a problem that has in no way been solved yet. None the less, the amount of empirical research in this field is overwhelming (see Kimberly 1976, p.572). A third important line of inquiry is that of the relation between organization structure and the characteristics of the environment. Here Lawrence and Lorsch and Thompson are important influences.

This superficial review of work done on the theories of organization might give the impression that it is relatively easy to categorize the different schools. This is not so. There is little or no consensus on who belongs in what category. Neither is there a clear indication as to what the mutual influences have been in the development of the different approaches. Most of them have influenced the formation of the theory presented.

NATURAL AND UNNATURAL SCIENCES

Parallel to the different schools mentioned in the previous section of this chapter, the distinction can be made between empiricists and rationalists. The empiricists rely on the formulation of empirically testable hypotheses in an attempt to provide an equivalent to the experimental method of the natural scientist. It is a fallacy to think that physical experiments are central to the development of theory.

Einstein had no explicit empirical indications to base his work on which led to the general theory of relativity; it was mainly a sense of aesthetics. Even in the theories that existed at that time no direct reason could be found to set him off in this direction in 1907. Einstein hypothesized that gravitation bends light but he could think of no feasible way to test it experimentally. By 1911 he had found a possible method. He calculated that a ray of starlight grazing the sun ought to be deflected by 0.83 second of arc. This deflection, Einstein suggested, could be detected during a total eclipse of the sun. It was not until 29 May 1919 that Eddington could perform the test during a total eclipse on the island of Principe off the west coast of Africa.

The predominance of empirical studies in the field of the social sciences is a fashion that is, in my opinion, based on a misunderstanding of what science is or should be. This misunderstanding is strengthened by the emphasis on the distinction between, on the one side, the natural or a-social sciences and on the other side, the social or unnatural sciences. As Medawar (1977, p.13) so sarcastically puts it:

> 'If a broad line of demarcation is to be drawn between them, it will at once be recognized as a distinguishing mark of the latter that their practitioners try painstakingly to imitate what they believe — quite wrongly, alas for them — to be distinctive manners and observances of the natural sciences.
>   Among these are:
> (a) the belief that measurement and numeration are intrinsically praise-worthy activities (their worship of what Ernst Gombrich calls *idola quantitatis*);
> (b) the whole discredited farrago of inductism — espeically the belief that facts are prior to ideas and that a sufficiently voluminous compilation of facts can be processed by a calculus of discovery in such a way as to yield general principles and natural seeming laws;
> (c) another distinguishing mark of the unnatural scientist is their faith in the efficacy of statistical formulas, particularly when processed by a computer, the use of which is in itself interpreted as a mark of manhood.'

The contention that the social sciences are too young for appropriate systemization does not seem tenable.

> 'The study of human society and human behaviour moulded by social instructions has been cultivated for about as long as has the investigation of physical and biological phenomena. However, much of the "social theory" that has emerged from such study, in the past as well as the present, is social and moral philosophy rather than social science, and is made up in large measure of general reflections on the "nature of man", justifications or critiques of various social institutions, or outlines of stages in the progress of decay of civilizations.' (Nagel 1961, p.447).

These reflections on the *nature of man* have even led large groups of social scientists to expound that this very *nature* makes it *impossible* to employ accepted analytical scientific methods of inquiry—a view not unlike that which was widely held during Copernicus' lifetime. This view does not give the theoretical approach the benefit of the doubt and in principle ignores possible results of attempts in that direction. When a theory is seen as a formal mode of representing knowledge on a certain subject in an ordered manner, one should be able to meet the same demands on such aspects as internal consistency, structural clarity and conciseness in both scientific areas. The validation of formulated theories is more difficult in the field of the social sciences, because of the difference in the possibilities of experimentation.

The reflections based on the nature of man categorically oppose a systematic representation of social reality. The combination of this view and the predilection for measurement has led to the proliferation of data-driven research and the relative scarcity of rational theoretical work. The absence of theoretical foundations makes the use of highly formal statistical methodology in the social sciences rather suspect, all the more because the process of measurement in this area is tremendously problematical.

The work that will be reviewed is nearly all empirically oriented, with the prominent exceptions of Thompson and Perrow. The theoretical concepts that should be the basis of empirical research have been left underdeveloped. This lack of understanding of the concepts themselves is the basis of the confusion about how technology and structure are related. After two decades of research we still cannot evaluate the importance of technology as a determinant of organizational structure (Comstock and Scott 1977, p.177). Also the concept of size has been little developed, nor has a theoretical rationale been specified as to why it should be included as a variable in studies on organizational structure (Kimberly 1976 p.573). In general, theorizing in this area occurs mainly during the interpretation of empirical research directed at the recognition of organizational regularities. The result of this poverty of the theoretical framework is a lack of criticism on the content of the studies, and an excess of research-methodological nitpicking. Instead of reappraising the deficient theories, studies are repeated using larger samples and more sophisticated analytical techniques.

None the less, a direct link is sought with work done in the past in this attempt to devise new theoretical concepts. Because the translation of such concepts into empirical indicators is problematical, it is worthwhile seeing how existing research can be reinterpreted to form a basis for the theory that is to be presented. It cannot be emphasized enough that measurement in the psycho- and sociological field should be regarded with the greatest suspicion due to the lack of underlying measurement theories. With this in mind, the review that follows will pay particular attention to those authors who have been most influential in the development of theories of organization. This review will be extensive because the concepts used by these authors form the basis of the new theory and an understanding of their origin and their role in existing theories simplifies the definition of new variables.

The review, and the criticism that seems to be inherent to it, must not be interpreted as a commentary on the authors' lack of success in reaching the exalted standards set by the reviewer. This would imply that if he has the temerity to present his own attempt at theorizing in the same field, this would reach such standards. No, it must rather be seen in a perspective of theoretical development over time, where the results of consecutive or parallel studies are compared with each other and possibly with a set of requirements formulated by the reviewer at a much later point in time. Thus part of the criticism concerns the lack of ability of the reviewer to see the reviewed studies against the backdrops of their own time rather than passing judgement on their theoretical status. Furthermore the requirements set by the reviewer are wide open to criticism.

Disparagement seems inescapable when reviewing previous studies, because dissatisfaction is being expressed and is in fact the motivation for a continued search for more satisfactory models or theories. This dissatisfaction is more a characteristic of the reviewer than of his material. Expressed dissatisfaction can be seen as an indication of arrogance. As Blaug (1968, p.1) remarks in this context:

> 'The danger of arrogance toward the writers of the past is certainly a real one, but so is ancestor worship. Indeed, there are always two sorts of dangers in evaluating the work of earlier writers: on the one hand, to see only their mistakes and defects without appreciating the limitations both of the analysis they inherited and the historical circumstances in which they wrote; on the other hand, to expand their merits in the eagerness to discover an idea in advance of their own times, and frequently their own intentions.'

Hopefully the expressed dissatisfaction is translated into a creative impulse leading to meaningful developments in the field of theories of organizations.

WOODWARD

Typological effort in the field of technology was stimulated tremendously by the work of Joan Woodward. She was one of the first to systematically study the relation between technology and structure and the economic success of organizations. She hypothesized that this success was the result of an appropriate combination of technology and structure. Such a theory is both simple and elegant. The concepts she uses are problematical, certainly when compared with later developments in this field of study. Some of these problems will be briefly highlighted.

(1) The success of organizations is evidently the consequence of many influences, both internal and external. For instance:

    (a) the market in which the organization operates;
    (b) the relative position to its competitors in for instance the development of new products;

(c) the geographical location;
(d) government policies towards the industry of which the organization is a part;
(e) marketing;
(f) the position of its product life-cycle;
(g) etc.

Every facet that can be recognized in an organization can influence its success. If one is of the opinion that the relation between the nature of the production process and the structure of the organization is the *decisive* factor, then one severely underestimates the above-mentioned and other environmental variables.

(2) Technology or the nature of the production. The division Woodward chooses is one of production technique (see Figure 3.1). It is a division based on evident exterior differences as can be recognized in production facilities. The motivation of this choice is vague. The way in which the method of production is related to, for instance, the product or the client system does not at all become clear. A superficial reflection on the difference between products for either a consumer market or a professional market shows that it can be of prime importance.

		Production systems engineering	Production engineering
INTEGRAL PRODUCTS	I	Production of units to customers' requirements	
			Jobbing
Units and small batch production	II	Production of prototypes	
	III	Fabrication of large equipment	
Large batch and mass production	IV	Production of small batches to customers' orders	
	V	Production of large batches	Batch
	VI	Production of large batches on assembly lines	
	VII	Mass production	Mass
DIMENSIONAL PRODUCTS	VIII	Intermittent production of chemicals in multi-purpose plant	Batch
Process production	IX	Continuous flow production of liquids, gases, crystaline substances	Mass
COMBINED SYSTEMS	X	Production of standardized components in large batches subsequently assembled diversely	
	XI	Process production of crystalline substances, subsequently prepared for sale by standardized production models	

Figure 3.1   Woodward's categorization of production systems

As can be seen in Figure 3.1, Woodward discerns three major technological categories.
(a) the division between those forms of production where a clear
    distinction can be made in the different steps in the production process
    and those forms where this is not possible;
    Integral versus *dimensional*.
(b) the timespan over which the same product is made or the series' length:
    jobbing, batch and mass, or *intermittent* or *continuous*;
(c) the grouping of production equipment.

The resulting eleven categories are seen as a scale of technical complexity
with which an indication is given of how controllable the production
process is or how predictable its results are. The manner in which
Woodward has arranged her categories might suggest that they are usable
as a scale for correlation analysis. This does not seem justifiable as they
have not been explicitly formulated in terms of 'controllability' or 'predictability', but more as a combination of the two, together with a grading
of throughput continuity. Furthermore these categories are not
independent of the following structural variables.
(3) The description of structure is less specific than that of technology. It is
    not defined but rather illustrated by a number of indicators based on
    Weber's bureaucratic ideal-type. Rational analysis shows that many of the
    indicators must be strongly related to the type of product that is made or
    the relation of the production organization with other organizations as in
    the case with a subsidiary or a division of a larger organization. In such
    cases the worker-staff ratio is bound to be different from other
    independent organizations which cannot fall back on the central services
    of their parent organization for specialist help.
(4) Woodward comes to the following conclusions:

    (a) There is a linear relationship between technology and structure as
        identified by several of her personnel ratios and organization chart
        aspects.
    (b) There is a curvilinear relation between technology and dimensions of
        social structure such as the tendency to break down the labourforce
        into small primary groups and the tendency toward organic, flexible
        forms of management.
    (c) Organizations are economically more successful when their structure
        fits their technology. Mass-production firms are more successful when
        they have a mechanistic management.

The study and its conclusions have been widely discussed in the sphere of
management research. Much methodological criticism has been levelled
primarily at the way in which Woodward's samples were drawn. Relatively
little criticism has been directed at the implicit theoretical basis of the study.

This is not so strange because there is a general lack of fundamental criticism in this field. None the less it is interesting to review some of the theoretical presuppositions that form the basis of this study. The most classical is that there is a strict organizational rationality, akin to Taylor's proposition that there is one best way to do everything. Because different organizations perform different tasks they should have different forms. For each type of activity there is one best way, in Taylor's logic, and therefore each technology is accompanied by its own structure. The technological imperative is: structure follows technology.

Very fundamental is the restriction of technology to industrial *production* programs, thereby excluding about 70% of western economic activity. Furthermore the superficial implementation of Weber's bureaucratic ideal-type makes reanalysis of these studies problematical.

Finally in order to make a comparison possible with other contributions, it can be stated that related to the methodological points presented in the previous chapter we may conclude that:

(A)　The study concerns only industrial production organizations.
(B)　There is no formalization apart from the presentation of empirical results.

(1a)　Woodward does not define the concept of organization as the domain of her theorizing. This has the consequence that the comparison of significantly different types of organizations (subsidiaries versus independents) obscures the relevance of her results.
(1b)　The means of explanation is not made explicit.
(1c)　The variables only concern the organization *in toto*. This presupposes homogeneity within the organization and the possibility of comparing subsidiaries with independents.
(1d)　Not applicable.
(1e)　Not applicable.
(2)　The influence of the environment is neglected, thus presenting a very limited picture of the possible influence on success.

THE ASTON GROUP

The Aston group had serious criticism about the samples drawn by Woodward and contended that the results of the two surveys in 1954–55 and in 1962–64 were not consistent. But it was not only on the basis of research-theoretical considerations that they decided to study the relation between technology and structure anew; they also took a more fundamental approach towards technology (Hickson *et al.* 1969) and structure. They constructed more systematic categories.
(1)　Within the concept of technology they distinguished between:
　　　(a) Operations technology: The equipping and sequencing of activities in

the workflow. This is common to both Woodward and Thompson, as will be shown further on in this chapter. The 'shape or form of the production process' is emphasized as one of the ways in which different production stages may be linked.

(b) Materials technology: A classification of different characteristics of the materials used in the production process.
(c) Knowledge technology: The distinction between the different kinds of 'search behavior' in the quest for solutions to problems inherent to the production process.

Sadly enough, the group concentrates solely on the operations technology in the same spirit as Woodward. Their approach is based on the definitions by Pugh *et al.* (1963, p.319) as consisting of 'the techniques it uses in its workflow activities that provide goods and service . . .' and also on definitions common to Thompson and Bates (1957, p.325) as 'those sets of man-machine activities which together produce a desired good or service'. They hypothesized that their technology concept consisted of a number of technological dimensions which could be operationalized independently. These were originally:

(a) *Automaticity*. The degree to which first energy (mechanization) and then information (automation) are provided by machines rather than man. Automated information and control systems do not fit here. The most automated category is 'self-measuring and adjusting machines using feedback'.
(b) *Workflow rigidity*. This characterizes the flexibility of the production process and is subdivided into eight subcategories.
(c) *Interdependence of workflows*. This is very closely related to the previous dimension.
(d) *Specificity of evaluation of operations*. This defines the measuring and supervisory methods that are used to check the products.

In their empirical tests these dimensions turned out to be highly inter-correlated, suggesting there might be an underlying common element or that their concepts each consisted of an only slightly different combination of other, more crucial dimensions. Through principle component analysis they arrived at a new overall variable which they called *workflow integration* which they defined as the degree of automated, continuous, fixed sequence operations. It was measured by adding up the scores of the constituent indicator scales.

(2) The structural variables are based on Weber's ideas on bureaucracy as was also the case with Woodward. Because Weber's bureaucratic characteristics are not readily translatable into empirical structural variables, the construction of such a multi-dimensional set of indicators proved problematical. Weber's description is based solely on formal, i.e. intended, characteristics and does not take into account the unintended consequences

which may be very important. Furthermore, bureaucracy is regarded as a unitary concept, as defined by the ten characteristics of Weber's ideal type (1947, pp.333–4). Udy (1959, p.794) finds that several of these characteristics, including hierarchical authority structure, are directly correlated with one another but not, even inversely, with several rational characteristics including specialization, which may be considered a primitive forerunner of technical expertise. Udy concludes that 'Bureaucracy and rationality tend to be mutually inconsistent in the same formal organization.' Heady (1959) distinguishes three aspects to bureaucracy:

structural characteristics;
behavioural characteristics;
achievement of goals.

Blau and Schoenherr (1971) contend that a fourth aspect is of prime importance and that is size.

Notwithstanding these problems of the distinction between these aspects, the Aston group conceptualized six elements which they considered to be dimensions or variables structure. Organizations can be rated on these six items and a profile can be constructed. These six dimensions are:

(a) *Specialization* refers to the division of labour within the organization and has two main aspects:
    (i) The number of specialists;
    (ii) The degree of role specialization which is concerned with the differentiation of activities within each function. It refers to the specificity and narrowing down of tasks assigned to any particular role.
(b) *Standardization* refers to the way procedures and roles are defined in the organization.
    (i) Procedures are standardized when there are rules or definitions that cover all circumstances and apply invariably. These rules would include how to proceed in cases not specifically covered.
    (ii) Standardization of roles is concerned with the degree to which the organization prescribes the role definition and qualification for office, the role performance measurement, titles for office and symbols of role status and rewards for role performance.
(c) *Formalization* distinguishes how far communications and procedures in an organization are written down and filed.
(d) *Centralization* concerns the locus of authority to make decisions affecting the organization. It is a measure derived from the authority located at levels within a given organization.
(e) *Configuration* is the shape of the authority structure as expressed in the organization chart.
(f) *Flexibility* expresses the change in organization structure. Its three main factors are:

(i)   the amount;

(ii) the speed;

(iii) the acceleration of change.

This last factor describes whether the changes were introduced slowly and continuously over a long period or in short sharp series with intermittent periods of no change. The two ideal types, 'organic' (continuous change) and 'mechanistic' (no change) as described by Burns and Stalker (1961) may be considered as examples of the extreme ends of the flexibility scale. In later studies (Pugh *et al.* 1968) this flexibility scale was dropped.

As the group noted, it was very much in question whether these single items could be added up to form, if not an equal-interval dimension, then a stable ordered scale, to represent the structural characteristics. Mansfield (1973, p.481) pragmatically justifies this addition with the remark that analysis would not be feasible if it were not done. However, if these variables are scaleable in a theoretic sense, Mansfield goes on, 'this implies a highly sophisticated theory of organizational development. Such a theory is nowhere made explicit.'

(3) The object of the original study (Pugh *et al.* 1963) was to test the proposition of the 'technological imperative' at the organizational level. They came to the conclusion that operations technology accounts for only a small proportion of the total variance in structural features and that size is one of the dominant influences on the structuring of activities.

Finally, related to the methodological points mentioned at the end of Chapter 2, for the sake of comparison, it can be said that:

(A)   The work contains a greater variety of organizations than Woodward's study. It is not restricted to industrial production organizations.

(B)   There is no formalization apart from the presentation of empirical results.

(1a) The Aston group does not define the domain of their research. Only those organizations where clearly distinguishable operations occur can be compared. The operations have to be homogeneous within the organization.

(1b) No means of explanation is made explicit.

(1c) The variables could be used for parts of the organization.

(1d) Technology and structure are analysed in terms of dimensions but not in the strict sense as defined in the second chapter.

(1e) The dimensions give an impression of being indicators rather than dimensions.

(2)   The influence of the environment is totally absent.

THOMPSON

This study (1967) is one of the most interesting and certainly one of the most influential for the development of theories of organization over the past ten years. It is highly original in its conception and form.

Thompson presented a quite different approach from previous studies. His was not an empirical study but rather a theoretical framework of propositions on the behaviour of organizations. The basic concepts in his study are: bounded rationality, structure, coordination and interdependence. The motivation of the choice of these concepts is not quite clear. It seems probable that they were made in order to come to a closed system of explanations for organizational behaviour and that they were not arrived at through 'systematic analysis of the concept of organization'. This can be illustrated by the lack of internal consistency of Thompson's definitions.

(1) Following the Simon-March-Cyert approach, the organization is seen as a 'problem-facing and -solving phenomenon'. The focus is on organization processes related to the choice of courses of action in an environment which does not fully disclose either the alternatives available or their consequences. In this view

'the organization has limited capacity to gather and process information or to predict consequences of alternatives. To deal with situations of such complexity the organization must develop processes for *searching* and *learning* as well as for *deciding*. The complexity, if fully faced, would overwhelm the organization, hence it must set limits to its definitions of situations; it must take decisions in *bounded rationality*.' (Simon 1957, p.198)

Within this concept Thompson defines his technology variables in the following manner.

'Instrumental action is rooted on the one hand in *desired outcomes* and on the other hand in *beliefs about cause/effect relationships*. Given a desire, the state of a man's knowledge at any point in time dictates the kinds of variables required and the manner of their manipulation to bring that desire to fruition. To the extent that the activities thus indicated by man's beliefs are judged to produce outcomes, we can speak of technology or *technical rationality*.'

It is strange that technical rationality and technology are presented as being identical. Rationality concerns the beliefs that cause–effect relationships are the appropriate constructions to explain or predict the manner in which phenomena come about. Technology concerns our ability to put this rationality to use and to help us to produce our desired outcomes. Apart from this criticism one would expect this definition to be the foundation of the ensuing categorization. This is *not* the case.

(a) 'Long linked technology involves serial interdependence in the sense that act Z can be performed only after the successful completion of act Y, which in turn rests on act X and so on' (p.15). Little indicates 'to which extent man's beliefs are judged to produce the desired outcomes.' His example of the mass assembly line is one that is based on great certainty that the manipulation leads to the desired outcomes. There are also serially interdependent production processes which are not based on a high certainty of the outcome but where one is, for instance, satisfied when reject rates remain within preset limits. The long linked technology has more to say about the way production is organized than about 'beliefs about cause–effect relationships.' Thus this technology characterization is closely related to Woodward's and concerns the choice of the organization structure rather than the knowledge of the production process.

(b) Mediating technology describes 'organizations which have as primary functions, the linking of clients or customers who are or wish to be inter-dependent.' This characterization, again, does not describe the state of man's knowledge of the production process. An indication is given of how the organization is situated between supply and demand. Thompson does give an indication of the basis of this technology. 'Complexity in the mediating technology comes not from the necessity of having each activity geared to the requirements of the next but rather from the fact that the mediating technology requires operating in *standardized* ways and *extensively*, e.g. with multiple clients or customers distributed in space' (p.16). As examples he uses banks and insurance companies. On the other hand nothing more standardized can be imagined than the mass assembly line — think of Charlie Chaplin in *Modern Times*. Furthermore, we also find many examples in banks and insurance companies that cannot be handled through standard procedures and which demand a unique approach. There are many mediating organizations that are specialized in handling such non-standard cases.

(c) 'Intensive technology signifies that a variety of techniques is drawn upon in order to achieve a change in some specific object; but the selection, combination and order of application are determined by feedback from the object itself. When the object is human, this intensive technology is regarded as "therapeutic" but the same technical logic is found also in the construction industry (Stinchcombe 1959) and in research where the objects of concern are human' (p.17).

With Thompson, it is a concentration of different techniques, whereas Stinchcombe distinguishes the *level* of technical skills as an important characteristic. The conceptual framework behind both descriptions is very different. Thompson goes on to specify:

'The intensive technology is a custom technology. Its successful employ-ment rests in part on the availability of all capacities potentially needed, but equally on the appropriate custom combination of selected capacities required in the individual case or project.'

Here too we find the obfuscating mixture of characteristics; the concentration on the organizational solution and the custom nature of the problem. Furthermore it is difficult to link this with his original definition of technical rationality.

(2) In the structural definitions we find a clear reflection of the three types of technology.

> 'The major components of a complex organization are determined by the design of that organization. Invariably these major components are further segmented, or departmentalized, and connections are established within and between departments. It is this internal differentiation and patterning of relationships that we will refer to as *structure*'.

Both the long-linked and intensive technology describe this internal differentiation and patterning of relationships. Thus it is extremely probable that with the use of these definitions structure and technology are closely related. Thompson explains this in the following manner; '. . . structure is a fundamental vehicle by which organizations achieve bounded rationality (Simon 1957). By delimiting responsibilities, control over resources, and other matters, organizations provide their participating members with boundaries within which efficiency may be a reasonable expectation. But if structure affords numerous spheres of bounded rationality, it must also facilitate the coordinated action of those interdependent elements' (p.54). Along these lines, the long-linked technology is, strictly speaking, a structural choice that has been made.

Another point worth thinking about is the analytical weakness that becomes evident in '. . . connections are established within and between departments' (p.51). This conceals the distinction between different levels which is so important to the concept of structure. Structure is the pattern or form of the possible relations at *one* level.

The division of labour is the medium by which bounded rationality can be achieved. Through this division, the units become interdependent. According to Thompson there are three types of interdependence which he describes as follows; '. . . all organizations have pooled interdependence, more complicated organizations have sequential as well as pooled; and the most complicated have reciprocal, sequential and pooled.' This rather seems like a description of organizational complexity where the types of interdependence are used as indicators. He goes on to add that in the same sequence the difficulty in coordinating grows and that different techniques become appropriate. 'With pooled interdependence coordination by standardization is appropriate; with sequential interdependence coordination by plan is appropriate, and with reciprocal interdependence, coordination by mutual adjustment is called for.' This makes for the conclusion that the three types of coordination are also 'nested'. The appropriateness of the mode of coordination is derived from the minimalization of the costs of coordination.

(3) Because of the tremendous overlap of the concepts presented it is not strange that Thompson does *not* go on to describe the relations between technology and structure. In the line of the total study it is unclear why he introduces his technology types at all. As the study evolves, the term technology takes on a quite different meaning, closer to technique or accepted programs and procedures.

(4) Thompson places a much stronger emphasis on the relation between *structural* and *environmental* variables. He indicates superficially that there are many kinds of environmental constraints such as those on finances, raw materials, energy, personnel, etc., and that there is a principle difference between 'environmental constraints located in the *geographic sense* or in the *social composition. . .*'

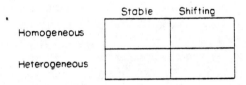

Figure 3.2   Thompson's environmental variables

The first are measured in transport or communication costs. For the second he presents, without clear motivation, a two dimensional representation of the environment (see Figure 3.2) based on Dill's (1958) study. With light-hearted opportunism, he defends this choice, using the following statement: 'There are undoubtedly other dimensions of task environments which have a bearing on organizational structure but these two appear at this moment to be quite crucial.' The difference between a homogeneous and a heterogeneous environment is not described but only illustrated by an example from Dill's study. The grave difficulties behind this distinction will be discussed in my own attempt to define environmental variables. Slowly but surely, Thompson introduces the concept of complexity without trying to define it, nor relating it to the previously employed typologies. This is a pity as it plays such an important role in many of his propositions.

In spite of his rather careless use of concepts but partly because of his semi-systematic presentation, he succeeds in presenting a highly acceptable theory of organized behaviour. It does not have the methodological coherence that one would expect from the manner of presentation.

Finally, again, related to the methodological points, for comparison:

(A) The work is applicable to a great variety of organizations.

(B) Apart from the *semi-systematic* manner of presentation using *propositions*, there is no real formalization. This makes it extremely difficult to find out if the propositions are internally consistent.

(1a) He does not define his theoretical domain, which in this case is not too important because his theory is of a *very general* nature.

(1b) A means of explanation, on the basis of bounded rationality, is employed but not explained.

(1c) The variables could possibly be used for parts of organizations.

(1d) Dimensions of variables are not mentioned nor can they be deduced from the given description of the variables.

(1e) Not applicable.

(2) The environment is an active influence on organized behaviour.

PERROW

The reviews get longer as the authors become more important to the development of the theory that is to be presented. It is for this reason that Perrow's (1967) *Framework for Analysis* is discussed at such length. Of all the studies in this field it comes closest to a theory of organizations as envisaged. The study is highly original and has formed the basis of many further developments.

> (1) 'Technology, or the work done in organizations, is considered the defining characteristic of organizations. That is, organizations are seen primarily as systems for getting work done, for applying techniques to the problem of altering raw materials—whether the materials be people, symbols or things. This is in contrast to other perspectives which see organizations as, for example, cooperative systems, institutions or decision making systems.
>
> Second, this perspective treats technology as an independent variable, and structure—the arrangement among people for getting work done—as a dependent variable' (p.195).

In this quotation we find the essence of the whole theory, including crude definitions of the variables. However, Perrow immediately weakens his point by stating, 'What is held to be an independent and dependent variable when one abstracts general variables from a highly interdependent and complex system is less of an assertion about reality than a strategy of analysis' (p.195). This seems rather an easy way out of the dilemma of making a choice of variables and their *mutual* relations. All the more, because the manner of analysis influences the perception and representation of reality. Here too, a lack of attention to the very fundamental problems of organization analysis becomes evident.

'By technology is meant the actions that an individual performs upon an object with or without the aid of tools or mechanical devices, in order to make some change in that object' (p.195). According to Perrow this definition facilitates the conceptualization of organizations as a whole instead of dealing only with specific processes or parts. It does make the description of all parts of processes possible. The internal heterogeneity of organizations as a whole makes it improbable that they can be caught in *one* type.

An interesting distinction in the definition is that between the raw material and the actions that the individual performs. This distinction is, sorry to say, not pursued further. It could be important because it indicates that certain actions are not appropriate for the change of certain materials. This can be translated to Thompson's cause–effect relationships. These can be learned through acquiring knowledge of the material form which one can deduce the possibilities for change, or one must have experience in these processes of change which is the result of a history of trial and error. This can be illustrated by the hardening of steel, originally mainly for swords. The ancient Egyptians understood the art of making swords. They knew that when steel was heated and then suddenly quenched this *could* result in a much harder material, making it possible to give it a sharper edge which also stayed sharp longer. However, there were a lot of unpleasant side-effects. Usually the steel became so brittle that the sword broke. The ability to make good swords was often attributed to magical powers, powers also attributed to the swords themselves, as can be deduced from legends. Even though the hardening process was used by the ancient Egyptians it took until the end of the nineteenth century to understand upon what physical phenomena the process was based.

Technology is concerned with the solution of problems in the widest sense. A specific manner of solving problems is called a technique or a programme. Such a technique can be arrived at without understanding the problem but through trial and error. Perrow states that there are two aspects important for solving problems:

(a) the number of exceptional cases encountered in the work, that is the degree to which stimuli are perceived as familiar or unfamiliar;

(b) the nature of the search process that is undertaken by the individual when exceptions occur.

This distinction is, as was also the case with Thompson, based on the *problem-solving* approach of March and Simon (1958, p.138) using the idea that 'choice is always exercised with respect to a limited, approximate, simplified "model" of the real situation'. According to March and Simon 'activity can usually be traced back to an environmental stimulus of some sort, e.g. a customer order or a firegong.' They distinguish routinized responses to these stimuli as opposed to 'problem solving activity toward finding performance activities with which to complete the response.'

The dimension of the number of exceptions is thus only based on the familiarity of the problem and is independent of the nature of the problem. It seems logical to think that an extremely complex problem is more readily perceived as unfamiliar than a simple problem. This is a moot point.

The second categorization, the nature of the search process, implies that certain types of search processes fit certain types of problems. It is also imaginable that certain individuals are predisposed to use certain types of search processes. Furthermore, it is doubtful if search processes are always exceptional, as Perrow states. It may very well be possible that an algorithm exists for the solution of a problem but that the execution of that algorithm itself is not easy. This may be illustrated by the fact that with the introduction of the computer many search programs have been developed. Many problems have become accessible to the computer although they remain unexecutable for the individual. We will return to this distinction later.

Perrow distinguishes two types of search process:

(i) A search process which can be conducted on a logical analytical bases.

(ii) A search process 'that occurs when the problem is so vague and poorly conceptualized as to make it virtually unanalysable. In this case, no "formal" search is undertaken, but instead one draws upon the residue of unanalysed experience or intuition or relies upon chance and guesswork' (p.196).

In this distinction it is interesting to note that in the first case there is no characterization of the problem, whereas in the second case the nature of the problem is the origin of the type of search process. If one turns the second description around, the search process can only be conducted on a logical, analytical basis when the problem is clear and well conceptualized. It is questionable whether it can then be unfamiliar! As was indicated previously, the search process depends on both the *searcher* and the *problem* or rather on the knowledge or the insight of the searcher of or into the problem and his inclination to employ certain types of search behaviour. This is the line taken in the theory that is to be presented.

As said, Perrow states that search processes are always exceptional, making this category difficult to combine with the number of exceptions that occur. Because of this, the distinction between the types of problems with which an organization is confronted and the manner in which solutions are found is obsured. Neither is this clarified by his description of the raw material variable.

'Techniques are performed on raw materials. The state of the art of analysing the characteristics of raw materials is likely to determine what kind of technology will be used . . . To understand the nature of the material means to be able to control it better and achieve more predictability and efficiency in transformation' (p.196).

The other characteristic of the raw material, besides the *understandability* of its nature, is its *stability* and *variability*, i.e. whether the material can be treated in standardized fashion or whether it needs continual adjustment.

The first distinction has a stronger relation to the manner in which the problem is solved than with the nature of the material. It seems unlikely that the 'state of the art of analysing raw materials' will be highly developed when the raw materials confront one with 'unanalysable problems'.

The second distinction is internally contradictory because it is quite possible that a material is highly variable but that the nature of the variation is so well understood that it can be treated in a standardized fashion. For example, the variability of raw material input in an oil refinery which is constantly monitored and reacted upon within the refinery process, or for instance the variability in demand in electrical power networks.

Perrow represents these two variables in two figures reproduced here as Figures 3.3 and 3.4.

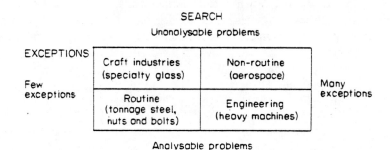

Figure 3.3   Perrow's technology variables

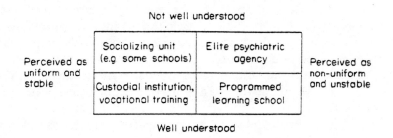

Figure 3.4   Perrow's raw material variable

(2) Perrow does not define structure more closely than in the statement at the beginning of this review. He does describe its two dimensions: control and coordination.

(a) 'Control itself can be broken up into two components. They are the degree of discretion an individual or group possess in carrying out its tasks, and the power of an individual or group to mobilize scarce resources and to control definitions of various situations, such as the definition of the nature of the raw material . . . discretion involves judgements about whether close supervision is required on one task or another, about changing programs and about the interdependence of one's task with other tasks . . . power affects outcomes directly because it involves choices regarding basic goals and strategies. Discretion relates to choices among means and judgements of the critical and interdependent nature of tasks.

The consequence of decisions in the case of discretion have no direct influence on goals and strategies' (p.198).

These definitions do not combine into a clear picture of what control is and why it should be a basic variable for the analysis of organizations. The way in which the concept of power is defined is unconventional to say the least, and makes it incompatible with studies such as that of Hickson *et al.* (1971) for which Perrow's technology variables *do* have an important meaning. What is more, both power and discretion, as defined here, seem to be a consequence of the task structure rather than its dimensions.

(b) The second task-structural dimension is coordinated. It

'can be achieved through planning and feedback, to use the terms proposed by March and Simon (1958, p.160). Coordination by planning refers to the programmed interaction of tasks, which interaction is clearly defined by rules or by the very tools and machinery or the logic of the transformation process. Coordination by feedback, on the other hand, refers to negotiated alterations in the nature or sequence of tasks performed by two different units'.

March and Simon (1958, p.180) however use a much more cybernetic description. 'We may label coordination based on pre-established schedules *coordination by plan* and coordination that involves transformation of new information *coordination by feedback*.' Perrow confuses these definitions with their area of application. For feedback it is necessary that information is used that is generated by the activities that are to be coordinated.

Whereas until this point the presentation of variables is relatively clear, Perrow now complicates the model unnecessarily by applying the four task structural dimensions — power, discretion, coordination within and interdependence between groups — to three organizational areas. The classification which he devises seems to follow logically from the division into four types of both the technology and material variables which he combines without further ado.

As a last structural variable Perrow schematically describes the bases for non-task-related interactions which he transforms into a social structural variable.

(3) The main criticism of Perrow's article is the lack of distinction between his variables and their mutual interdependence. This may take the form of an overlap or, more probably, that each variable is a collection of interrelated though not in principle distinct concepts. However, this criticism mainly concerns the definition of the concepts. The structure of the framework itself and the ideas behind it are by far the most inspiring I have found anywhere. Furthermore he clearly indicates in which direction to look for possible solutions when he states:

'. . . it says that structure and goals must adjust to technology or the organization will be subject to strong strains. For a radical change in goals to be a successful one, it may require a change in technology, and thus in structure, or else there will be a large price paid for the lack of fit between these variables.'

He indicates a causal relation rather than one of mutual interdependence. The price that is to be paid for the lack of fit between these variables is the very point to which this study is directed.

Finally, related to the methodological points it may be said:

(A) The domain can be said to be universal.

(B) There is little or no formalization.

(1a) The domain of the theory is defined quite clearly by the (general) definition of organizations that is supplied.

(1b) No means of explanation is made explicit.

(1c) The variables can be used at all levels of an organization.

(1d) The dimensions of the variables are explained.

(1e) It is unclear if the dimensions described by Perrow are dimensions in the sense as described in Chapter 2.

(2) The environmental influences are neglected but could be translated to the variables employed.

LAWRENCE AND LORSCH

Lawrence and Lorsch (1967) have a more ambitious objective than the previous authors. They seek to answer the question: 'What kind of organization does it take to deal with different environmental conditions?' (1967, II, p.3) Instead of using technology as the independent variable they use sub-environmental uncertainty as perceived by different members of the organization's management team. The total uncertainty score they use, is the sum of three individual scores they have devised:

clarity of information;

uncertainty of cause and effect relationships;

the timespan of definitive feedback.

The definition of uncertainty used in conceptualizing the characteristics of different subenvironments is not altogether clear. In another publication (1967, II, p.7) they mention the rate of change of conditions over time in the subenvironment, instead of the uncertainty of cause and effect relationships. As internal variables they use differentiation and integration, of which they give the following description:

(a) *differentiation* is the state of segmentation of organizational subsystems, each of which tend to develop particular attributes in relation to the environment. Differentiation, as Lawrence and Lorsch use it, includes behavioural attributes of members of organizational subsystems. This represents a break with the classical definition of the term regarding the division of labour. The term is used more in the sense of *differences* between departments when comparing them. Lawrence and Lorsch have identified 'three specific dimensions of the differences in ways of thinking and working that develop among managers in these several functional units.' To this they add a fourth dimension, the formality of structure. They describe the first three dimensions as follows:

—*orientation towards particular goals*: to what extent are managers in different units concerned with different objectives (e.g. sales managers with sales volume and production managers with low manufacturing costs)?
—*time orientation*: do different managers deal with more or less immediate problems (e.g. production engineers with more immediate problems than design engineers who deal with longer-range questions)?
—*interpersonal orientation*: in other words an orientation either towards task accomplishment or towards social relationships; the difference between getting the job done in dealings with others and paying attention to maintaining relationships with peers.

As said, the fourth dimension is the *formality of structure* which concerns formal reporting relationships, criteria for rewards and different control procedures. They summarize their concept of differentiation as follows:

'. . . when we refer to differentiation among units we will mean differences in orientation and in the formality of structure. While these four dimensions are not all-inclusive and homogeneous, they do provide us with shorthand measures of differentiation as we define it in this study — *the difference in cognitive and emotional orientation among managers in different functional departments*. When we describe pairs of units of organizations as having more or less differentiation, we will be referring to whether the managers in the various units are quite different (more differentiation) in these four attributes or whether they are relatively similar (less differentiation).'

Differentiation seems to be the opposite of homogeneity where it concerns different subunits. Intra-departmental homogeneity then seems to be taken for granted.

(b) *Integration* is the process of achieving unity of effort among the various subsystems in the accomplishment of the organization's task, or 'the quality of the state of collaboration that exists among departments that are required to achieve unity of effort by the demands of the environment' (1967 II, p.11). *Task* is defined as a complete input–transformation–output, cycle involving at least the design, production and distribution of some goods or services.

Lawrence and Lorsch (1967, II, 47) predicted 'an inverse relation between the degree of differentiation between any two departments in a single organization and the quality of the integration between them' and they found this to be true. Later they give a slightly different interpretation of the relation between integration and differentiation. '. . . it does suggest that the inverse relation between differentiation and integration may not be a straight line. Instead it may be curvilinear, with both high and low differentiation being associated with poor integration. High differentiation leads to problems of communication between units and makes integration difficult to achieve. Extremely low differentiation means the units have begun to deal with the same part of the environment and are basically in competition' (1969, p.32, footnote 6). This statement is based on only one observation and it is dangerous to generalize on such evidence, as Lawrence and Lorsch state themselves. Furthermore differentiation does not seem the same concept as was originally defined. Here we are concerned with 'low differentiation means the units have begun to deal with the same part of the environment . . .' and not that there is but a small difference in orientation of its members and that there is a slight difference in their formal structure.

Differentiation was seen as an independent variable, initially leading to this straightforward inverse relation with integration and eventually to a rather more complicated curvilinear relation. However in the footnote an interesting opening has been created, to view these relationships in a more relevant perspective. Between differentiation and integration there seem to be *intervening variables : communication* when differentiation is high and *coordination* when differentiation is low. This line of thought is central to the theory that is to be developed in this study. It may be seen as a further development of the initiatives as displayed in the studies of Lawrence and Lorsch.

Finally, related to the methodological points, it may be said that:

(A) Lawrence and Lorsch do not treat the domain as being universal.

(B) There is no formalization.

(1a) The domain of the theory is not defined, only general descriptions are given.

(1b) No means of explanation is made explicit.

(1c) The variables are used at different levels of the organization simultaneously. This happens because an awkward definiton of differentiation has been chosen.

(1d) The dimensions of the variables are described more in the sense of indicators than in the sense of theoretical definitions.

(1e) It is unclear if the dimensions described by Lawrence and Lorsch can be compared to the dimensions described in Chapter 2.

(2) The environmental influences form an integral part of their 'theory', but are difficult to analyse independently of the organization's activities.

OTHERS

Khandwalla (1977) further develops the ideas presented by Lawrence and Lorsch. Apart from the link between differentiation and integration, there is an indication of an intervening variable; the profitability of the firm. This is in line with Woodward's original study. Khandwalla (1977, p.583) notes: 'There is substantial evidence . . . that suggests that structural variables *in association with* situational variables affect the performance of the organization.' He considers three categories of organizational (structural) variables:

(1) Uncertainty reduction variables, i.e. 'vertical integration, and staff market intelligence and uncertainty absorption services like R & D, use of electronic data processing, long term forcasting and planning, etc.'

(2) Differentiation variables, i.e. 'decentralization of authority by the chief executive, divisionalization and functional departmentalization.'

(3) Integration or coordination variables; i.e. 'participative or team decision making of the top levels of management, and the extent of use of sophisticated management controls.'

The situational variable is represented as technoeconomic uncertainty and operationalized as perceived competition and technological change. Khandwalla hypothesizes that 'the greater this uncertainty—that is, the broader the range of issues about which the organization's decisionmakers experience uncertainty—the more use the organization will make of uncertainty reduction devices. Once the key areas of uncertainty are identified, the organization will get differentiated to respond more appropriately to each area of uncertainty. To keep its activities coordinated, the differentiated organization will invest considerable resources in integration activities. Thus, the greater the technoeconomic uncertainty, the greater the use of all uncertainty reduction, differentiation, and integration devices.' The key findings relating to the three structural variables and the technoeconomic uncertainty to performance were the following:

(1) None of the individual organizational variables was associated with profitability.

(2) 'The degree of *covariation* between the three classes of variables was a predictor to profitability . . . Thus, a certain specific pattern of relationships between elements of organizational structure, not the individual elements of structure, was a predictor of performance.'

(3) For the relatively highly profitable firms the two measures of techno-economic uncertainty had substantially higher positive correlations with the three structural variables. This implies

'that in technoeconomic environments high in uncertainty, it is necessary for the organization to employ uncertainty reduction, differentiation and integration mechanisms to a considerable extent. On the other hand, in technoeconomic environments low in uncertainty, it is better for the organization to avoid any significant use of these' (p.590)

These findings seem straight forward. It should be clear that the term differentiation as Khandwalla uses it is different from the manner in which

Lawrence and Lorsch use it; it comes much closer to the way it is usually used, i.e. the number of departments into which an organization is divided. Due to this difference in concepts the two studies are difficult to compare.

Khandwalla is mentioned here because he is one of the few who presents a model with a clear intervening variable.

Harvey (1968) defines his technology variable as a continuum from 'technical diffuseness to technical specificity.' This is derived from the number of product modifications that have occurred in the last ten years. For the structure he uses a description of 'properties essentially internal to the organization' which are mainly concerned with the decision taking process in the organization. He defines the following aspects:

(1) Subunit specialization: the degree to which groups of individuals within the organization are charged with a formally defined set of responsibility.
(2) Levels of authority within the organization.
(3) Rates of managerial supervisors to total personnel.
(4) Programme specification. Programmes are defined as the mechanisms or rules in terms of which an attempt is made to give direction to organizational activity. There are three major areas of organizational programming:
(i) *Role programming*. The formalization of duties and responsibilities as in sets of job specifications.
(ii) *Output programming*. The formal delineation of steps through which material pass in the course of becoming outputs.
(iii) *Communication programming*. The formal specification of the structure, content and timing of communication within the organization.

If the organization scores high in all three dimensions Harvey calls it 'mechanistic' and if it scores low 'organistic', According to Harvey the degree of innovation and the nature of the structure of the organization are related, thereby confirming the results of the earlier study by Burns and Stalker (1961). They pose the question of whether the rate of innovation may be changed by changing the structure to a more 'organistic' one. They give a positive answer.

Shull et al. (1970) have also presented a very interesting study covering nearly the same domain as mine. Because their efforts are directed at the departmental level, they escape from the dilemma of organizational homogeneity and facilitate the analysis of interdepartmental differences. This study will not be discussed further because it does not present a new view on concepts that are used. Also it will be referred to further on in the study. In a footnote V. A. Thompson makes the following remark regarding their model: 'It is not completely clear whether you are describing or prescribing. Have we really evolved beyond bureaucracy? Not for most people. However interesting movements are occurring.'

A last important set of contributions to the structural analysis of organizations can be found in the research on the relation between the organization's size and its structure. Kimberly (1976, p.581) succulently describes the opportunism of many researchers in this field. Certainly the theoretical framework that can explain the relationships sought is blatantly absent and gravely complicates the problem of defining the variables. One of the main problems is that of definitional dependence. That is when one of the independent variables in an equation is also a component of the dependent variable. In the way many indicators for organizational size have been designed, this may very well be the case. Kimberley (p.586) concludes 'that the concept of size as it has been generally used by organizational researchers is too global to permit precise determination of its importance to structure.'

SUMMARY

Summarizing it may be said that:

(1) There is a tremendous amount of literature and empirical research available on the relation between technology and structure.

(2) The authors do not present formalized theories of organizations.

(3) The definitions of variables are methodologically problematical. Stanfield (1976, p.489) remarks on the confusion about technological variables. There are two factors which blur the distinction between variables:

(a) The generalization of the findings of one's study by drawing conclusions about variables not measured.

(b) The failure to set boundaries between categories.

Both of them result from unrationalized categorization of variables, which is the practice of providing no substantial, explicit explanation of one's conceptual groupings and separations, as if the system of categories had consensual validity. Therefore homogeneous categories are assumed, which is evidently not the case where both the technological and structural variables in most studies are aggregates of variables. What may even be more important is that the dimensions of technology and structure tend to overlap each other, greatly diminishing the meaning of hypothesized relations.

(4) Most assessments of technology and structure rest on the implicit assumption of homogeneity, uniformity across and within departments.

(5) There are indications that there are intervening variables that go unmentioned in the hypothesized relations.

(6) The theories do not illustrate what phenomena influence the process of change within the organization. They only present a static interpretation of structural variables. Thompson *does* define that *under norms of rationality* organizations try to minimize certain influences and consequences of organizational activity, but these are hardly related to his definitions of technology.

(7) Little or no attention is paid to the methodological criteria for scientific statements. Apart from criteria on the appropriateness of using certain statistical methods, little or no attention is paid to the *form* of the material or its presentation.

Chapter 4

Towards a Theory of Organizational Dissonance

INTRODUCTION

The previous chapter presented a critical review of authors who wrote about the relation between the nature of the work done in an organization and its structure. The problems in the colour TV tube factory, described in the first chapter, seemed to be of a structural nature. It was for that reason that an attempt was initially made to find out what solutions were presented in the literature on this subject. That was much too heavy a demand to make on the theories that were presented. Therefore, the next possibility was to find out which authors presented a framework for analysing the problems that could be recognized within the organization. It seemed that the technology employed by the organization was an important aspect that should be taken into account. It is for this reason that the relation between technology and structure is further examined.

In order to comply with the requirements that were formulated, attention must first be paid to the intended domain of the theory and to the variables and the dimensions in which they are to be expressed. This leads us to consider how structural complexity can be represented in a consistent manner.

The mode of representation that has been chosen is then applied to the variables of the structural aspects of organizations. This is done by formulating a theory of organizational dissonance.

To begin with, technology as it is treated in the literature on organizations will be reviewed.

Technological Inhomogeneity

If we look at the organizational settings that were described in the first chapter, the two technologies, seen as a whole, were not very different. The colour TV tube factory was a mass production organization. The lighting fixture plant was somewhere between a mass production and a large batch production organization.

If we look at the second case more closely, we see that we are not only concerned with the lighting fixtures plant, but also with the automation

56

department. We are concerned with two organizations employing quite different technologies. The automation department cannot even be characterized using the typologies of some of the authors as described in the previous chapter. The problems of contact between organizations, i.e. *interorganizational* problems, fall completely outside the scope of those studies.

Even if we restrict ourselves to the colour TV tube factory, we are confronted with different departments—the production department, the engineering department, the product development department and the sales department—each employing quite different technologies. This leads us to the conclusion that organizations do not employ a homogeneous technology, as is often implied. Studies such as those of Bell (1967), Grimes and Klein (1973), Hrebiniak (1974), Van de Ven *et al.* (1976), Hall (1962) and Mohr (1971) assume that organizations are composed of different subunits with different types of technologies. They do not use the difference of technology between departments to describe their relations, nor as the origin of conflicts between departments. These *intraorganizational* or *interdepartmental* conflicts were the main motive for my original study.

The difference in technology between departments is often based on characteristics of tasks performed by individuals. This might lead to the conclusion that because all the tasks performed within a department are not of the same nature, the technology of that department is not homogeneous either. If a difference in technology influences the relations between the units employing those technologies it seems likely that we will be confronted with *intradepartmental* problems based on this difference.

The theory as presented in this chapter does not assume homogeneity at any level. Even the tasks of individuals are not necessarily homogeneous.

The distinction as presented between interorganizational, interdepartmental, and intradepartmental problems leads to the conclusion that a *hierarchy* of analysis is necessary. This hierarchy needs to be structured in the opposite direction to that presented above: from specific problems via individual tasks consisting of solving a variety of possibly inhomogeneous problems, via groups, subdepartments, divisions to whole organizations. Depending on the direction we look in we can discern two orientations. The first, looking up from the individual towards institutional structures one might call bottom-up or *anascopic* (Zijderveld, 1973, p.188). The second, looking down towards the individual, top-down or *katascopic*.

Organizational Harmony

Whilst looking for an analytical framework for describing the problems I was confronted with, I realized that another basic assumption was made by most authors—an assumption that seemed inappropriate to the problems as they presented themselves.

The approach of the authors that were presented in Chapter 3 can be summarized as follows: In trying to understand why organizations operate in the way they do and why they are more or less effective, the central themes are that organizations have certain goals and that they use specific technologies to achieve these goals. The authors presuppose a consensus within the organization on the objectives of the organization, and a harmonious form of collaboration to achieve these objectives. In that perspective it could be said that it is a logical consequence that structure follows technology — to paraphrase Chandler.

If we see what happens in reality, this seems to be only part of the picture. Organizations certainly have such objectives as putting certain types of goods on the market or supplying certain kinds of services. But this is not achieved only by harmonious collaboration. In reality we are confronted, at best, with coalitions within the organization, each coalition having its own objective which may very well be in conflict with the assumed overall objective of the organization. We are confronted with both *collaboration* and *conflict*. A theory of organizations should at least be able to describe them both. It would be even better if it could explain how they come about or can be influenced.

Theories and Practical Application

In order to clarify the foundations of the theory from the point of view of its development in time it is appropriate to show how what the authors had to say fitted into the problems as we saw them in the first chapter.

Woodward's typology, concerned with mass production, large batch production, etc. applies only to industrial production organizations as a whole. It sheds no light on intraorganizational problems. As we saw earlier in this chapter, both the TV tube and the lighting fixtures plants fell in the same integral category of mass and large batch production. However, the nature of the products and the stability of the demand were totally different, as well as the nature of the production process. As was said in Chapter 3, the possibility of production organizations belonging to a much larger conglomeration has a strong influence on the structure of the organization. This could be seen clearly in the two organizations. The TV tube plant was to a large part independent of its technical environment, whereas the lighting fixtures plant was but a small unit in a much larger division. As for the automation department in the second case, Woodward's theory gave no foothold whatsoever.

The Aston Group's theoretical approach at least supplied a framework of concepts or dimensions which one could use for describing the structure of the organizations or the different parts. Their hypothesized relation between technology and structure gave little help.

Thompson, with his emphasis on the minimization of coordination costs, certainly directed the attention to the interfaces between the different units of the organization. The analytical approach to technology, however, partly because of its internal inconsistency, was of little help.

Perrow's approach turned out to be valuable. His technological typology, based on the nature of the problems that were solved within a unit, could be applied at all levels. Furthermore it supplied a basis for remedies to specific problems. Using his theory one could try to come to a design of more fitting structures for the different departments. Using this approach one could imagine that the tensions *within* each department would ease off. What the consequences would be for the relations *between* departments remains unclear.

Lawrence and Lorsch's ideas on integration might provide indications for solutions to some of the interdepartmental problems. They describe a number of integrative devices that might be applicable. For instance

> 'a special department, one whose primary activities was integration of effort among the basic functional units. In addition, this organization had an elaborate set of permanent integrating teams, each made up of members from functional units and the integrating department. The purpose of these teams was to provide a formal setting in which inter-departmental conflicts could be solved and decisions reached' (1967, p.137–8).

At least Lawrence and Lorsch clearly referred to intraorganizational conflicts.

Shull et al. proposed solutions which might well be practicable by providing four ideal types of structure or rather strategies. For the analysis and the explanation of the existing situation they were difficult to use.

None of these theories supply the concepts that could aptly describe the situations that were found, partly because of their basic assumptions on homogeneity and harmony.

In this chapter an attempt will be made to supply the theoretical framework that can describe and explain these problems and they may form the foundation for possible solutions.

Conflict and Collaboration

Stated bluntly, most organizations are rife with minor and sometimes even major internal conflicts of one sort or another. Tensions abound between the commercial departments and the production departments of most firms, between product developers and the production department, between the production department and the engineering group and between the engineering group and the product developers. And last but not least between book-keepers and everybody else. Exaggerated though this might seem, there is almost certainly a degree of tension at some time between any two individuals or groups. Still, organizations work. They build and sell cars, they treat patients, they pass laws and they commit organized crimes. Persons or groups who are performing a task not only set demands on themselves, but also on their direct environment just as the environment sets demands on them. But also within groups tensions abound as well as between individuals and other groups. It is the object of this study to give a plausible explanation of the origin of *some* of these tensions or conflicts, and a description of where they might be productive and where they become disruptive.

Organization

After formulating requirements for acceptable theories in Chapter 2 it is wise to fulfil them. The first of these requirements is the description of the domain of the theory. As the objective is to formulate a *general* theory it will not be necessary to describe the type of organizations, but it is necessary to specify the concept of organization itself. Such a description can be seen as a purely arbitrary statement, as long as it is used consistently, it is not empty and it is discriminatory. However, a specification can also be more or less *expedient*. The considerations of expediency are subtle and cannot be seen independently of the use to which the specification is to be put.

A description of the domain of intended application of a theory is important, for it can restrict inappropriate generalizations. In the theories that were presented in Chapter 3 much is taken for granted as to the consensus of the domain. Implicitly organizational specializations have been assumed which restrict the application of the theories and make application to other types of organizations inappropriate. For instance, the domain of Woodward's theory is restricted to industrial profit-oriented organizations, the Aston group does not present clear restrictions, but it is hard to imagine that the whole set of their analytical dimensions applies to a mental hospital.

It may also be possible that the domain of a theory is the consequence of that theory itself. The clarity of the presented theories makes such a distinction difficult.

Because the ulterior objective of this study is a *formalized* theory of organizations, the description will be as explicit as possible. Most intuitions of what an organization is, are incorporated in the following description of the intended domain of application.

An organization is seen as, at least, a set of individuals who, by coordination of their individual behaviour and effort try to reach a joint result or common objective.

For the theory that is to be presented the intended application should include any *set of individuals who attempt to solve coordination problems by agreeing to certain conventions*. In the widest possible meaning, such a set could consist of the users of a common language in a dialectical region or in a biological sense of a flight of starlings, or in a more recognizable form, of four missionaries in a canoe.

Conventions are the Essence of Organizations

Next, within the previous description, an organization can be seen as a result of an explicit organizing activity. In order to show that there is some order in the different meanings of the term organization a further analysis is appropriate. The Webster *Dictionary* (1966, p.1580) defines the verb to *organize* in the following manner:

'(1) To put into a state of order: to arrange in an orderly manner;

(2) To arrange elements into a whole of interdependent parts;
(a) to arrange or constitute into a coherent unity in which each part has a special function or relation; (b) to unify into a coordinated functioning whole;

(3) To arrange by systematic planning and coordination of individual effort;

(4) To set up an administrative and functional structure.'

Order and Organization

The first definition implies that there must be a *standard* by which 'ordering' is feasible. All those things that are to be ordered must have recognizable properties that can be related to each other such that ordering is possible. In principle, ordering can only be done by means of one characteristic at a time. The definition of the characteristic that must be ordered is often hard to give, as can be concluded from the studies reviewed in the previous chapter. To be able to order or rank things in a linear manner, values must be attributed to the ordering characteristic. These values must meet the following requirements:

$$\text{if } a < b \text{ and } c < c, \text{ then } a < c.$$

If this is not the case, but

$$\text{if } a < b \text{ and } b < c \text{ and } a > c,$$

then these three elements cannot be ordered or ranked.

The ordering characteristic may itself be a *specified combination* of other subcharacteristics, but their mutual relation must be defined in such a manner that they can be used operationally as one.

Objects may also be ordered by specifying their relative position in, for instance, a circular fashion. A walks behind B, B walks behind C, C walks behind D, and D walks behind A. When this form of ordering is combined with a ranking according to length, supposing that

$$L_A > L_B > L_C > L_D,$$

then we see that the two types of ordering show an inconsistency at the point where A and D meet.

The next description speaks of interdependence, i.e. certain relations exist between different parts. There are more or less appropriate positions for the parts to be in. This is narrowed down further to functional requirements.

In the third description individual effort is mentioned, and the last definition the creation of an *organization* in the sense as it is used in theories of organization is first presented. In the light of the previous definitions the character of such an organization would be functional.

Analysis, Systems and Elements

Before we go on to describe or define organizations further it is appropriate to pay attention to the analytical vocabulary used here. In what is often referred to as systems theory, it is not unusual to define a system as a collection of elements that are related to each other. This does not clarify much as long as we have no idea of what an element is. An element is by definition the basic unit of analysis. The external characteristics of an element can be interpreted as the relations the element *can* have with its environment. What occurs *within* this unit of analysis should *by definition be excluded*. When one accepts the method of stratified analysis, one must be very conscious of the level of analysis one is working on.

The use of the concept of element makes a stratified approach necessary. The strata are defined by the inclusiveness of the definition of its elements, as described on p.26. Thus in the case of analysing an organization at the most basic level, the individual is taken as the elementary unit, thus excluding his psychological motives.

This does not mean to say that individual psychological variables are not taken into account—on the contrary. They are, however, only to be expressed as possible characteristics of the interaction between individuals, instead of the result of interior mechanisms which are on another level of analysis. If these interior mechanisms or motives were taken into account then one would unwittingly shift the level of analysis to a more elementary or basic level, inferring new more basic variables that have not yet been specified.

It is also possible to use a group or department as a unit of analysis when we are concerned with interdepartmental conflicts, thus excluding individual behaviour and interaction within the group or the department.

The distinction between different levels of analysis is extremely important; it is so easy to make casual remarks concerning different levels, thereby mixing them up.

The Two Main Aspects of Organization

The definition of organization on p.60 mentions individual *behaviour* and *effort*. They are indicators towards its dual nature, as will be described in this theory. Furthermore an organization was specified as having a function. This function can be described in the following manner.

Organizing is the attempt to find a rational solution to the problem of handling large and complex tasks.

From the point of view of this study, *the most important aspect of executing tasks is the solving of problems* that are inherent to the results that are to be achieved.

An organization distinguishes itself from other social groups by its purposeful or functional nature. This functional nature leads to the distinction of two independent aspects of organization(s), as mentioned before, as seen as a set of individuals.

The *first* is the nature of a social group. By a social group is meant a group of individuals having common traditions, institutions and collective activities and interests. A group is distinguishable by particular patterns of behaviour.

The *second* aspect is that of the purposeful, functional nature of some of their activities.

This distinction has on the whole been neglected in the literature on organization although it seems important for the following reasons:

(1) Different organizations place different emphasis on the two aspects, leading to a strong difference in organizational character. For instance, consider an organization of retired persons set up to organize communal trips abroad for its members. The objective of the organization is the establishment of mutual social relations between its members. Travel is one of the means to accomplish this. On the other hand one can imagine a travel agency specialized in organizing trips for elderly customers. Here the means have become ends. In the first example the functional organization is the means to attain the social ends. The classical examples of the human relations school of organization theorists specify that attention must be paid to the social setting in which the functional work is performed, turning the sequence around. The social organization is a means by which products can be produced more 'efficiently'. An assembly line for automobiles does not necessarily operate as a social group, but human relations advocates contend that it works better, more efficiently, if the 'social' group characteristics are enhanced.

(2) Within an organization the choice of the *forms* given to both the 'social' and the 'functional' organization may be conflicting. This will be the main subject of study.

Experience shows that the two aspects are not easily distinguishable. There is a wide penumbra of mutually interacting organizational attributes. This complicates the analysis of these two aspects. These attributes will prove to be the most interesting, because they can be in conflict with each other. In the classical theory of organizations, only the functional nature is taken into account. This rules out analysis of conflicts between the functional and the social aspects. In this theory they are essential. This type of conflict has been ignored or neglected and has certainly never been translated into quantifiable costs. Because the cost accounting is still the mainstay of the assessment of organizational efficiency, the neglect of this translation of these conflicts to recognizable costs has resulted in their neglect as variables on which one may base considerations of organizational design.

Organizational Aspects and Orientations

Parallel to this distinction of social and functional aspects, we find the distinction in level of analysis (see also p.26) from the individual via groups, etc., to the total environment. This results in the two analytical orientations as presented in Figure 4.1. Looking up from the individual to institutional structures one might call it *anascopic* (Zijderveld 1973, p.188) and downward towards the individual *katascopic*.

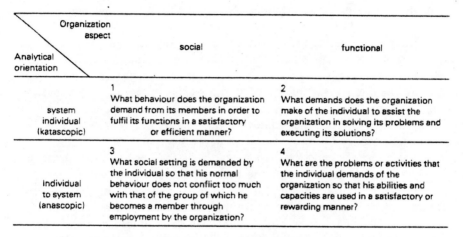

Figure 4.1   The analytical orientations and aspects of organization

To illustrate Figure 4.1 a number of examples will be given, one for each cell, numbered appropriately. It would have been more to the point if the examples referred to the two cases presented in the first chapter. It was too difficult to find striking and clear examples there, so others were chosen.

(1) Airlines, in their selection for cabin personnel, have often set clearly defined criteria as to comportment, language, dress and looks. In this case the criteria are based on possibly imagined demands of its client, giving these criteria a functional tint. We do see, however, that not only standards of effectiveness or efficiency of activities are demanded, but also social characteristics which lie outside the direct functional field. Another well-known example is that of executives who are judged very severely as to their behaviour in and outside the organization, or even physical characteristics (Gofman 1959, p.47). Demands may also be set on the characteristics of their wives, their cars, their social activities, etc. In those organizations or functions where the 'technical' demands for the capacities of the functionary are not

clear enough to set unequivocal selection criteria, social characteristics are also often used. This may be called the co-optation process. New members of a group are selected on the basis of the unlikelihood that they pose a threat to the 'culture' of the group.

(2) Organizations set demands on the abilities of their members, be it mentally or physically. If a member has to perform heavy manual labour, he must be strong. If a member has to perform tasks that require agility in the solution of complex quantitative problems, he must have the ability for it. These demands are often expressed by specifying the level and direction of formal education that is required.

· (3) An example that springs to mind is that of students who, in order to gain experience, must serve short apprenticeships at the base of an organization that employs members of their profession. They are confronted with social situations, among the shopfloor workers with whom they have to work temporarily, which are strange to them or at least quite different from those in their educational environment. They accept it, or have to accept it, because it is temporary. For long-lasting employment they would probably choose a social environment in which behaviour, language and interests are closer to their own.

(4) Not only will a person choose a social setting close to what he is used to or to which he aspires, but he will also want to exploit his own functional potential. On the whole it is unsatisfying to do work for a long time which is uninteresting because it does not make use of the abilities of the performer. A mechanical engineer will not, on the whole, find it satisfying to be lastingly employed as an automobile mechanic nor a qualified surgeon as a nurse.

Partial Inclusion at Different Levels ·

These four examples should only give an impression of the two aspects of an organization and the analytical orientation at one intersection between two levels; that is, the individual as a member of an organization. However, there are more levels as illustrated in Figure 4.2. The same kind of mutual influence can be discerned between the organization and its social environment (7, 8) and the individual and his social environment (5, 6). Society sets demands on the organization and the individual, as regards both behaviour and activities. If the individual is socially integrated he complies with these social demands and through this compliance is a transmitter of these 'societal' values to the organization.

That these mutual influences can have disrupting effects is poignantly illustrated by Naipaul (1976, p.10) when describing how Indian society can kill off the individual's use of his own abilities. He gives two examples. One is of a doctor in medicine, a Nobel prize winner who is invited back to India after having become famous in America, and because of the social environment (combined with his own personality, partly formed by that society) finds he cannot be what he has become. The second example is the following:

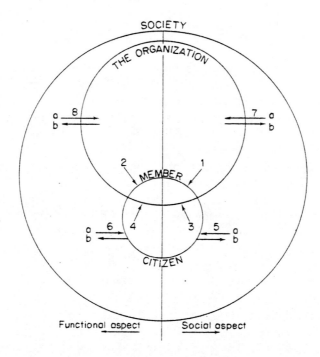

Figure 4.2   The individual as a member of an organization and as a citizen; the organization as a subsystem of a society

'A foreign businessman saw that his untouchable servant was intelligent, and decided to give the young man an education. He did so, and before he left the country he placed the man in a better job. Some years later the businessman returned to India. He found that his untouchable was a latrine cleaner again. He had been boycotted by his clan for breaking away from them; he was barred from the evening smoking group. There was no other groups he could join, no woman he could marry. His solitariness was unsupportable, and he had returned to his duty, his *dharma*, he had learned to obey.'

Granted, our society is much less stratified and social mobility is much greater. This makes it unlikely that we will find such striking examples in a western situation. However, a general theory of organizations must fit both a European situation and an Indian one. There may, of course, be a shift in emphasis of interrelated variables.

Society may also set demands on an organization, either directly or through other organizations (7 and 8). For instance, the rising level of education in western Europe has led to a prolific growth of the educated labour force. Workers are no longer satisfied with performing menial unskilled tasks that do not utilize their capacities. This has not only led to a shortage of unskilled labour necessitating the importation of foreign workers (inverted colonialism), it has also set off a systematic demand from 'society' for a change in industry towards a high knowledge and skill content in jobs. Thus when the higher demands of the individual cannot be met, he may prefer to stay unemployed. There is even a clause in the Dutch unemployment law concerning 'fitting labour'. When this becomes prevalent, society at large demands changes in the functional structure of organizations, partly because it becomes necessary to do so from an economic point of view.

Authority Outside and Inside the Organization

By the term 'social structure' we commonly understand the internal institutionalized relationships built up by persons living within a group, especially with regard to the hierarchical organization of statutes and rules and principles regulating behaviour. We can see in western societies that a change has taken place in the acceptance of authoritarian relationships. This is not the place to analyse to what this can be attributed, but hopefully it can be agreed upon that it is true (evidence to the contrary may be found in *Time Magazine*, of 6 August 1979, formulating the demand for a national leadership in the USA, as well as a similar issue five years earlier). The authority of the church has declined, the authority of the social and political authorities has been put to severe tests and the authority of scientists is doubted.

The individual, on becoming a member of an organization, may well resent the internal authority structure and the manner in which it manifests itself. This can lead to insubordination within the organization by the individual, possibly resulting in overt conflicts with the organization which may resort to coercive activities. It may also lead to 'societal' influences that try to change the way in which the organization is run. This may happen through the formulation of corporate laws. Such a process can be recognized in the Dutch army where, first through personal insubordination which was later organized by the nascent labour union of armed personnel, the conflict became evident. This resulted through other external pressures in a changed attitude of the army towards its own social structure. At a later point we will return to the complicated matter of the authority structure.

This is analytically complicated because it transcends the boundary of the social and functional aspect of the organization.

Systematic Analysis and the Individual

The analytical orientation, as described earlier, is not restricted to the distinction between the individual and the system. It concerns the whole array of distinctions between the individual and society. It concerns the way organizations are shaped by both individual effort of, for instance, managers or management consultants and the influence from society on the organization. It is hypothesized that these influences on the *shape* of organizations, as opposed to the content of their activities or their domain, can be described in a systematic manner. More specifically, a *theory* is presented which should explain how different influences on organizations interact or are mutually related.

Such a systematic approach could easily lead to a dehumanized analysis. That is not our objective. Organizations are intrinsically human constructions. The role of the individual is central to this study, but one has to restrict oneself to certain approaches. In this study the three propositions of March and Simon (1958, p.6) concerning humans, can be recognized.

(1) They are partly passive instruments capable of performing work and accepting directions, but not initiating action or exerting influence in any significant way.

(2) 'They bring to their organization attitudes, values and goals; they have to be motivated or induced to participate in the system of organization behaviour; there is an incomplete parallelism between their personal goals and organizational goals; actual or potential goal conflicts make power phenomena, attitudes and morale centrally important in the explanation of organizational behaviour.' It is doubtful if it is necessary, or even appropriate, to emphasize goal orientation in this manner.

(3) They 'are decision makers and problem solvers'. This last proposition is the most relevant aspect of the individual in purposeful organizations. But in order to make this clear and to comply with the requirements of the second chapter, it is necessary to present stricter definitions or descriptions of the most crucial concepts that will be used.

Complexity

In the philosophy of science no theories on complexity are available. Because it is a concept which is central to this study an attempt will be made to characterize it. Therefore I will have to operate on a rather informal plane and depend mainly on giving examples to illustrate the characterization. No formal or complete definition should be expected.

Complexity is a concept that is widely used in all fields of scientific activity. It is difficult to find descriptions of what most authors mean by it. It may be said to be an attribute of every phenomenon that has more than one characteristic. Such phenomena are usually described as *systems, networks,* or *fields* (Lewin 1963, p.45).

A close relation can be found with Perrow's descriptions of material and technology variables (see p.48). Furthermore, it is closely related to Ashby's concept of variety, but here too, no explicit definition could be found. Another example of the use of the concept of complexity is found in Emery and Trist's (1975, p.38-56) description of four types of environment. Their subdivision is not principally of an analytical nature.

Let us start by looking at a mathematical example. In mathematics a problem can be described by a set of differential equations. Such a set of equations may be said to have three dimensions of complexity. They are:

(1) the number of variables;
(2) the degree of the equations;
(3) the order of the equations.

This does not mean to say that all problems can be described in such a set of equations. It should be unnecessary to emphasize this; such a formulation of a problem places great demands on such aspects as continuity of the variables and the deterministic nature of the relations. Therefore the mathematical metaphor generally applies to theories that are not highly sophisticated or complicated, and are not of a very general nature as illustrated by Lewin (1963, p.43–59).

Received or Perceived Problems

A problem can be characterized as a number or quantity of phenomena or variables that are perceived as related, but where the relations are not yet understood and need clarification. Because it concerns a perception it is a characteristic of both the perceived and the perceptor. This duality between perceived and perceptor is inescapable.

Four missionaries, while trekking through a tropical forest are taken by surprise by a number of savages. However, through an intelligent ploy they succeed in escaping from the boiling pot and flee to the river. There they find a canoe with paddles in it. They push it into the river and step into it while the crocodiles lazily float by. The canoe is very narrow and tips over easily, so the missionaries realize they have to be very careful if they do not want to be eaten either alive or boiled.

How complex is the problem of propelling the canoe in their attempt to escape?

'Complexity is in the eye of the beholder.'

Initially the missionaries might think there are only five variables — the four paddles and the canoe — in which case it would be a very simple problem. However, further analysis, following attempts to paddle in a haphazard fashion, would show that there were a large number of variables which would prove to be closely related. The distribution of the weight of the paddlers over the canoe, the rhythm of their movements, where and in what manner the paddles are plunged into the water, etc.

The more the observer understands about the problem, the larger will be the number of variables that he will take into account. At a certain point he may be content with the solutions he has found, and will not describe the problem any further.

Because there are certain problems that have been widely studied, it is possible to formulate statements on the state of the art of understanding those problems: the received view. This state of the art makes it possible to distinguish between the individual perceptor and the phenomenon that is perceived. A motor car is quite a different object to a mechanical engineer who is familiar with automobile construction than to someone who has no idea about how it works. The mechanical engineer can give an idea of the difference in technical complexity between a motor cycle and a car, whereas somebody less knowledgeable will find this difficult.

THE DIMENSIONS OF COMPLEXITY

As said, a problem can be described as a number of phenomena that are perceived to be interrelated in a manner which is not yet fully understood. The complexity of the problem is the result of the number of different phenomena or variables (elements) that are interrelated and the nature of these mutual relations. Presented in a more systematic fashion, it can be said that *complexity has three dimensions*.

(1) The *differentiation* of the problem is the number of different elements that are perceived to be interrelated.
(2) The *interrelatedness* of the problem is the number of different ways in which the elements are perceived to be linked or related.
(3) The *variability* of the problem is the manner in which these relations can change.

These three dimensions coincide with those in the mathematical example as given above.

A consequence of the chosen approach is that complexity is not only a characteristic of a problem, but also of its solution. One might imagine that once a solution has been found for a problem, its complexity has been reduced. This is not so.

Problems and solutions should be identical to each other as far as complexity is concerned. The solution of a problem often reduces perceived uncertainty. Complexity is often identified with uncertainty. This might lead to the conclusion that if the uncertainty is reduced this also applies to the complexity. This is not so. A *partial* solution to a problem may be more simple. That does not mean to say the problem itself is therefore simple.

Complexity can be attributed to any form of composition or structure.

Complexity and Organizing

But why should complexity be central to the understanding of organizations? Organizations are the attempt to find an answer to large or complex problems that need to be solved.

If the problems were not so large or complex, an individual could handle them on his own, he would not need an organization to help him.

For example, a person can handle a small canoe. He must organize others if he has to move a large one. If a number of people step into a large canoe they cannot help but organize themselves.

It is alleged that the human mind can only relate a small number of things at a time. To prevent the mind from boggling, certain constructions are employed, systematizing the manner in which one can think of complex phenomena — constructions of differentiation and coordination, the same kind of constructions that form the basis for the division of labour. For thinking, one of the most accepted constructions is that of formalized models or theories. For the division of labour, formal organizations are the equivalent. For thinking about organization a formalized model of the manner in which labour can be divided is appropriate. As such, a theory must be of a very general nature and the concepts employed similarly so. From this viewpoint nothing more general can be thought of than complexity.

Only certain kinds of complexity can be handled in the process of problem solving and it is interesting to see how problems which are too complex to solve are reduced in complexity by introducing simplifications. There are strong indications that Ashby's law of *requisite variety* is based on the same concept as presented here. This law can be interpreted for organizations to mean that the variety (complexity) of an organization's reactions must be large enough to fulfil the different demands of its environment. In other words, the variety of the possible internal reactions must be larger than the variety of the external influences.

Last but not least, complexity is the central issue in statistical thermodynamics, and as such may be influential in the explanation of the evolutionary development of organization towards greater complexity. From a more methodological point of view, the choice of the concept of complexity is closely related to the phenomenon of analysis in the sense of 'resolution into simple elements'. It consists of the breaking down of the object of analysis into interrelated parts, and the description of these parts and the relations between them. In a mathematical sense the combination of the number of different parts and all their possible relations and the number of times each different part exists in the system of analysis *defines* the number of possible states the system can be in. Of course, the system does not have to be fixed in time and therefore the time aspect has to be taken into account.

Representing Complexity

From a very formal point of view it could be said that the elements can only be defined by describing the possible relations they can have with other elements or groups of elements. Thus the combination of the R and T dimension in Figure 4.3 is definitive for the complexity of the elements, and the N

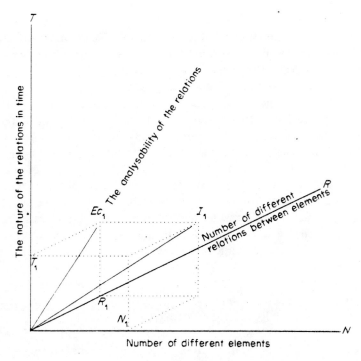

Figure 4.3   The three dimensions of complexity

dimension is definitive for the complexity of the system when seen independently from the contribution of the constituent elements. It is an extensive dimension. The combination of the R and T dimensions describes the complexity of the elements themselves. It is an intensive dimension, independent of the size of the system. Because we are only beginning to formulate an approach towards the analysis of organizations by means of complexity, a simplification is proposed. Because the R and the T dimensions characterize only the elements — are part of the *intensive* dimension — and the N dimension characteristics the system of elements, it is thought to be permissible to use only this main distinction between elements and system. This simplification leads to the combination of the R and T dimension, to one *intensive* dimension.

The analysis of organizations along the lines that are proposed is complicated enough as it stands. Therefore, for a purely pragmatic reason this combination is proposed to simplify the description of the difference in complexity of two structures. However, when using the two remaining dimensions one should always keep in mind that one of them is a composite dimension and that in certain cases the distinction between its two elementary dimensions may provide important clarification. This is certainly the case when one is confronted with highly *dynamic* situations.

Dissonant Complexities

The description of complexity makes it possible to describe differences in complexity between systems. By definition these are called dissonances. From Figure 4.4 it should become clear that there are esentially three types of dissonance:

(1) $(N_2 - N_1)$ quantitative dissonance;
(2) $(R_2 - R_1)$ relation dissonance;
(3) $(T_2 - T_1)$ variational dissonance.

As said, for simplicity's sake the last two will be combined into what we call a qualitative dissonance $(Ec_2 - Ec_1)$. These dissonances will later be applied to the different variables of an organization — variables that are to be presented in this chapter. The proposed reduction from three to two basic dissonances greatly simplifies the description of the relations between the different variables.

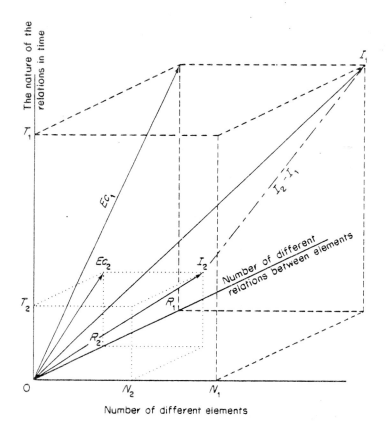

Figure 4.4   The three dimensions of dissonance

It must be stressed that the 'technique' described here only facilitates the description of *relative* complexity and it is by no means intended to create an absolute categorization. It can best be compared to the concept of entropy as used in thermodynamics, and is only relevant in a relative sense.

The description of differences in complexity should not present grave problems when the phenomena are *clearly comparable*. For instance, a dishwasher is a more complex machine than an icebox, or a computer chess program is more complex than a computer draughts program if it is to operate on the same level of either game. A difficulty arises when comparisons are made between for instance specific types of problems and the ability of problem solvers to solve them. In the case of human problem solvers this ability is much more difficult to assess than in the case of, for instance, a computer, or rather the combination of a computer and its programs. In this instance there are derivative indicators such as memory space required, central processor time demanded for certain operations but also the sophistication of the solutions, which gives an idea of the fit between the problems and the solutions. Usually these indicators are translated into costs and benefits, a translation in which most details which could help in the analysis of the fit between the nature of the problem and its solutions are lost.

A Theory and its Terms

From a methodological point of view, certainly where it concerns the consistency of the theoretical structure, it is interesting to see how the dimensions of the different variables were arrived at. The concept of complexity can be traced back to both:

(a) system theory's concept of variety (Ashby);
(b) thermodynamic's statistical analysis of the different states in which a system can be.

The influence of the thermodynamic point of view, especially when viewed as a specific form of organization theory, was dominant for this study. The choice has been made so that dimensions of *all* the variables could be reduced to one set: the three dimensions of complexity. What remains is the application of those dimensions to the different interpretation of the elements of the different variables. This still poses a difficult question. It is the basic difficulty of theory formalization, as also mentioned in the second chapter. Theory and the meaning of the terms that occur in them are indissolubly linked, as are also concepts and the manner in which they are expressed. In a formalized mode they are expressed using dimensions. The application of the dimensions to the elementary variables is the essence of theoretical endeavours.

For example, in physics, or rather Newtonian mechanics, the three basic dimensions are length, time and mass. We recognize the importance of the application of these three dimensions to the concepts of force, mass and acceleration in Newton's law.

$$F = Ma.$$

The consistent use of dimensions makes dimensional analysis possible when we are confronted with complex problems. Newton's law not only defines the relationship between mass, force and acceleration, but at the same time, it defines the concepts themselves in terms of the dimensions in which they are to be expressed: length, time, and mass.

Content versus Structure

In this Section, where a general description is given of the approach that is taken by using complexity as the main analytical concept for the theory of organizations, it is appropriate to clarify the distinction between content and structure.

Let us again start with the mathematical example. A system of differential equations can be said to have three basic dimensions.

(1)   the number of variables;
(2)   the degree of the equations;
(3)   the order of the derivatives

These three dimensions describe the basic *structure* of the system. The *content* of the system consists of the actual existence of the possible terms within the system and the manner in which these terms occur. This can best be described by the values of the coefficients of each possible term. Usually many of them are zero.

In the case of the four missionaries in a canoe, the structure of the problem concerns the number of variables. In the case of the canoe it would be paddles, weight, movement, etc. Were all four of them to flee on one bicyle, the structure of the problem might be just as complex, but its content would be different.

The Purpose or Goals of Organization

Until this point no criteria have been given or referred to for the effectiveness of the organization or the appropriateness of its structure or form. Such criteria are usually based on a teleological rationality. One of the most widely used criteria is what could be called the *goal paradigm* (Georgiou 1973) — a criterion that is attractive for its simplicity. If a system is viewed as being a complicated network of cause–effect relationships, then the efficiency of the system is most easily assessed when one ultimate effect is chosen and each relationship can be judged for its contribution to that final effect. Simon's analysis views the organization as a decision-making structure leading to a means–end chain, where the decisions in the organizations are reduced to the selection of the best means for achieving the ends as defined higher up in the structure (essentially the basis for management by objectives). This analysis seems possible only where the ends of the organization can be made fairly clear at the higest level of the organization. The idea that different individuals or different groups can have different or even mutually imcompatible objectives does not fit this idea. I would, however, never contend that organizations are not purposeful at all. They are purposeful to such an extent that they operate in certain domains and that they try to guarantee their own existence in one way or another. They are in a sense structures which try to remain viable in an environment which is on the whole not very encouraging to their existence. They share an essential characteristic with all other forms of life, they transform energy into structure and try to keep this structure intact against the odds of the second law of thermodynamics. In the sense of organization theory, organizing is the natural reaction to complex environments. In the sense of a theory of organization, another dimension is added to organizing; it is the rational solution to the problem of handling large or complex tasks, tasks generated both inside and outside the organization. The concept of a task makes the organization necessarily purposeful with respect to the achievement of the results of the tasks.

Differentiation

How do organizations handle complexity, and what are the main variables to which complexity can be applied? From this viewpoint organizations are not different from other natural systems. The problems organizations have to solve are *partly* of their own making, but *mainly* the consequence of the interaction between an organization and its environment. It is for this reason that organizations will be compared to natural systems.

The principles behind this solution to the problem of handling extremely complex tasks are: differentiation, specialization and coordination. The process of differentiation in biological systems lies at the basis of evolutionary theories.

(1) Every form of life can be seen as a thermal machine turning energy into structure. The structure, in order to exist, needs at least a constant flow of energy (food).

(2) Every form of life exists in an aggressive environment; it needs to be aggressive in order to maintain itself in such an environment. Those who defend themselves successfully can stay alive. It is not survival of the fittest, but extinction of the least fit. Possibly, fitness should not only be defined by, for instance, physical fitness, but rather by fitting into available niches of a total biological structure.

When existing flows of energy (resources) are threatened or thwarted, new flows have to be developed. The ability to do this can be called differentiation. Thus, those species with the greatest access to resources of which none are individually vital is least vulnerable to extinction through loss of resources.

The dependence on the aggressive environment is neatly expressed in the relation between prey and predator, as described formally by Lotka (1956) and later further illustrated by Nicolis and Prigogine (1977). Assuming that there is at least a random process of mutation, they show there is an intrinsic tendency to diversify, filling as many ecological 'niches' as possible. This will turn out to be important in Chapter 5 when it will be shown that there is an irreversible process of change in technology if one only adheres to a teleological development theory.

In a rational study, as this sets out to be, the organization (structure) is first of all conceived as an instrument *deliberately* established for its continued existence. The consequence is that the actual domain is not of principle interest to the ways in which the organization can react to external influences. The organization meets the demands of the environment in its domain, within the constraints set by the environment. When either the demands or the constraints change, the organization has to change too. Thus in the study when the 'attainment of goals' is mentioned it usually means the demands and constraints set by the environment. This does not mean to say that an organization has no way to influence these demands and constraints. There are even social scientists who claim that large organizations are mainly instrumental in creating new demands in their own domain of activities (Galbraith 1967). The viewpoint can also be taken that individuals or groups of individuals create their own environment in the sense of an enacted environment (Weick, 1969, p.64).

Goals and Irrationality

The classical idea that an organization is 'an instrument, a deliberate and rational means of attaining known goals', is central to the scala of management theory literature. This idea leads to a weakened Tayloristic view that there is one best way. The nature of the goals may differ as well as the way in which they are defined, but they are known to the organization and its members. A logical conclusion to this description is that an organization then demands 'deliberate and rational' behaviour of its members directed at attaining these known goals or contributing towards the possibility of their attainment.

Empirical analysis has shown how inadequate this concept of organizational rationality proves to be. Such a 'consensus' view is contradicted by the abundance of intraorganizational conflicts up to the highest levels of the hierarchy. As is shown in the second case study, members of organizations are not always sensitive to the rational solutions of the functional problems of the organization as they are perceived by either the management or by experts. This 'irrationality' is further exemplified by the general resistance to decision-making aids, devised by operation research scientists and other rational management experts. The purposeful nature is often most clearly recognized at the level of the organization where the 'technical production processes' take place. Here the rationality of the technical process and the results which are demanded and the constraints that apply, is usually much more clear. In the case of the engineering department one would expect such highly rational behaviour in, for instance, the choice between different mechanization projects. This proved untrue. There were a number of, often conflicting, sometimes rational but usually rationalized criteria leading to certain preferences.

In the rational organization models, the individuals in it are means to execute transformations (or solve problems) necessary for the achievement of goals. This monistic approach has proved to be not too fertile. The human relations group (Roethlisberger and Dickson, 1939; Mayo 1945 etcetera) emphasized the multidimensionality of people in organizations. (For an interesting analysis of this see R. Atkin, 1981.) The changes in organizations resulting from the resistance to prescribed behaviour, limit the degree to which organizations can be understood through their goals. This is exemplified by the phenomenon of 'bureaucratization', the members of an organization subordinate the goals to the means that have become accepted. Rules become ends rather than means. An interesting review of this 'rational' approach is given by Georgiou (1973). He opposes this with the *incentive theory*. This theory applies more to the motivation of the individual as a prime-moving force than to the effect of goals on organizations as a whole. It helps us very little towards a new approach to the theory of organizations. Furthermore it seems to neglect the fact that the human being is a social animal and is thus by nature inclined to act in an organized manner. What is more it reduces the individual to a goal-attaining mechanism.

The purposeful nature of an organization is mainly defined by the domain of the organization. In it, it must reflect the behaviour of the environment. This behaviour of the environment is usually expressed in demands set within the domain, primarily in the form of goods or services and the economic constraint within which they have to be supplied. The satisfaction of the demand for goods is usually achieved by transforming available resources into the goods demanded. The services are either in the form of the ability to solve problems which the environment cannot or will not solve, or making available individuals who are willing and able to perform tasks that cannot be met by individuals in the environment not connected to such an organization. These activities of an organization can be split into two distinct categories; the physical processes where human 'mechanical' activity is demanded, and those informational processes where information is processed in such a manner that new meanings or interpretations are generated to existing information. It is mainly the latter aspect that will be treated in this study, where *individual effort* is concerned as in the description of an organization as given on p.60. The effort is directed at change in either a material or an informational sphere. This change can be expressed in the trinity of the input–transformation–output sequence. The subdivision is an artificial one, but for the sake of analysis it is appropriate. The combination of the three is defined as the technological variable.

THE STRUCTURE OF THE DISSONANCE THEORY

In the previous section of this chapter two main perspectives have been presented:

(a) *The analytical orientation*, which was either system to individual or vice versa. This will for the time being be reduced to two levels, the lowest being the individual, the next being the department of which he is a member.

(b) *The functional and the social* aspects are described on the two above-mentioned levels. The functional aspect of the individual is described in terms of his *cognitive structure* and the social aspect in terms of his *personal norms and values*. On the departmental level the functional aspect is described as the *task structure*, and the social aspect as the *control structure*.

The *functional links* between the different parts of the organization are formed by the *technology* employed to remain active with the domain of the organization. All these distinctions can be represented in Figure 4.5, where different sets of variables form recognized concepts used in the theory of organizations.

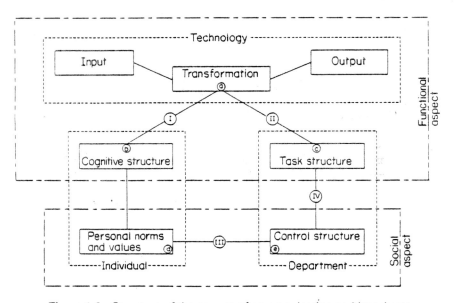

Figure 4.5   Structure of the aspects of an organization and its subsets

The intention is to describe variables within the framework in such a manner that it is *not* necessary to define *all* the variables at the beginning. In order to let the concepts of dissonances prevail, the definition of the variables and their intermediate dissonances will be described segmentally, as indicated by the letters and the numerals in Figure 4.5

Thus technology will be described first, then the cognitive structure will be treated, i.e. the ability of the individual to handle complexity. The next step is the comparison between the two: the ability of the individual to solve complex problems is compared with the complexity of the problems that the organization confronts him with.

In order to build up the theory in a systematic manner, the next variable that is treated is the task structure; the manner in which the division of labour is achieved within the organization. This makes it possible to match this *task structure* with the *transformations* that are performed and see if this leads to dissonances that can be recognized in existing organizations. When this has been completed, we will have described the functional aspect of the organization (see Figure 4.5).

The next step is to describe the social aspect of the organization. This is first done on the level of the individual member and then on the organizational level. The two are again matched to see if incompatibilities can be recognized leading to normative dissonances. As a last step in the construction of this theoretical framework the relation between the functional and the social aspect is presented. That is, between the task structure and the control structure. The structural dissonances are described and illustrated.

This completes an outline of the main framework of the theory.

The dimensions of all the variables have been chosen to represent the complexity of their structures, and the intermediate dissonances are then the difference in complexity of the related variables. In order to clarify this rather complex construction, an attempt has been made to schematize the different types of relations and the different levels so that they become more easily distinguishable.

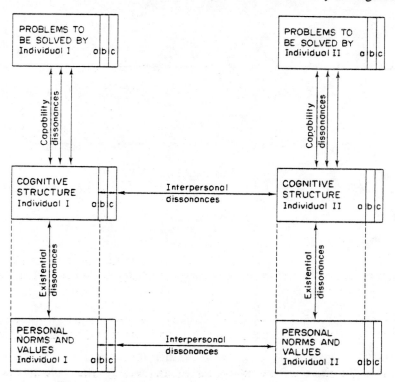

Figure 4.6   Dissonances at the level of the individual

In order to explain the multi-level nature of the domain the following figures present an indication of the analytical orientation that can be recognized and the manner in which they are related to the different variables.

In Figure 4.6 the relations at the level of the individual are represented. All dissonances indicated in this plane are between either an individual and the problems he has to solve or between individuals. These dissonances are situated at the lowest level of inclusiveness. The small rectangles containing the letters b and c signify that in the same plane more than one individual can be represented by superimposing their images.

In Figure 4.7 the same has been done at the departmental level. Thus all dissonances represented in this (higher) plane are at the same level of analytical inclusiveness. As shown, the functional relation between the departments is represented by the flow of materials and information.

In Figure 4.8 we see the result of the superposition of the two previous diagrams, resulting in an axonometric depiction of two levels of analytical variables and their dissonances. Because there is no *direct* relation between the cognitive structure of the individual members and the task structure of their department this is not represented in this figure. Thus only the dissonances between the personal norms and values and the control structure, and the dissonances between the nature of the problems that a number of individuals can solve and the technology of their department remain. In this figure an indication is also given of the three possible directions in which structural dissonances can be found.

In the next section a more complete description of the variables and their dissonances will be presented.

TECHNOLOGY: THE KNOWLEDGE OF GETTING THINGS DONE

As we have seen there is considerable confusion about the meaning of technology in the literature, a confusion partly based on the *lack of distinction between what is done and what arrangements have been made to do it*. In the sense used in this study, the technological variable must be independent of the structure of the organization. It pertains to the knowledge in the organization about the change processes that are to be executed. This change process is influenced by all three subaspects mentioned above.

Inputs

'The state of the art of analysing the characteristics of the raw materials (inputs) is likely to determine what kind of technology (transformation) will be used.'

'To understand the nature of the materials means to be able to control it better and to achieve more predictability and efficiency in transformation' (Perrow 1967, p.196–7).

These descriptions concern the state of the art at the location of the transformation process. For example, the knowledge of the nature of the

82

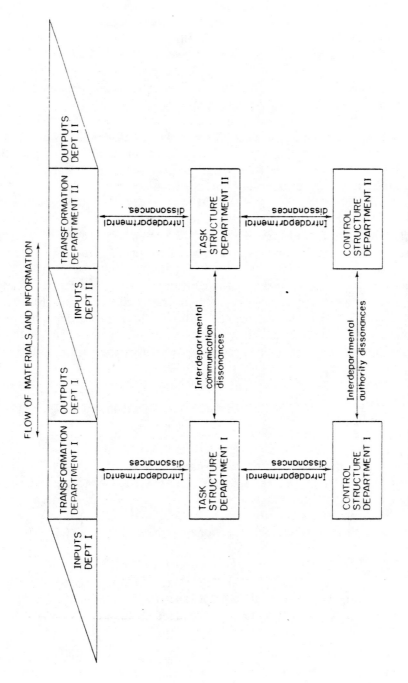

Figure 4.7 Dissonances at intra and interdepartmental level

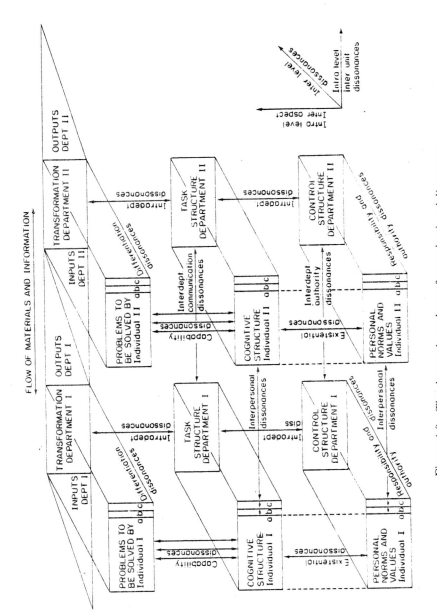

Figure 4.8   The three orientations of organizational dissonance

supercooled liquid that is known as glass is quite different in the case of a craftsman blowing art objects or in the case of the laboratories of the Corning or the Pilkington companies specialized in producing all types of glass and related products. Both types of glass production, based on such different levels of knowledge, can exist side by side, possibly because they are not in direct competition with each other.

In the case of the automated information system the knowledge of the nature of the formal planning problem was much more thorough on the part of the specialists from the automation department than on the part of the men in the factory. The factory planners had a deeper knowledge of the related problems within the production departments, such as personal preferences and individual characteristics. Thus, when we speak of inputs and their relative complexity, this is as perceived by specific groups. In essence it concerns the model the actor has of the material or input. The complexity of the model can be represented in the three-dimensional manner as described, but for simplicity's sake this is compressed in two dimensions.

The structural dimension is characterized by the number and the nature, in time, of the relations between the different elements in the model, and the quantitative dimension by the number of different elements. This approach certainly helps the analysis of the information flow in organization, but in my opinion, it also works for the physical and material flows. However, the most fundamental application is for the nature of problems or phenomena that have to be understood; basically, an informational question.

This structural dimension is clearly related to Perrow's analysability dimension, but an attempt has been made to dissociate it from the ability of the problem solver, by quantifying the number of the relations and by indicating, possibly in classes, their relation to time.

For the planning department of the lighting fixtures plant, the quantitative aspect could be inventoried by keeping account of the different orders and their parts lists. The structural dimension would be more difficult, i.e. the relations between the different orders in the production process, the relation between different products using the same parts, or time delays when ordering, throughput times, etc. The specialists from the automation department used a much more *complex* model on which to base their activities than their counterparts in the factory. They inventoried the relevant information categories and the relations between them and from this, constructed a formalized cybernetic model.

Outputs

The description of the outputs must necessarily be only a minor variation of that of the inputs.

To understand what is needed for the appraisal of the change from one state to another, one must be able to control this transformation better and to achieve a higher predictability and efficiency in researching the results that are demanded.

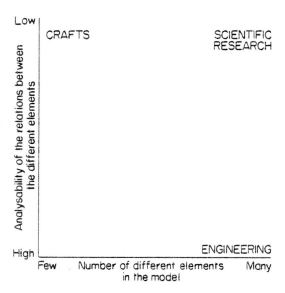

Figure 4.9 Complexity of the model of the domain that is used to solve task-related problems

It therefore involves the physical definition of objects or the appropriateness of the supplied information.

In the case of the information system, the specialists could show more clearly what demands should be set for the specificity of production planning information. Because of their more complicated model of the cybernetic system of the production facilities, they could also analyse where the system is most sensitive to a shortage of information. This does not necessarily mean that the results *must* be better. The content of the model can be quite different, and issues that are taken into account in an intuitive manner in the simpler model may be left out in the more complex model (possibly because they are not easily quantifiable) and this omission may have drastic effects.

In the first case, the outputs of an engineering department are quite different from those of a development department. In the former the outputs are dictated by the knowledge of mechanical tolerances and of the technique of producing mechanical parts. In the latter the results were based on a scarcely formalized field of techniques where solutions were often based on intuitive choices out of many alternatives. The nature of the constraints and their mutual relations were often not clear.

The smaller the unit of analysis, the easier it is to define the demands and the constraints on outputs. When total organizations are taken as objects of analysis, the main origin of these demands and constraints lies in the domain and the environment of the organization. They are aspects such as markets in which they operate, finance, available personnel and its characteristic, etc. This brings to the fore the importance of viewing the organization, at *every* level of analysis, as an open system. But such openess is difficult to tackle analytically. Therefore a technique is used to close the system and create openings through which the system can communicate with the environment —

openings not in the sense of physical channels of communication, but rather in domains of contact. Thus the environment influences the outputs of organizations: in the most literal sense where it concerns the physical products which are brought into the market, but in a more oblique sense also in the way organizations treat their employees or what kind of work they have them do. This environmental perspective will be looked into further at a later point. It suffices to say here that it has a major influence on the nature of the outputs of every part of the organization, because the output, as the word strongly implies, is one of the media by which the organization communicates with its environment.

Transformation

For the purposes of this study the concept of transformation is defined much more formally than elsewhere.

Transformation is defined as the change from one state into another. The knowledge necessary to accomplish this is an important aspect of this change.

It concerns our ability to change material along pre-established lines in the widest sense of the word, independently of how such a change is organized in a social setting.

In my opinion the knowledge of the change process is inextricably related to the knowledge of the materials or things to be changed. I am well aware that this opinion is based upon a philosophical presupposition that is widely disputed, especially in the field of social science. As was already stated in the introduction, structure defines which processes are appropriate, but the structure is not sufficient to deduce specific processes from it.

The transformation has both a knowledge aspect and a skill aspect. Whereas in the knowledge aspect the insight is based on scientific knowledge of the materials that have to be transformed, in the skill aspect the insight in this transformation process is mainly based on experience, often gained through trial and error. Both concern the predictability of the outcome, but knowledge is based on a set of general explicit explanatory theories or models.

In the second case study, the transformation of information on parts and production schedules was processed as a matter of rule of thumb. The sheer amount of information that was available made it impossible for the few employees whose job it was to plan the production, to transform this into an accurate plan. Whereas the specialists from the automation department could, by using a computer to process the information, on the basis of their model of the cybernetic system of production control, restrict themselves to programming the *manner* in which the information should be mutually related. Due to the fixed nature of the model, influences not accommodated in the program were necessarily neglected. The original means of scheduling was based on an implicit model used by the planner which was strongly influenced by his own here and now perception of his direct environment and allowed ad hoc changes. This perception changed with the changing circumstances (see Figure 4.10).

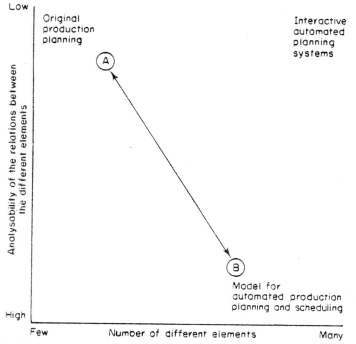

Figure 4.10 Planning systems described as specific forms of transformation in the two modes of planning in the lighting fixture department

In the first case study we can also describe the way the problems were solved by the different departments, although it must be made clear that the transformation process within each department was *not* homogeneous. The mechanization department, by means of the long established engineering culture, had a highly standardized process of transforming designs into blueprints for the actual physical machines, whereas the development department was forever searching for alternatives that were difficult to compare with each other in a reproducible rational way. There exists some knowledge of the physical processes that take place while the product functions, but this knowledge has not been translated into 'received' solutions.

Technology Summarized

If technology is defined in terms of the ability to get things done, then it could be seen as a combination of the three subaspects that have just been presented. Thus when we speak of *high technology industries* it concerns industries that operate on complex materials using complex transformation processes to change these materials into complex products. On the whole it must be stated that this is not necessarily the only combination of these three subaspects and that these three do not necessarily fit together in such a simple manner. It is not necessary for this study to treat this in detail as it would lead us too far astray.

The domain of an organization describes the area of primary activities it undertakes. These primary activities demand a certain technology, a certain knowledge about the processes that are necessary to maintain one's position in that field of activities. The manner in which such technology is put into operation in the organization is largely a question of task structure—the subdivision of the field of activities into smaller parts that are to be treated by organizational units.

The technology thus describes the general ability to solve the problems that are inherent to the activities undertaken in a certain field; it concerns the state of the art rather than the ability of a specific organization or a unit of an organization. There can be a difference, a gap between the state of the art and the actual implementation within an organization, there can be a technological lag between the *available knowledge* and that which is *applied* within organizations or between the sophistication of the knowledge applied in different organizations.

It is *important* to emphasize that when employing the concepts of technology and transformation in a structural analysis, this presupposes that the technology and the transformation themselves can be characterized by their own structure. Thus in this study, where technology or transformation are mentioned, the reader should identify them with the structure of the technology or the transformations.

The Individual as Member of an Organization

As in the previous paragraphs the emphasis has been put on the complexity of problems and the appropriate manner of their solution, it seems fitting to treat the individual member of an organization as a problem solver. It is an aspect which is very difficult to speak of with authority, not being a psychologist and knowing that specialists in the field attribute such different meanings to the same words. However, for the sake of a systematic approach, but also because it is of the utmost importance to the functioning of organizations, I will have to make my way gingerly across this slippery slope. This by no means implies there are not many other interesting and important aspects of the individual from an organizational point of view. This study has in no way the objective to give a *complete* picture of human organizational phenomena. A choice has been made in the line of the *structural* approach.

COGNITIVE STRUCTURE

The Individual's Ability to Handle Complexity

In organizations, individuals perform actions in order to alter raw materials (people, symbols or things). This performance is one of the main reasons why he is a member of an organization. There are two sides to these individual's actions:

(1) mechanical actions;
(2) problem-solving activity.

The development of industrial production and the increasing price competition focussed attention on the productivity of human activities and opened the road to mechanization. The historical development from the industrial revolution to the completely automated plant is not only fed by our technological progress, our increased understanding of production processes, but also by an increasing emphasis on the minimization of the work content of industrial products in an environment where labour costs are high in relation to both capital costs and wages in other geographical locations.

The approach to production as a 'mechanistic' form of labour made the similarity evident between the principles of mechanization and 'scientific management'. Automated information processing nowadays presents a similar influence on the decision-making and problem-solving activities of humans in organizations. They may be viewed as *misplaced metaphors* with lives of their own. People are treated as machines and the criteria used to design machines are transposed to human social organizations.

Manual or physical work is of gradually decreasing importance. Nowadays the main activity of the individual in organizations is to solve problems and to make decisions and their execution possible. Because the individual has to solve problems, his ability to do so can be seen as an important variable. This ability is described as his *cognitive structure*. It is to be described in the manner that was explained under the heading of complexity.

In this instance the *quantitative* dimension refers to the amount of raw uninterpreted data an individual can use when solving problems.

The *structural* dimension refers to those broad characteristics of intelligent activity which virtually define the very essence of intelligent behaviour, i.e., ability to recognize relations between different phenomena or classes of phenomena and to draw conclusions from those assumed relations.

Viewing the individuals as problem solvers, where the problems are posed either by the individuals themselves or by other functional groups within the organization, *information is the main commodity of organizations*. Instead of the raw materials and the consumers of transformed raw materials, available information and the ability to process it is taken as the central issue. This also fits more closely the definition that is used of technology as the knowledge of getting things done. Knowledge is essentially a specific form of information or its availability and not a physical object. Following this line it is apt to treat an individual as an information processor or a problem solver. It is by no means my intention to treat him *only* as a problem solver, as will be seen later on. The shift of attention from physical action to problem solving or information processing is also reflected in a shift of attention from mechanization to automation or automated information sysems.

The individual is confronted with a wide range of problems. These can be characterized as extremely simple problems, such as encountered in assembly line situations, to very complex problems, as is the case with research scientists trying to solve problems which are not yet clearly defined. By defining the nature of the complexity of problems, as in the previous paragraphs, insight can be gained into the ability the individual needs to solve them.

The Reduction of Uncertainty

Nyström describes problem solving as the reduction of uncertainty. The nature of the uncertainty is a direct consequence of the type of problem. Nyström (1974, p.134) defines the nature of the perceived problem as 'cognitive structure'.

He says that it

> 'may be defined as a set of partially ordered cognitive elements—notions or ideas—which are viewed by the decision maker as relevant for determining the outcome of a contemplated decision. The relations between elements may be either an implicit—that is intuitive—or viewed as being an explicit cause and effect relationship to each other.
>
> There are two dimensions of cognitive structure that would appear to be of particular interest in this connection. One is the degree of detail which a certain structure contains or in other words how *differentiated* it is. The other is the extent to which a certain structure is *causally linked*, i.e. how interrelated different elements are.'

This definition contains the same methodological approach as was used to treat the previous variables. It should be remarked that it is a combination of the perception of the problem by the problem solver, and the nature of the problem itself. The proposition is to distinguish between the two: on the one hand, the problem as perceived by a specific individual, and on the other hand (from the point of view that may be regarded as more scientific) as also seen by others who are also concerned with the same subject. Admittedly these two are extremely difficult to distinguish, but it is worth our while to try.

I prefer to call Nyström's definition of cognitive structure the cognitive model of the problem which the individual uses in order to grasp the problem. Nyström introduces the 'uncertainty gap'; it 'is experienced by the decision maker, with regard to a specific cognitive structure (cognitive *model* in my own terminology—J.K.). The less his belief in the cognitive structure (his *model* of the problems—J.K.) as an adequate representation of relevant factors, the greater the uncertainty gap.'

The experiencing of an uncertainty gap in relation to specific problems can be viewed as a factor of the personality of the problem solver as well as the manner in which this uncertainty gap tends to be reduced in the process of solving the problem. This comes much closer to the description of the individual's cognitive structure as it is used in this study.

As experiencing an uncertainty gap is professed to be unpleasant, the problem solver is also apt to define the problem in line with his problem solving ability. In order to close the remaining uncertainty gap, information on the problem will be selected and processed. Nyström goes on to describe the manner in which this is done as cognitive styles: intuitively oriented versus analytically oriented.

'Intuitively oriented uncertainty reduction may be viewed as depending mainly on differentiation, that is the number of elements in a structure may be seen as more important than the explicitly recognized relationships between them. Analytically oriented uncertainty reduction, on the other hand, may be regarded primarily as dependent on establishing causal links between existing cognitive elements.'

Systematic versus Intuitive Styles

A more thoroughly researched and defined description of this distinction between the systematic (analytical) and intuitive approach can be found in Keen's work: 'The Implication of Cognitive Style for Individual Decision-Making.' He combines this distinction with a typology of information gathering distinguishing between *re*ceptive and *pre*ceptive individuals.

He describes systematic thinkers in the following manner (Keen 1973, p.13–14).

'Systematic thinkers' analysis is basically sequential, zeroing in on a solution through steps of increasing refinement; they try to set up their definition of the problem so as not to have to repeat any step in the solving sequence. This systematic mode of response is thus marked by several distinctive features.

(1) a conscious awareness of where any substeps fits within the overall plan;
(2) an ordered sequence of search and analysis;
(3) justification of a solution largely in terms of method.

The systematic thinker's plan amounts to a program, all the rules for action have been specified so that the rest of the problem solving process is mainly computational and analytic; in a sense, the methodology guarantees the solution.'

Because the systematic thinker's plan amounts to a program, the problem must be programmable in order to find a solution. With problems of a vague or 'qualitative' nature this is not the case. They are by definition more difficult to analyse.

An intuitive thinker is much more difficult to describe. This is partly due to the fact that intuitive thinking lacks conscious definition and scores low on recognizable structure.

Keen gives the following characteristics of each mode of cognitive style. *Systematic thinkers tend to:*

(1) look for a method and make a plan for solving a problem;
(2) be very conscious of their approach;
(3) defend the quality of their solution largely in terms of the method;
(4) define the specific constraints of the problem early in the process;
(5) move through a process of increasing refinement of analysis;
(6) complete any discrete step in analysis that set out on.

Intuitive thinkers tend to:

(1)   keep the overall problem continually in mind;
(2)   redefine the problem frequently as they proceed;
(3)   rely on unverbalized clues, even hunches;
(4)   defend a solution largely in terms of 'fit';
(5)   consider a number of alternatives and options simultaneously;
(6)   jump from one step in analysis or search to another and back again;
(7)   explore and abandon alternatives very quickly.

Keen used eleven different tests to measure the difference between individuals. The scaling is less concerned with absolute capacity than with relative performance on one test in comparison with another. If he scores highly on all tests his style cannot be identified, in fact, he does not have a style, but operates comfortably in both modes.

Keen's distinction does not differ too greatly from that of Zangwill (1970). He distinguishes between divergent and convergent thinking. 'In divergent thinking, the aim is to produce a large number of possible answers, none of which are necessarily more correct than the others though some may be original. Such thinking is marked by variety and fertility rather than by its logical presentation.'

Divergent thinking is related to intuitive and convergent to systematic.

Styles of Information Gathering

The intuitive-systematic duality is only one of the dimensions of Keen's model of cognitive style. The other is the manner of information-*gathering* described in terms of *re*ceptiveness and *pre*ceptiveness.

'Preceptive individuals tend to bring to bear concepts that they use to filter data; they focus on patterns of information, look for deviations from or confirmation with their expectations. Their precepts are both cues for information-gathering and heuristic for cataloguing what they find. By contrast the 'receptive' thinker is more sensitive to the stimulus itself. He will focus on detail rather than on pattern and tries to derive from its fitting his precepts.'

I think the distinction between problem solving and information gathering is not a basic one. They prove to be highly correlated. They both have something to say about the 'structural' aspects of problem solving. Differences in models of problem solving are nutured by the type of environment that is encountered in the individual's upbringing and education, or perhaps his early work experience. The individual develops a manner of information gathering and evaluation, and a manner of problem solving that relieves his cognitive strain (Bruner 1956).

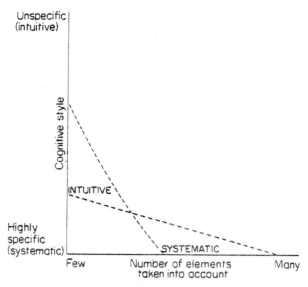

Figure 4.11   Cognitive Structure

The Distinction between Structure and Content

Piaget distinguishes three characteristics in the learning process, as is described by J. H. Flavell (1963, p.17)—function, structure and content. 'Function' refers to those broad characteristics of intelligent activity which hold true for all ages and which virtually define the very essence of intelligent behaviour. Interposed between function and content, Piaget postulates the existence of cognitive structures. They are organizational properties of intelligence, which explains why a certain content rather than some other emerges. They could also be described as the nature of the relations between the different contents. Where memory is seen as a file of index cards, content describes the amount of information on the cards (the number of cards) and structure the number of the nature of the cross-reference between the cards.

I propose to define the description field of cognitive structures as a synthesis of these approaches, where the structural dimension goes from systematic to intuitive and the quantitative dimension concerns the number of elements that the individual takes into account when solving problems (see Figure 4.11).

Structure and Quantity

In the first case study the distinction between different cognitive structures within the departments concerned is problematic. A common technical or scientific education and organizational background should not breed structural difference. However, on considering more deeply, one might say that the developers, basing themselves on a systematic insight in the variables that are of importance to their problems and their possible solutions, pick one out in an intuitive manner as being important and then through analysing and varying the variable within certain boundaries they look for solutions. In the engineering department the solutions were mainly sought by conscientiously applying 'received' design techniques. But also here, in the engineering group, new developments are based on intuitive hunches or ideas.

In the second case study the most clear cognitive structures could be found among the specialists from the information department. They were thoroughly analytic, resulting in tremendously large and complex models of the cybernetic control system of the production department. Their counterparts in the factory were much less analytic; their model of reality was much less explicit and much more intuitive and they did not have the means to handle large quantities of data. The computer itself is of course the apogee in systematization, in the sense that all its activities are programmed. The use of a computer compels the user to define his problems in such a manner that they can be approached systematically. That this need not necessarily be so for the whole problem that one sets oneself, but only for that part of the problem to which one applies programmed intelligence, will show in the next chapters and was also indicated earlier in my critique on the quantitative empirical approach to the social sciences on p.33.

This method of describing cognitive structures is by no means meant to be interpreted as a possibility for ranking individuals along a two-dimensional scale. It rather indicates the styles in which individuals can operate and their preference for a specific mode. This becomes clear when we realize that most people can be taught to translate certain problems into prespecified programs of solution, as is done in many schools.

Vickers (1978, p.145) gives a lucid description of the two-different modes, which I would not like to withhold from the reader:

> 'My thesis is that the human mind has available to it at least two different modes of knowing and that it uses both in appropriate or inappropriate combinations in its endless effort to understand the world in which it finds itself. One of these modes is more dependent on analysis, logical reasoning, calculation, and explicit description. The other is more dependent on synthesis and recognition of pattern, context and the multiple possible relations of figure and ground.'

Both are necessary and a mixture is used in most mental operations.

Needs versus Abilities

As was said earlier, the individual tends to define the problem to fit his mental structure. But the state of knowledge may already be such that an accepted definition of the problem exists, and the individual is no longer free to choose. The existence of operations research and cybernetic models of production control systems decreases the freedom of individuals in organizations to solve their planning and scheduling problems in a simplistic or outdated manner. The more is known about certain phenomenon the greater the chance that systematic approaches will lead to more certain solutions. However, the *first* step towards a new understanding of phenomena is usually the consequence of an intuitive insight. Further development of this insight into a more formal representation demands a more systematic approach. A fine example for this can be found in Einstein's autobiography. He gives us insight into his own experience. His general theory of relativity was developed from introspection and a sense of 'fit'. Much of what he postulated came from a tentative feeling that he admitted could not be justified or explained. He tolerated ambiguities and imprecision of ideas that were almost a contradiction of 'scientific method'. But he also makes clear the underlying tenacity and lucidity of thought that made his intuitive sense disciplined and in its own way methodical. It is also true that his intuition was very vulnerable. He largely pointed the way to quantum theory in physics and then spent the last years of his life trying to refute it, despite the massive accumulation of experimental and theoretical evidence supporting it.

It is a grave misconception that natural scientists are necessarily cool and systematic thinkers. Their creativity too depends on an emotional intuitive dissatisfaction which leads Hoffer (1952, p.57) to remark that '. . . the genuine writer, artist and even scientist are dissatisfied persons — as dissatisfied as the revolutionary — but are endowed with a capacity for transmitting their dissatisfaction into a creative impulse.' But for the result of the creative impulse to be communicable it will have to be systemized in such a manner that it can be understood by others. Thus when an 'individualistic' approach has been used to solve certain problems it often takes some time before someone else can translate it into such a comprehensible statement. Mathematics facilitates this translation in the physical sciences because it proceeds from the consensus of the syntax and only the interpretation is left to be agreed upon.

Generalizing versus Individualizing Problem Solving

The methodological point of view that was stated in Chapter 2 leads to the following distinction in scientific approaches. A scientist is confronted with complex phenomena which he tries to understand. This means reducing the complexity in such a manner that it becomes acceptable, describable and possibly usable to effect changes in his environment. This last is the technological aspect of science. There are different approaches to this reduction of complexity.

'The generalizing method divests reality of all its random differences and unique aspects by reducing qualitative differences to precisely measurable quantities which can serve as a basis for a general and legitimate postulate. The individualizing method, on the other hand, neglects generic elements and concentrates its entire attention on the qualitative and particular features of phenomena. In this sense both depart from reality to serve the needs of conceptualization without which scientific knowledge is impossible' (Freund 1972, p.40).

I do not think it is strictly necessary to state that the generalizing method demands quantification. The basic distinction lies in the different manner in which they try to diminish the experienced complexity. The individualizing method does it by reducing the amount of elements that are taken into account and constructing complex relations between them; the generalizing method by reducing the number of elements as little as possible but simplifying relations between these elements. In mathematical models this often leads to linearization, as is so popular in, for instance, econometrics. Each method should appeal to another cognitive structure: the generalistic method to the systematic thinker, the individualistic method to the intuitive thinker.

It is interesting to note that the mathematic representations of problems leads to different examples of the reduction of complexity. As mentioned, the linearization of higher degree equations reduces complexity by leaving many possible solutions, or else the decomposition higher degree equations into a larger number of lower degree equations; substituting quantitative complexity for structural complexity. And in differential equations, the reduction of the order of the equation is achieved by creating new variables which are representing the higher order differentials. Thus creating new variables and raising the structural or qualitative complexity (see Willis 1962, pp.369-82). It is contended that the individual can operate in a 'field' of cognitive styles, and he can switch between them to a smaller or larger degree depending on his training or natural abilities. Applied to the above-mentioned mathematical techniques, this may mean that he will choose a technique that fits his perception of the problem and which will also be influenced by his own preference.

Problems, Solutions and Decisions

At this point it is important to make a small detour to the distinction between problem solving and decision making. The latter is used in many organizational studies. The distinction is not one of major importance, and is mainly one of the degree of rationalization. Problem solving is concerned with generating a field of acceptable answers to more or less clearly formulated questions. The relation between the question and the manner in which the satisfactory answer is reached is more (systematic) or less explicit (intuitive). Decision making is often seen as a more complex activity of which problem solving can be a part. It consists of gathering, assimilating and evaluating information, assessing risks in various interrelated fields such as political or interpersonal relations, financial or personal consequences. The problem of the decision maker is to discover the meaning of the information with which he is confronted, to sift out relevant information and to store it in such a manner that he can easily find it when he has chosen a strategy for analysis. Bruner (1956) identifies those strategies and points out that their overall direction is towards economy and efficiency and away from redundancy.

Decision making is not the same as problem solving. Essential differences are the emphasis on the choices that have to be made and the link that is laid with the execution of the decision — the activities that have to be undertaken in order to put the decision into effect. The distinction is certainly not straight-forward. They are not mutually exclusive. In the process of problem formulation decisions are taken which restrict the problem description and which make whole classes of alternative solutions to the problem impossible.

In this study when problem solving is mentioned, it does *not* concern the application of solutions. It only concerns the description of a number of possible courses of action that *may* lead to the desired consequences. The choice between the different courses of action and the command to set off on the chosen course are only part of the decision.

The choice itself can be based on a range of different motivations or techniques. The choice can be made with dice or any other stochastic mechanism at one end of the range, or at the other end the choice is a direct consequence of the formulation of a formalized problem and the application of an explicit optimization technique. The alternative solutions are weighed and ordered and only when there are two or more solutions leading to identical results will there be any choice left. In this case, problem solving and decision making become identical. Systematic problem solvers will tend to view decision makers in the latter perspective.

Decisions, Solutions and Stress

The cognitive structure thus gives an indication of the abilities of the individual to handle problems which are part of the decision-making process. It does not say anything about the ability to cope with the mental stress associated with assessment and taking of risks. The origin of such stress may be a characteristic of the individual or, and that is more important in the perspective of this study, it may be the consequence of the way the individual is suspended in a network of organizational relations. This latter aspect is treated by Kahn *et al.* (1964) in a manner that analyses the nature of the demands that are set by the organizational environment and the possibility of the individual to meet these demands.

Their theory distinguishes between several types of role conflicts:

(a) *intra-sender conflicts* arise from *different* prescriptions and proscriptions from a single member of a role set which are *incompatible*;
(b) *inter-sender conflicts* arise when the membership of one organization produces pressures which are incompatible with pressures from memberships or another group;
(c) *person-role conflicts* can occur when role requirements violate moral values (Kahn *et al.* 1964, pp. 18–21).

These distinctions are based on a difference in *context* of the role expectations between role senders and/or receivers. In the theory as presented in this study the basis of dissonances, which may eventually lead to conflicts, is found in *structural* differences between an individual and the organizational set in which he operates. The differentiation between structure and content makes the presented theoretical analysis complementary to that of Kahn *et al.* rather than contradictory.

Dissonance

In the previous part of this chapter two distinctly different subjects have been treated.

Technology, the ability to get things done, the state of the art, was treated as a description of the nature of the problem that must be solved.

Cognitive structure was treated as the ability of an individual to handle complex problems.

It should be clear that these two subjects are, although different, closely related. They are variations on the term variety in Ashby's law. (The variety of the problem and of the problem solver do not fall in the same range, and this may well be the origin of a conflictual situation, as was hinted at on p.65 where it was stated that a mechanical engineer will not find it satisfying to be permanently employed as a motor mechanic.)

It is hypothesized that there are 'fitting and non-fitting' combinations between the problem and the problem solver.

Based on the two-dimensional representation of both the complexity of problems and the cognitive structure of the individual, the following diagram should make clear that there are four principally different types of dissonances between the problem and its solver, which can be subdivided into two subcategories.

They will be illustrated by means of the two cases presented at the beginning of this study.

COGNITIVE STRUCTURE–TECHNOLOGY DISSONANCE

This is the first of many descriptions of structural dissonances that can occur if we assume that the variables that were chosen to describe organizations are appropriate.

These descriptions are the result of a combination of the abstract formulation of the difference in complexity of systems as represented in Figure 4.4 and the interpretation of the structural dimensions for the variables that have just been described. It was for this reason that first a description was given of the technology and the cognitive structure variables so that they could be combined in the following manner.

(1) *Under-utilization dissonance.* The individual is presented with problems that are 'too easy' or rather not complex enough. This can result in a sense of boredom or in a quest for more interesting problems. In the automation department the second option was often found and was also widespread in other such departments. When prospective clients came with their problems to which there was a relatively easy though uninteresting solution, the automation boys most often tried to blow up the problem to such complexity that building a solution became interesting. This resulted in the design of

highly complicated and sophisticated large-scale control sysems which were extremely hard to implement and therefore not very successful.

In the engineering department the same tendency occured in mechanization projects, resulting in a form of technological imperative. Individuals want to work at the forefront of their abilities using new techniques and knowledge where, for the wishes of the client, existing and well-tested solutions would have been more effective. This became quite clear when studying the sequence of mechanization projects. Usually, new projects were causally linked to previous projects creating possibilities of a more thorough exploitation of ideas already used in the previous project. For the client, a study of bottlenecks, or inefficiencies in the production process would have resulted in much more effective mechanization projects. In other words, the technician is likely to define his problem to fit his interest in certain solutions, a process that undoubtedly leads to technical progress. This progress is based more on an automatic technical change than on a demand for technical solutions to problems experienced.

(2) *Overload dissonance.* The individual is confronted with a problem he cannot solve. The usual tactic is to simplify it to such an extent that he can solve it. The question remains of whether the solution is a satisfactory one. In the first example, the development department was often confronted with problems of great complexity where solutions were hard to find and results difficult to predict or plan. The solution technique is necessarily one of trial and error by means of varying variables which are thought to be important.

Apart from the distinction between underutilization and overload the structural approach results in two different types of dissonance.

(a) *Quantitative dissonances* result from a difference in the quantitative aspect in cognitive structure and technology. In this sense people can be confronted with more (relatively simple) information that they can handle. Systematization (or automation in the sense of data processing) can be the solution to this.

(b) *Structural dissonances* result from a difference in the structural aspect of cognitive structure and technology. The problem is either unanalysable in the sense of Perrow, and trial and error techniques do not lead to the result hoped for. This was often the case in the development department where certain variables were *known* to influence the phenomena that had to be mastered, but their mutual relations were such that solutions were extremely difficult to find. The *ceteris paribus* manner of experimentation is often employed to try to solve such problems. But when one does not know which other things have to be kept equal this can be very frustrating.

In the area of production planning, where there are many mutually influencing production units, the planning of the product flow leads to such dissonances. This results in long throughput times and low flexibility. Both can have important consequences for the production organization. Solutions to such overload problems are often sought in the uncoupling of interrelated variables by means of creating buffer stocks between the different production units. The higher degree of utilization of the production units compensate the higher costs of keeping stocks and the longer throughput time. Such a solution is achieved by reducing the structural complexity of the planning problem by raising the quantitative dimension by adding extra elements (the stocks between the production units).

The combination of the two directions of dissonance between the cognitive and the transformation structure can be illustrated in a diagram by super-imposing the cognitive structure field on the transformation field, as is done in Figure 4.12.

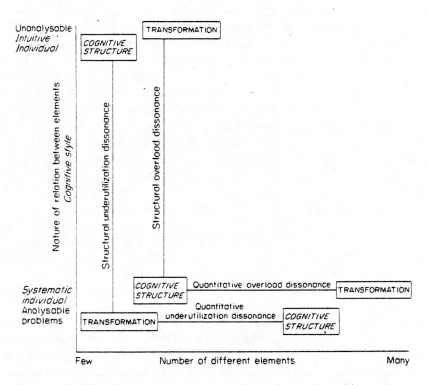

Figure 4.12   The dissonance between transformation and cognitive structure

It will be clear that most real life situations are a combination of the two dimensions (structural and quantitative) of dissonance. It is even possible that the individual is both overloaded and underutilized, each on a different dimension of complexity.

Computers with the appropriate software (programs) can be viewed as problem solvers. The capacity of the computer to store and retrieve information can be represented as the quantitative aspect of its cognitive structure and the complexity of the cross references in the programming as the structural complexity of its cognitive structure. The programs can be too complicated for a specific situation, but the capacity may also be too small or the capacity too large and the program not complicated enough. The two dimensions are independent. An interesting aspect of the computer example is that the quantitative aspect is one of hardware whereas the structural aspect is basically one of software or programming. But here too we often see that structurally complex programs also use a lot of memory space.

Some Consequences of Dissonance

The dissonances that have been defined solely in terms of a combination of two independent aspects of the model are important to the individual because they place him in a situation of stress which can have consequences for his own well-being. They are also important to the organization in a technical sense i.e., independent of the fact that the well-being of the members of an organization is of importance to that organization. It is technically important because existing problems do not get solved in a satisfactory manner. This results in a deficient functioning of the technical organization.

We will now pursue our systematic course through the field of organizational variables in the same manner as in the previous part of this chapter. However, a switch will be made from the level of the individual to a higher level of aggregation.

TASK STRUCTURE

The main characteristic of an organization is the coordination of specialized and differentiated individual effort. The source of organizational surplus is commonly attributed to specialization of effort, the division of labour, the differentiation of instrumental roles or tasks among its members. This differentiation is often most clearly visible at the executionary level, as in Adam Smith's example of the production of pins. This would be called horizontal specialization, as opposed to vertical specialization. In the literature on management theory, organization structure is largely concerned with responsibility in the sense of approving decisions made within the organization, with vertical specialization. It emphasizes the leader as a decision maker and the operator as a 'doer' or follower. It is apparent that a leader cannot emerge in an organization unless the members assume differentiated responsibilities. Within this condition a leader is 'a person who becomes differentiated from other members in terms of the influence he exerts upon the goal setting and goal achievement activities of the organization.' (Shull et al. 1970, p.173). This distinction is probably founded on historical political examples concerning cultural divisions such as tribal chiefs, kings, presidents and bosses of the Mafia. In reference to this it is not so strange that Etzioni (1961) tries to base his typology on the medium of control, using compliance as a major source of differentiation between organizations. The significance of compliance lies more in the relevance to the problem of social order than to the coordination of differentiated labour. Compliance is a relationship consisting of the power employed by superiors to control subordinates through a reward and punishment medium and the orientation of the subordinates to this power. This aspect will be returned to when treating the control structure of the organization.

Horizontal and Vertical Differentiation

In the context of the task structure, vertical specialization is equally important, even when dissociated from its power aspect. As Knight (1933, p.16) remarked, 'The gain from superior direction is so much more important than that from superior concrete performance that undoubtedly the largest single source of increased efficiency results from having work planned and directed by the exceptionally capable individuals.' Now, nearly fifty years later, a less personal approach seems appropriate. The gist of the statement still rings true.

The differentiation of problem-solving activities or decision making along a line of the inclusiveness of the area or the domain of the problem is one of the main characteristics of vertical differentiation.

Problems with far-reaching and profound consequences will usually be handled in another place in the organization than superficial routine problems. The word 'hierarchy' is too often used in the sense of a rigid boss–slave relationship with control passing unidirectionally from top to bottom. In the context of the task structure it has a nearly inverse meaning, for here it is the interlocking of smaller problems that generate larger over-arching structures. *The smaller problems are inherent to the execution of particular tasks and the over-arching structures those concerned with coordination and planning.* Task structure concerns both the differentiation of the executionary tasks as well as the executive task. That cannot be seen independently of each other as each form of differentiation demands coordinative activity if more is required of an organization than random reflection accommodation to the environment.

One of the first problems that has to be solved when describing the task structure is a semantic one. In the organizational literature the distinction between role, task and function seems difficult to define. For this study the choice has been made for the term task structure, where task is equivalent to an instrumental role. With the description of the individual in an organization not only the set of activities with he performs is described, but as a logical consequence also the instrumental relation between affiliated task performers. The task structure describes how all the transformations inherent to operating within a specified domain are distributed over the units of analysis.

The variable employed to characterize the task structure is its complexity, as defined previously. This will have to be translated to this specific subject.

The *quantitative* dimension concerns the differentiation of the work that has to be done. It concerns the number of different tasks that are performed. Because the differentiation and the size of the domain of the organization cannot be specified beforehand it is not possible to equate differentiation and the sequence length of each task. (see the end of this chapter).

The *structural* dimension is the combination of a qualitative and a temporal dimension.

The first is the specificity of each task itself. Is it clearly defined? Are only the in- and outputs defined or is also the exact manner in which the transformations are to be executed defined? Highly specified tasks are found in assembly line situations and are analogous to a high degree of routinization (Blau 1974, p.626). This means that the range of tasks is narrowed down, simplifying jobs. It implies that activities (or rather the solving of related problems) can be programmed. This in turn implies that possible problems are known and the solutions incorporated into the design of the task. Highly specified tasks are also found in automated information-processing departments.

The temporal dimension can also be called the stability or, as an inverse description, the dynamic nature of the task. Does the task change often and are the changes predictable? As was done previously, these last two dimensions are combined with the implicit assumption that dynamic or unstable tasks are not very liable to be highly specified.

I am well aware that examples can be found, as for instance with pilots of aircraft, where the combination should not be made. Their work is highly routine. But their task is one of reacting to unforeseen circumstances. The less often these circumstances occur the better.

The task structure is definitive for the complexity of the relations between different tasks in a group and therefore also concerns the way in which the tasks are to be coordinated. The higher the task specificity of the individual, the clearer the relations can be between the different tasks that must be performed within a group.

The specificity is a parameter of the analysability of the relations between different tasks and of the amount and the nature of the information that needs to be processed in order to perform the set tasks effectively (Galbraith 1973).

The difficulty in keeping transformations and task structure apart, becomes evident when we realize that the nature of the task structure of other departments is the origin of the transformations performed by a planning or coordinating group within an organization.

As was stated at the beginning of this section, the use of the task concept poses a semantic problem. Not only is the distinction between task, role and office not quite clear, but that between task and transformation is even more difficult.

Task and Transformation

Transformations are often referred to as the task in organizational literature. Transformation and task are closely related but can nevertheless be the origin of organizational conflict. The mixing of these concepts becomes clear when we realize that Perrow's description of technology, 'the number of exceptional cases encountered in the work' coincides with the task variability of Van de Ven *et al.* (1976, p.324). And likewise Perrow's analysability concept coincides with Van de Ven's task difficulty. On the other hand, Perrow distinguishes two dimensions in the task structure, control and coordination, whereas Van de Ven *et al.* hypothesize a theoretical relation between the different coordination mechanisms and modes and the task uncertainty, inter-dependence and unit size. Terminology in this field proves to be very ambiguous, so it seems wise to be thorough in one's description of concepts.

Task, Role and Office

Because the concept of 'role' is originally one employed in sociology and anthropology, the main accent does not fall on the instrumental activities. Linton (1936, p.113) proposes a classic distinction between status (position) and role.

> 'A status, as distinct from the individual who may occupy it, is simply a collection of rights and duties . . . A role represents the dynamic aspect of a status. The individual is socially assigned a status and occupies it with relation to other statuses. When he puts the rights and duties which constitute the status into effect, he is performing a role!'

Kahn *et al.* (1964, p.13) modify this into

> 'a role is the set of activities associated with each office, which are defined as potential behaviour.'

Here too the office and the role are inseparable.

In the concept of *task* as it is used in *this* study, only those activities that are instrumental to the functioning of the organization or rather to the processes executed within it are taken into account. It is very much a question of whether they are explicitly linked to an office or status. That would be so if one took a very formal Weberian view of organizations. In practice, however, large parts of the tasks performed by individuals are defined by themselves. In an organization the specialization and definition of tasks is only partly one of *design*. As in society at large, it is also an effect of cultural evolution and development. The design is possible when the goal paradigm or the purposeful nature of the organization is taken for granted. Without this, differentiation would also come about in organizations in the same manner as Blau (1974, p.627) describes: 'society's division of labor is the emergent result of the actions performed by many people pursuing diverse ends.' The generative mechanism of this increasing differentiation is a most interesting subject that is only in the first stages of being studied or understood. (see Chapter 5).

In this study, the complexity of the task structure is represented diagrammatically by a two dimensional field with along the quantitative axis the number of different tasks that can be recognized within the unit of analysis, and along the structural axis, the specificity of the individual tasks.

Task Homogeneity

It must further be noted that an individual may perform a variety of subtasks which are not necessarily homogeneous, in the same sense as he uses different cognitive styles to solve different types of problems. Even in organizational environments where extremely complex and widely different problems have to be solved and individual tasks are largely unspecified, where no programs for solving these problems exist, the actual individuals performing such tasks are for a certain part of their time occupied with *routine* activity.

Routinization versus Specialization

The task specificity is the product of two components that are widely used in organizational literature: routinization and specialization. The distinction is not always clear. In this study, the distinction is made on the following basis.

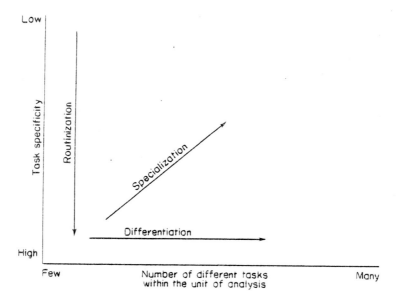

Figure 4.13 Task structure

Within an organization or a subpart of it, certain activities must be performed. These activities are the domain of the organizational unit. This domain may be subdivided in many smaller domains *without* specifying the manner in which problems in that subdomain have to be tackled. Quite often the opposite is the case. By narrowing down the domain, possibilities are created for acquiring greater skill, knowledge or expertise on the specific problems within that domain, often demanding increased training. This is called *specialization*. With *routinization* the domain is usually also small but the most distinctive characteristic of the task is that the solutions to the problems are programmed. Thus the distinction mainly has its origin in the knowledge or the state of the art of the transformation process. This means that most of the problematic situations that can occur are known and understood. Therefore the fashionable trend of job enlargement, making the domain of the job larger, does not necessarily influence its routinization. It only makes the program that has to be executed longer. *Within a routinized task, differentiation reduces task related training. With a non-routinized task, differentiation may make increased training necessary.*

Thus routinization contributes to the quantity of the achievements and specialization to the quality. Under the assumption that labour costs are related to the level of skills necessary to perform them, routinization improves productivity by enlarging output at lower costs. Specialization may also improve productivity, but this depends on other conditions. Time and resources are needed to train specialists. *Routinization has in the past helped to supply the manpower resources that specialization demanded, and specialization supplied the programmed solutions to the production problems, making routinization possible.* Specialization supplied the know how for mechanization and automation, they in turn supplied monotonous routinized jobs. From a technological point of view, these jobs should be the first to be mechanized or automated. It is very much in question whether the economic criteria, as they are predominantly used, weigh in favour of such substitution. From a social or psychological point of view the substitution of automated production apparatus for highly routine tasks is attractive (see also Chapter 5).

Coordination

Until now the main field of the task structure has been the horizontal differentiation aspect. However, every form of differentiation demands a form of coordination. This in an organization the 'coordination of individual effort' is one of its central problems. The complexity of that problem can be defined in the same three-dimensional manner as all the previous areas to which the concept of complexity has been applied: the number of units that have to be coordinated in so far as they are manifestly different from each other, the nature of the relations between the different units, and the predictability of the activities of these units are all elements that influence the problem of coordination and its possible solutions. In this sense coordination can also be seen as an aspect of integration (Lawrence and Lorsch 1967).

Blau (1974, p.621) says it seems paradoxical that 'structural differentiation is the condition that brings about integration, . . ., in as much as differentiation is conceptualized as restricting social intercourse and integration as contingent on it.' This does not seem so paradoxical when segregation and not differentiation is taken as opposite to integration. *Both* integration and segregation are impossible without differentiation. Blau's paradox may be the consequence of his conceptualization of differentiation as restricting social intercourse. This will be true when the domain of communication is made smaller, but not necessarily when the depth or quality of the information that is to be communicated becomes more extensive than in the previous situation.

Coordination is the activity or task that is designed to link or integrate other differentiated tasks. The effectiveness of these coordinating activities is by no means easy to assess; widely different norms to judge it by can be thought of. We will return to this presently. The coordinative aspect of the 'vertical' organization structure has overwhelmingly been interpreted in a superior/subordinate relationship, as interpretation we do not wish to follow at this point. The vertical differentiation must be seen, in the perspective employed here, as concerning the domain or the scope of the problems that have to be solved. As the scope becomes wider, it seems probable that the task specificity will decrease (as opposed to the length of the program in the routinized task).

Planning is, of course, one of the most widely applied coordinating techniques and automated management information systems may well have an influence on these tasks, tending to make them more specific. These planning techniques presuppose knowledge of the nature of the individual tasks and the manner in which they are related to each other. Planning as a form of coordination, in this sense, expresses a wish for routinization of the solving of problems concerning coordination.

Tasks or activities become more difficult to specify as the timespan increases, over which the results of decisions made higher up in the hierarchy of the organization become clear. More formal models of the field of the problems in which decisions have to be made have a positive effect on the specifiability of executive or policy-making tasks.

Summing up the concept of differentiation, it can be said that there are two main directions in which it can take place:

(a) horizontally, pertaining to the delineation of tasks through reduction of domain;
(b) vertically, pertaining to the scope of the problems solved or decisions taken, in respect to the influence on horizontally differentiated units.

Examples of Differentiation and Coordination

In the engineering department of the first case study, both task differentiation and the specificity of the tasks were high. The design was mainly given form by the chief designer and then consequently worked out in greater detail down the echelons of the design department. When the total design was approved, the blueprints were sent to either their own workshop or the machine factory. It was then analysed on work content and materials were ordered by the purchasing department and the work was split up and differentiated according to the different skills or machines that were necessary. Then the whole was fit into a schedule in which most specifications were reflected. The people in the workshop were in reality no longer treated as craftsmen, but as machine tenders. They translated information from the work instructions into input signals for their machines, a step that could quite easily be left out when employing numerically controlled machines to which programs could be fed. The high degree of task specificity, the strong interrelations between the organizational positions resulted in a heavy coordinative structure and therefore a relatively low flexibility. Routinization is high in this 'old' branch of the industrial organization. *Specialization occurs only in functional areas at the forefront of the designing process.*

In the development department differentiation in tasks was much less outspoken. Differentiation in product area did, however, take place, so that many jobs were duplicated in the different product-oriented departments. In other words, *differentiation within the time dimension of the development program was low. Specialization within specific areas of the development problem was much higher.* Individuals with specialized training or experience in a narrow field worked in parallel to find solutions to marginally related problems. As a consequence, there was little or no coordinative activity within a specialized function in that department. At departmental meetings the different specialists discussed their problems and their *hopes* for finding solutions. Differentiation in the vertical sense was mainly based on the range of scientific solutions for practical or instrumental experimentation or testing.

In the factory, both differentiation and routinization were very high. Since the industrial revolution the philosophy in industrial production has been one of the predominance of mechanized production in which the worker is seen as an appendix to the machine. The task of the individual is a direct consequence of the technical process taking place in the machine and the chosen solution to that process, specified by the design of the machine. From a task structural aspect the 'vertical' differentiation is low. *Coordination is built into the production process itself.*

Apart from the controlling functions analysed in the following sections of this chapter, the task remains of solving exceptional problems left unsolved by the workers in the production process and of firefighting when sporadic disruptions in either the flow of materials or in the production process takes place. The whole production process in the case study was designed for uninterrupted production of uniform products and had become extremely inflexible over time.

The automation department in the second example can beset be characterized by a medium differentiation and a low degree of task specificity. People were to a certain extent interchangeable although their training level was remarkably high. Little or no specialization coordinative activity took place. On the other hand, the clients were a highly differentiated, highly routinized organization which had an important differentiated subdepartment concerned with the coordination and planning of the industrial production. The tasks in this subdepartment were to a large extent routinized, but *routinization was not evident* in their own organizational environment.

The manner of planning and coordination worked according to simple patterns. These were judged by the planning department as flexible, but turned out to be rigid when analysed by outside specialists. Through organizational slack, i.e. excess capacity of certain parts of the organization, disruptions due to a lack of coordinative activities of the planning department were smoothed out. Thus from a *technical* point of view the planning system was rather routinized. From a social point of view, the planning department fulfilled a different role–one which was only slightly less routine, but one which would be lost when an automated planning system would be introduced. The contrast between the social and the functional role of this department will be treated further on in this chapter.

TRANSFORMATION–TASK STRUCTURE DISSONANCES

On the assumption that both the transformations and the task structure can be analysed in the manner outlined in this section, it must be possible to define the four basic types of dissonances as explained on p.73 and first illustrated in the case of the four technology-cognitive structure dissonances. The dissonances presented here will show a great similarity to the previous ones.

The technology of building machines is an old one and that of designing machines is only slightly less old. They have been at the centre of our attention since the industrial revolution. The innovative impulses are mainly to be found in the first stadia of the design process and only as far as the designers are willing to step outside the accepted techniques. This well-designed technology has been reflected in the highly differentiated and routinized task structure. This leads to inflexibility and complex coordination problems, which are both difficult to translate into calculable costs.

In the case of the TV tube factory it might be suggested that an independent subdepartment of the engineering department should be created in order to supply the flexible service that the development department demanded. The consequence would be the creation of a service department with highly skilled members, and this department would hardly be differentiated in tasks in order to keep the coordination problem between the different tasks comparatively simple. The planning would only be one of general capacity, i.e. determining whether anyone would be available at a certain time. This would have as a consequence that the man-hours would be much more expensive, assuming a relation between the level of training or skill and the pay, and also that the members of such a department would have to master the whole trajectory of design to the installation of the finished machines or tools. This sets very high demands on the breadth of experience and skill of such individuals or groups of individuals. This high demand is called *program-overload dissonance* (see Figure 4.14). It can best be described as the consequence of a quantitatively

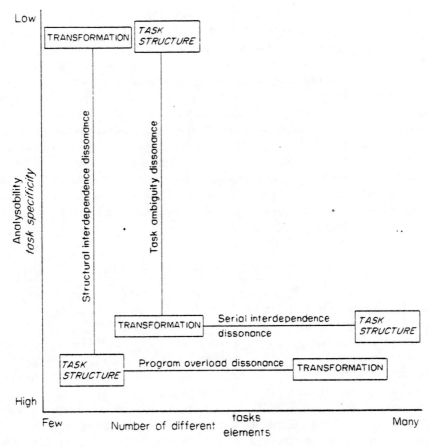

Figure 4.14 Dissonances between personal norms and values and the control structure

complex problem that is *not* split up into sufficient different tasks. A clear example would be the assembly of a whole car. The program of activities would be long and therefore time consuming to learn, whereas it would not necessarily be difficult to understand. In the example of the engineering service department, the breadth of skill was combined with great depth. This can lead to *task ambiguity dissonances*. From an outsider's point of view the transformations are well understood and are thus susceptible to routinization. Because the tasks within the group are hardly specified, it leads to the dilemma of *who* will do *what* and *when*, if the cooperation of more than one member of such a department is necessary.

The opposite to program-overload dissonance is *serial interdependence dissonance*. This is when a transformation is to be executed which is not of an extensive quantitative complexity, and this is done by designing extremely narrow tasks. One could speak of *over*-differentiation. An inordinate amount of attention has to be paid to coordinating the different tasks. In assembly line technology this leads to strict programming activities. This can partly be restricted by creating buffer stocks between the different places on the assembly line. However, this is detrimental to the amount of material in the production process. In processes that are not characterized by serial inter-dependence, but rather by a structurally much more complicated inter-dependence, such as can be found in engineering workshops for instance, coordination becomes problematic. In such situations many different working stations have to be passed in highly variable sequences. This lengthens throughput time and the amount of work on the shop floor.

The fourth and last type of dissonance can be found in organizations that *want* to routinize transformation processes that are *not yet* well understood. Tasks are created that function only when the process runs as it should. When something exceptional occurs (and this happens often because the transformation process is not well understood) the exception is ignored and a faulty decision or a defective product is made. Indications in this direction are highly specified task structures which produce a high defect rate in the production process or a low effectiveness in an area of problem solution. Such a situation existed in the early years of integrated circuit production. Because of the strong demand for these circuits production had to be stepped up, making laboratory production methods infeasible and uneconomical. An industrial production method was created resulting in high reject but low labour costs. Under the existing circumstances this was probably the most economical solution.

The Old and the New Structural Approach

In essence, what has just been presented is part of the classical technology structure theoretical approach. The main difference in this presentation is that a 'fit' between technology and structure can be described. When such a fit is not found, an intervening variable emerges on the level on which the 'fit' has been described. Thus there will be no correlation between technology and structure, as is hypothesized in the classical theories. Instead there is a relation between the *difference* in the structure of the technology and of the task structure on the one hand and a recognizable form of dissonance on the other.

I hope it has become clear that there is a great similarity between the cognitive structure — technology relation and the technology — task structure. This is due to the fact that the *cognitive structure* concerns *problem solving by the individual*, whereas the *task structure* concerns the manner in which problem-solving activities are *distributed over a set of individuals*. This will be dealt with more explicitly when treating interlevel dissonances. In order to complement the presentation of the *technostructure* we will now go on to treat the *sociostructural* aspect of organizations.

ROLE AND CONTROL STRUCTURE

It is again with the greatest hesitation and the utmost caution that I step into an area on which there is as yet so little scientific consensus — the sociology of organizations or organizational anthropology. I would not have the temerity to state that I intended to practise anthropology were it not necessary to approach the positions of individuals in an organization in an anthropological manner. Gross *et al.* (1958, p.23) stress that determining cultural patterns is a major task of the anthropologist.

'Deeply embedded in the "culture" of ideology of the anthropologist is the belief that one of their major tasks, if not their primary one, is to uncover the covert behaviour patterns or "blueprints for behaviour" of the society they study. Just as the detective feels he must find the motive if he is to resolve a crime, so the anthropologist feels he must isolate culture patterns if he is to make sense out of the myriad bits of behaviour he observes in society. It is for these regularities in social behaviour that he searches.'

In the context of this study it is not our object to isolate and describe culture patterns, but rather to define which characteristics of the culture form the dimensions of these patterns. Before this can be done it is necessary to pay attention to the concepts as they are frequently used pertaining to culture. They prove to be problematic. What Neiman and Hughes (1951, p.149) observed when reviewing the role concept is still very true:

'The concept of role is at present still rather vague, nebulous and non-definitive. Frequently in the literature, the concept is used without any attempt on the part of the writer to define or delimit the concept . . . the assumption is that both writer and reader will achieve an immediate compatible consensus!

I am afraid that definitive concepts in a field as complex as this one (as yet) not possible. Still I will try to give an impression of what is meant by these concepts in order to facilitate the possibility of consensus. Linton (1936) provides a link between culture and social structure that can help us to gain some clarity in this matter. He says three separate elements are prerequisites for the existence of a society:

'an aggregate of individuals, an organized system of patterns by which the interrelations and activities of these individuals are controlled, and the *esprit de corps* which provides motive power for the expression of these patterns' (*ibid*, p.107).

In his opinion a society is a cultural phenomenon, which minimally includes 'the knowledge, attitudes and values shared by the members of the society' (Linton 1947, p. 25).

In a more or less purposeful organization the tasks that the individual has to perform are only a part of the interrelations and activities that can be recognized. The necessity for earning a living is partly substitutable for the esprit de corps. What is most interesting to this part of the study is how the interrelations and activities are *controlled*, how individuals are kept at performing their tasks and how they are also brought to show common forms of behaviour outside the performance of their tasks. In other words, what is the generative mechanism that leads to these common forms of behaviour?

Power Media

As was stated on p.106 'differentiation is the condition that brings about integration' and it is this integration that is such a specific characteristic of *social* behaviour. Without trying to explain why differentiation is a natural consequence of interactive open systems, it is hypothesized that differentiated roles are a prerequisite for social behaviour. *A consequence of this differentiation is mutual dependency and a need for coordination.* This dependency creates the possibility of influencing each other's behaviour and is thus the basis of mutual power relationships. As this dependency can occur in many different areas, be it physical, mental or otherwise, it is possible to speak of different power media. This can result in a situation that person *A* dominates *B* through the possible use of physical force whereas person *B* dominates person *A* through the use of social ridicule. This combination can result in a relatively stable situation. In this context Etzioni's (1961, p.5–6) organization typology based on the use of compliance distinguishes three media: physical, material and symbolic.

(a) the infliction of pain, deformity or death (coercive);
(b) material resources and rewards through allocation of salaries and wages, commissions ·· and contributions, 'fringe benefits', services and commodities (remunerative);
(c) social recognition through the allocation and manipulation of symbolic rewards and deprivations through employment of leaders, manipulation of mass media, allocation of esteem and prestige symbols, administration of ritual and influence over the distribution of 'acceptance' and 'positive response' (normative).

He suggests that the typology is exhaustive because every type of power that has been encountered so ·far can be classified as belonging to one of the categories or a combination of them. It is the last phrase of this sentence that makes it doubtful if it is efficient as a *typological* distinction for organizations, as they often employ two or more of the media to keep it functioning. It thus may be exhaustive but not sufficiently discriminatory to characterize an organization. What is more, because the different media can be used by different parties or actors in an organizing structure to influence each other, it is more appropriate to use it as a tool of analysis for intra-organizational relations than as a characteristic for whole organizations. It is therefore proposed that a different approach should be taken, not incompatible with Etzioni's.

NORMS AND VALUES

The origin of this approach lies in the classical interpretation of role behaviour as can be found in Parsons' (1951, p.38–39) *The Social System*:

> 'A role . . . is a sector of the total orientation system of an individual actor which is organized about expectations in relation to a particular inter-action context, that is integrated with a particular set of value-standards which govern interaction with one or more alters in the appropriate complementary roles.'

Interpreted freely one could say that an individual's behaviour is based on his expectations of possible reactions of the environment to that behaviour. These expectations are expressed in terms of the norms and values of the individual and of the social environment. If these norms and values coincide, the individual can be called socially integrated.

The activities and interrelations of an individual can take place in diverse environments of which an organization as a place of work is only a specific one, his home environment another, etc. The individual's expectations are based on experience and learning. Within the first twenty years of his life, the individual is shaped and formed in the family, the school, university and all those other institutions of which he becomes a member in the process of growing up. All this time a large number of claims have been laid upon his activities and thus on his behaviour. From all these influences he has retained a 'blueprint for his behaviour'. Or if he is a flexible person, a number of blueprints that allow him 'to do as the Romans do when in Rome'. He has developed a set of norms and values that is largely the product of his past. Usually there are a number of clearly recognizable influences of which his family background is one of the most evident. Thus we can state that norms and values are not hereditary in the strictest sense of the word, but that they have been communicated to the individual by his social environment. They are a heritage of his own past.

In this sense it may clarify matters to illustrate the forms of influence of the social environment as they can be recognized in some articulate sectors of society. In particular, religious sects can have a strong influence on the patterns of behaviour of its members, in clothing, customs and, for instance, eating habits. A common identity derived from a religion has often been a strong medium for the conveyance of formalized norms and values, as given form in the Jewish rules on food, the Ten Commandments, etc. But religious backgrounds have also been *important for the acceptance of authority*, an aspect that can be important for the *coordination of organized activity*.

The pattern of norms and values of the individual is the reflection of his social environments. They have been acquired by interaction with a higher level of aggregation. Most individuals 'fit' themselves to their social environment in the process of growing up. If they have not done this, or if they do not 'fit' in a new environment, we are confronted with an interlevel dissonance.

Normative Complexity

In the manner that should by now be familiar, the complexity of the structure of the norms and values can be described in a two dimensional fashion:

(a) the number of different norms and values that can be recognized within a social unit;
(b) the specificity or explicitness of these norms and values.

The first distinction is not too problematic. It concerns the differentiation of the norms of a (sub)society, the number of aspects of behaviour that are regulated. The second distinction is more problematic. Its origin lies partly in Weber's bureaucratic ideal type, in the form of formalization and standardization, but more clearly in the frequent experience that one knows that certain rules are assumed implicitly to exist, leading to specific behaviour. These norms are in no way made explicit. There are many things which 'simply aren't done'. Many of these norms lead to an organization's identity. Members are not judged explicitly on their adherence to these norms, but they are made to understand that they don't 'fit' in the organization. Every society has its 'outcasts'.

Referring to Figure 4.2, we saw that the individual is a transmitter of societal norms and values towards the organization, but that the organization is also directly subjected to societal norms.

Furthermore, the differentiation of norms and values, when they 'fit', can lead to integration of the individual in his social or in his organizational environment.

Interlevel Dissonance

Because of its emphasis on coordination of individual effort, an important aspect for an organization is the control of individual behaviour. *Coordination implies constraint;* the knowledge of *what* the constraints are or *who* can instigate them is the main aspect of the constrol structure. The organization specifies part of the individual's behaviour, his activities through the definition of his tasks. Why does he agree to fulfil these tasks? Why does he agree with the manner in which he has to fulfil them? Why is he willing to do what his superior tells him without significant motivation? What makes him accept a certain position in a hierarchy of authority? The answers to these questions are embedded in the norms and values of the individual as he has acquired them in his past. This leads us to our first presentation of interlevel dissonance. This is a form of lack of 'fit' between different levels of aggregation, i.e. between the individual and the group or organization in which he has to operate. It is hypothesized that the individual's norms and values can be so different in both content and structure that it is problematic for him and/or the organization to function in a mutually satisfactory manner. Apart from giving a few examples we will not go into the differences of content, only those of structure. An organization may implicitly or explicitly demand for instance the wearing of white shirts. If the employee persists in wearing a blue shirt, this is a conflict of content. It is not the complexity of the system of norms and values that differ, only a specific instance is given a different meaning. Such a difference of content can usually be discussed because both parties employ norms or values in this area of behaviour even though they are different. With differences in structure it is much more difficult because where the one has but few regulating rules the other has many, or where the one has clearly delineated norms and values, those of the other are vague.

Examples of Normative Types

In the two-dimensional descriptive field, an illustration could be given of certain (ideal?) types, for example:

The local. This pattern of norms and values is formed in a small closed system of social relations, as exemplified by rural communities until the beginning of this century in Europe. Often a direct religious influence is evident as well as a clearly delineated and simple social structure demanding certain types of proto-typical behaviour. Furthermore, within the closed society there is a strict hierarch of authority. There are few rights and many duties.

The bureaucrat is modelled mainly after Weber's ideal type. His norms and values are also formed in relatively closed social systems with a much more complex structure which is nevertheless still quite clear. Authority is differentiated along different domains, as are also the duties of the individual. Such individuals can be found among people who have for a long time been a member of complex organizations and have internalized the organizational norms and values and have possibly even transmitted them to their familiar environment. Early examples can be found in religious circles, families from the armed forces, and expatriate families in the colonies. Examples occur in general in environments where, due to the occupation of the head of the family, the social environment and of that of the primal organization have to a large extent merged.

The cosmopolitan's pattern of norms and values is complex. Due to a varied background, derived from membership of a large number of different social groups, he has internalized many different sets of norms and values which are not necessarily consistent or compatible. Behaviour is mainly influenced by the relation of the present circumstances to a number of circumstances in the past which seem appropriate. Thus the behaviour of the cosmopolitan is only predictable as far as the predictor has knowledge of the past of the cosmopolitan and of his present situation. Here cosmopolitan means 'Belonging to all parts of the world or free from national limitations' (Oxford). This does not mean to say that the orientation towards either the organization or the profession, as described by Gouldner (1957) is not of interest. To a large extent both distinctions run parallel. The professional, if he is to be integrated in the dual environment of his profession and his employing organization, will necessarily have to differentiate his personal norms and values to the extent that he can comply with the wishes of both environments.

Local in the description given above will also tend to be organization oriented. This is not due so much to a theoretical relationship between the organization and a closed social system such as rural communities, but rather to the fact that many organizations are organized in a strict manner in view of the necessary conditions of individual activities. The orientation towards leadership or hierarchy of authority is in this instance a common denominator.

The professional orientation bears upon the existence of outside reference groups and even suggests predominance of these outside reference groups over the influence of the employing organization, just as the cosmopolitan refers to divers reference groups which can be chosen to fill the circumstances.

In reference to Parsons' definition (1951, p.2), where the value standards are related to 'particular interaction contexts', it will be clear that the origin of the complexity of such a system of norms and values may be found in the number of different 'interaction contexts' that have been important enough, in the past, for the actors to internalize their specific sets of norms and values.

The main emphasis has been on the acquisition of a set of norms and values by the individual through interactions with his environment, especially in the more formative years of his life. We will now turn our attention to the organization.

CONTROL STRUCTURE

For a set of individuals we could establish the highest common factor of the individual norms and values of the members outside the organizational context and then see if the common behaviour inside the organization is a reflection of this common set. The contention is that this would not be the case. Many individuals show a markedly different behaviour when functioning in an organizational context in comparison to, for instance, their home surroundings. It can thus be said that inside the organization a specific set of norms and values is operational. They concern not only the division of labour as was treated in the task-structural aspect, but also such things as dress, language, behaviour towards colleagues and superiors, the expression of criticism on colleagues or the organization in general, the way in which the functioning of the individual member is judged by his superiors and how their (lack of) appreciation can be expressed, or what facilities the members have to counter the evaluation of their activities by their superiors or other groups within the organization. Many things spring to mind when thinking of the difference in behaviour at home or at the office, but also between at home or at the country club, another *organized* social setting.

Within the organization quite different behaviour patterns may be demanded of a member when interacting with other members of a different hierarchical status: he may be very deferential towards a member of the board of directors, behave as an equal towards someone of his own level, and be rather formal, possibly even patronizing, when dealing with a subordinante. In his home surroundings deference towards one's parents is no longer the norm because open communication and equality is emphasized. This can lead to a split between a person's working and private behaviour. This split can be infuriating to youngsters of college age, for they are apt to see it as hypocrisy. The individual however, has two sets of values, functioning in two different roles, which operate in two different environments. It is more like schizophrenia than hypocrisy.

NORMATIVE DISSONANCES

We now come to the point where we can diagrammatically present the dissonance between the structure of the individual members' norms and values and those of the organization or the group of which he is a member (see Figure 4.15).

The nature of the control structure with its inherent distribution of authority and power in the group or the organization is a strong determinant for individual behaviour. It is not only the member–leader relations that are influenced but also inter-member relations in a peer group. The common norms and values that are prerequisite for the existence of a social group, together with those necessary for the coordination of the technological processes in the organization demand that, in order to fulfil his role as a member of a group, the individual must temporarily adjust his own norms and values or substitute those of the group.

Coordination demands conformity.

Authority ambiguity exists when the individual member of an organization has a set of very explicit norms of what is done and what is not and the organizational norms are vague in that area. This becomes most evident in a hierarchical relation when it takes the form of a *perceived* authority ambiguity. For the individual in a lower hierarchical position it is difficult to find out how he can comply with the wishes of his superior. These can easily give an impression of arbitrariness. In the sense of Kahn *et al.* (1964) it is a

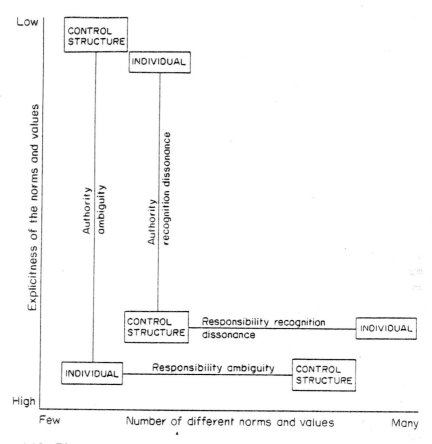

Figure 4.15 Dissonances between personal norms and values and the control structure

dissonance that can lead to an intra-sender conflict, not so much because different prescriptions and proscriptions from a single member of a role set are incompatible, but rather than they are unclear or ambiguous.

In the engineering group, as is described in the first case, the people working in the workshop were used to an explicit control structure. Clear rules existed on how to behave, and what reactions a difference in hierarchical status demanded. In the experimental workshop, which worked for the development department, there was hardly any hierarchical differentiation. It was not clear what reactions were demanded from subordinates by their supervisor. When somebody switched over from one department to the other the problems inherent in this situation become evident. The worker coming from the ordinary workshop would be at a loss on encountering the equalitarian attitude of his superiors, on whom he still depended for his annual job evaluation, increases in pay or promotion. If a worker were to return from the experimental workshop to the regular workshop he would find the explicit directives and relationships unsatisfactory, he would experience an *authority recognition dissonance.* He would find it difficult to identify with the overt regulations for his behaviour.

Along the quantitative dimension we will find a strongly *bureaucratically* tinted type of dissonance — a type that can be recognized in the armed forces. For every situation there is a specific rule or regulation to fit the circumstances. Due to the complexity of the norms and values of the organization a simple individual finds himself very uncertain as to the way those complex norms and values relate to himself. He may even have difficulty in recognizing the difference in circumstances to which different norms and values apply. We will call this in the most general case a *responsibility ambiguity*. The opposite can also be the case, in which the individual has a highly differentiated set of norms and values, whereas the organization operates with a much simpler set; we will call this a *responsibility recognition dissonance*.

Usually dissonant situations are a combination of both dimensions. The most disturbing example of the combination of authority and responsibility ambiguity can be found in Kafka's *Trial* where tremendously subtle but inexplicable demands lead to a paranoiac situation.

Another point to keep in mind is where *fashion* plays a role in the definition of norms and values. This means that the third dimension of structure becomes important; the *stability over time*. In political organizations a change in political dominance can have such normative consequences as to demand different forms of behaviour from its members, or forms which are impossible to comply with which can have disastrous consequences, as illustrated in Koestlers' *Darkness at Noon*. The same thing may be said in the social environment of young people. Norms on dress and language change quickly. Not being able to keep up with the changes in norms excludes the individual from group membership.

Anomie

This lack of fit between the norms and values of the individual and his social (or in this study his organizational) environment is also a basis for anomic phenomena. Merton (1957, p.162) defines the organized *set of normative values* governing behaviour which is common to members of a designated society or group as its *culture structure*. The social structure is that organized set of social relationships in which members of the society or group are variously implicated. *Anomie* is then conceived as a *breakdown in the cultural structure*, occurring particularly when there is an acute disjunction between cultural norms and goals and the socially structured capacities of members of the group to act in accordance with them. In this conception cultural values may help to produce behaviour which is at odds with the mandate of the values themselves.

In the domain of society studied here, the social relationships are mainly defined by the interaction of tasks. Mertons' anomie description points at an intrinsic relation between the task structure and the control structure. When these two do not fit, this can have anomic consequences. These are to be described in the next section. Before we do so, it is appropriate to pay some more attention to the concept of anomie as it concerns not only the above-mentioned fit between task and control structure but also that between the structure of individual norms and values and the control structure. This leads to the remark that *anomie is both a sociological and a psychological* phenomenon, a reaction of an individual to his social environment. It is a state of mind which can lead to physically recognizable results but which are not immediately or only traceable to a lack of normative fit.

Cooptation

Organizations make use of this fit in their selection procedures especially where positions higher up in the hierarchy are concerned. Social origin or background is an important factor not only for the initial selection but also for further success. In France only the cadres from Grandes Ecoles and with a *better* social background stand a good chance of becoming top executives. (see Benguigni and Monjaudet 1970). It is the result of cooptation; the process of absorbing new elements into a system as a means of retaining an internally stable structure. Although nepotism in its original meaning may no longer be widespread in larger public organizations, in a more subtle form is still readily recognizable. Where originally the family or relatives were homogeneous in respect to their social norms and also dependent on the family hierarchy, now it is still worthwhile to search for similar social backgrounds or reference groups such as the professions. What is more, according to the hypothesized relations between personal and organizational norms and values, it is an effective method of keeping this type of dissonance, which might lead to disruptive conflicts, within acceptable boundaries.

Given the lack of discriminatory abilities of most personnel officers or managers in this direction, it still leaves open certain paths for development of the control structure through the influence of new members.

Selection and Change

The discriminatory information on which selection procedures are based is mainly derived from personal interviews by organization members with applicants for certain jobs. If it were to operate as a rational selection mechanism, more or less formal criteria should be available. Usually this is not the case apart from criteria of formal education and/or experience. An important non-formalized criterion is the opinion of the interviewer of the ability of the applicant to function in the social network of the department. This results in the use of criteria based on the assessment of the probability that the applicant may challenge acquired social positions in the network. Applicants who are judged to threaten existing equilibria are on the whole unattractive for an organization. It should be clear that they *can* be used by individuals responsible for selection of applicants as instruments for change.

Authority

An important aspect of the norms and values of both the organization and the individual is the approach to authority. It should be clear that this is certainly an aspect of *content*, but as will be shown, also one of structure. Authority is a characteristic of interpersonal relationships, *recognized by both parties*. Authority that is demanded by one of the parties but not accepted by the other is *no* authority. If for the moment the power aspects of authority is ignored, as well as the aspect of reward and punishment, then there only remains the aspect of the norms within a society that describe or define the accepted relations within a differentiated social structure. That the acceptance of these norms may largely be due to the possibility of punishment or reward is unimportant at the moment. In this light we can view for instance the role of the church in many societies, but also the authority of the landowner or the industrialist. Individuals have been brought up in the belief that such difference of status is natural and that authority is a God-given privilege in the sense of:

'Theirs is not to reason why
Theirs is but to do or die'.

In this perspective the question of authority in organizations, concerning who is allowed to *decide* the acceptability of individual behaviour, but also over the division of labour, is a cultural problem. It is hypothesized that there can be a tremendous difference in the differentiation *and* the recognition of authority. It is for this reason that the difference between problem solving and decision making was emphasized (see p.96). Decision making implies the restriction or the direction of behaviour (of others). Problem solving implies the description of appropriate courses of action given specified objectives or goals.

A research scientist may well accept the authority of somebody working for him where it concerns a subject of which he has the impression that his subordinate knows more or has a deeper understanding, whereas that person will have no say in the distribution of the resources over different areas of work. The same research scientist will not recognize any authority of his superior over decisions concerning the content of his own work because he is under the impression that his superior is not as well informed as he is himself. But he will accept decisions on resource allocation.

The hypothesized differentiation of areas of authority has two interfaces with the organization model as it is presented here. The first is the acceptance of authority by individuals as illustrated in the above example and also widely discussed in the literature on organizational leadership. The second is the relation with the division of labour or the task structure. This leads us to the last set of organizational dissonances on an intra-departmental level.

TASK STRUCTURE–CONTROL STRUCTURE DISSONANCE

Because the division of labour is the most fundamental characteristic of organizations, coordinative activities are called for. On the whole, every form of differentiation demands coordinative activity. Coordination demands restriction of behaviour — restriction of both a social and a functional nature. If an organization is to achieve the results that are demanded in reaction to the stimuli from both the environment and from inside the organization, it will have to control its activities in such a manner that these demands are met. Part of the control is achieved by defining tasks in such a manner that interface problems are solved at the level of task performers. The remaining activities have to be performed by individuals with tasks directed at controlling the activities of others. The *functional coordination* of the different tasks that must be performed can itself be viewed as a *task with a highly technological*

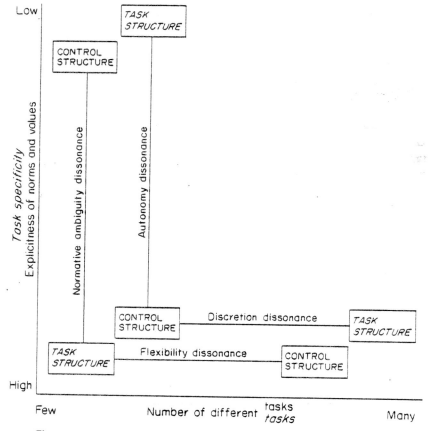

Figure 4.16   Dissonances between task structure and control structure

characteristic. That technological characteristic becomes all the more evident when the coordination is built into the production process, as is the case with an assembly line production, or is done with the help of automated information systems.

When the results of the task performances are easily recognizable and quantifiable, the problem of coordination can be presented as a formal one. This means that the coordinative technology is analysable. However, when the content of the tasks are more vague, the appreciation of their execution more problematic, then a different type of coordination is called for. These problems can be analysed by superimposing the two-dimensional representations of both the task structure and control structure in one diagram and defining the structure dissonances (see Figure 4.16).

Discretion Dissonance

When the task structure is highly differentiated, meaning that a large number of different tasks are performed within a group, the variety of norms and values that are necessary to influence and compare individual behaviour must also be large: If this is not the case the control activities will not be specifically related to the specialized task and will probably only be effective for influencing a small part of the individual's behaviour. This is called a *discretion dissonance.* Discretion is used here in the sense that Perrow (1967, p.198) employs it. 'Discretion involves judgements about whether close supervision is required on one task or another, about changing programmes and about the interdependence of one's task with other tasks.' In this case the discretion of the individual task performer is too large for him to be able to perform effectively. If he is to do so, he will have to *add* to his task such coordinative activities as to adjust his performance to those on which he is dependent or who are dependent on him. Such situations can be found in small fast-growing organizations where the development of the control structure lags behind the development of specialized roles and tasks. This happens because the founders or owners of the organization are still the main controlling or coordinative influence.

An example of this can be found in the case of the colour TV tube plant. In the design sub-department of the engineering group a dissonance of this type could be recognized. The classical highly differentiated task structure, ranging from chief designers specialized in certain types of machines to draughtsmen performing the more routine tasks, demands a fitting control structure. This is needed not only to coordinate the activities in time, but also to set the standards for the transfer of work from one level to the next. Within the sub-department this did not pose too great a problem as the head of the design group was a rather prim and meticulous man bent on detail and order. The next step in the hierarchy proved to be problematic, the norms for the evaluation of the activities of the sub-department as expressed in the contacts between Mr Ripple and the head of the Design sub-department were not of the same finesse and regularity as used within the sub-department. This resulted in friction between Mr Ripple and that sub-department, and often in the expressing of the opinion that their organization was not flexible enough, and that the design process took too long. The head of the design group did not have the discretion which was *appropriate* to his job.

Flexibility Dissonance

The opposite of the above-mentioned type of dissonance occurs when the control structure is more highly differentiated than the task structure. This is called a flexibility dissonance. Of course this also pertains to the discretion allowed to the task performer, but it becomes perceptible by the lack of flexibility of behaviour and activities of the task performer as demanded by the control structure. It is more easily recognizable than the previous type of dissonance. Staff departments with little differentiated task structures have to function within the control structure of their organization. This control structure 'fits' the highly differentiated task structure of the departments employing the 'core' technology. The *difference* in task structure and the similarity of the control structure leads to conflicts. The nature of tasks performed in the staff departments do not permit such strict regulations of activities and behaviour.

The classical example in this field is of the research laboratories where the control structure, in order not to thwart the creativity of the researchers, is kept restricted to minimal proportions. When the economic situation deteriorates and financial resources are restricted, the call is often heard for a better 'management' of research facilities. The same techniques as used in the other parts of the organization are demanded in order to bring the costs and the results closer together. Such a swing towards more 'bureaucratic' control structures never lasts very long because it proves to be detrimental to the results of research departments.

Normative Ambiguity Dissonance

A normative ambiguity dissonance exists when the task structure is highly specified (one can speak of a strongly routine task) but the norms for the evaluation and control of the individual's behaviour within that context are not. The individual is kept uncertain of what behaviour is demanded from him and how his performance will be evaluated.

Autonomy Dissonance

A low specificity of tasks implies that the individual is, to a large extent, autonomous in defining his own activities. The boundaries of his autonomy are created by the demands set on the results of his task performance by individuals with functionally related tasks. Highly explicit control structures strongly restrict individual behaviour and lead to conflict situations. The individual is not allowed the autonomy which the execution of his task demands. Such situations can be found in small organizations with clear role structures that fit a simple technology. When in such an organization a professional specialist is introduced in order to further certain developments which lie outside the abilities of the present non-professional personnel, the execution of such an autonomous task is hampered by the explicit control exerted by the leader of the small organization. Anticipating the development of the presented theoretical structure this example presents a first step towards the mechanism of differentiation of the control structure in a small organization. Because the execution of the specialist's task is hampered by the explicit control relationship with his superior, it can lead to conflict situations. In order to avoid this, withdrawal from everyday contact with members of the organization is often attempted, thus creating an exceptional position within the organization. The specialist builds his own mini-organization outside that of his employer.

Before we close the description of the relations between the task and control structures it may be interesting to place these concepts in a historical perspective.

The Weberian Assumption

This brings us to the assumption inherent to the Weberian bureaucratic archetype. It concerns the differentiation and explicitness of *both* the task and control structures. It *presumes the coexistence* of similar structures, excluding conflicting situations between the two. Only under the assumption that organizations minimize such intra-structural dissonance would the neglect of this distinction between task and control structures be permissible from an empirical point of view and would the combination of measurement scales not lead to too grave misrepresentations. However, when such minimization is also influenced by other forces outside this bilateral relation, as is hypothesized in this study, then this lack of distinction leads to an unworkable situation, in which such structural dissonances as described above cannot be recognized.

This brings us to the end of the description of intra-departmental dissonances based on the distinction between technology, the individual's characteristics and group structures.

Alienation

Before we go on to the last set of dissonances, those between departments, a problem that is inherent to the manner in which this theoretical framework has been constructed must be explained.

For clarity's sake one more set of dissonances will be added to the array, although it is not essentially of the same nature as those already presented. It is a combination of two sets which have already been described. It is the cognitive structure-task structure dissonance, which can be viewed as a combination of the cognitive structure-technology dissonance and the task structure–technology dissonance. These dissonances are on the same level as the personal norms and values versus the control structure. They are dissonances on the interface between the individual and the next higher level of inclusiveness. Even though it was not presented explicitly as a set of *inter-level* dissonances, the *normative dissonances* are between different levels of aggregation. In the case of normative dissonances, *behaviour is the medium through which the two structures are matched*. In the case of task structure-cognitive structure, the medium is the solutions that can be or are given to problems which are central to the domain of (that part of) the organization that is studied. Where, in the personal norms and values versus control structure dissonances it was possible to relate to the wide range of literature on anomie, in the case of the cognitive structure–task structure relations a link can be found with the concept of alienation. When interpreting Marx's discussion in the light of being concerned with the workers' loss of control over the means of production, not only in the economics and political sense but more in the sense of the essential conditions of their work, this link becomes evident. The worker loses his grip over the process of his labour when he has to execute tasks that do not engage his interests nor challenge his abilities. He loses control over both the production process and the product, as is made clear in the early writings of Marx (1964, p.124–5).

'What constitutes the alienation of labor. First, that the work is *external* to the worker, that it is not part of his nature, and that, consequently, he does not fulfil himself in his work but denies himself, has a feeling of misery rather than well-being, does not develop freely his mental and physical energies but is physically exhausted and mentally debased ... . His work is not voluntary but imposed, *forced labour*. It is not a satisfaction of need, but only a *means* for satisfying other needs.' (Italics mine–J. K.).

The work usually demands little thought, initiative or judgement and can often be characterized by close supervision, high routinization and low complexity. It is not in the line of this study to analyse the direct economic and political grounds for the loss of control over one's work. The content of the work in the sense of the substantive complexity of the problems the worker is confronted with is one of the foundations on which this study is built. It can thus be hypothesized that a lack of 'fit' between the nature of the individual, as far as the content of his work is concerned (cognitive structure) and the way the work is organized or split up (task structure, division of labour) leads to alienation in the sense as described by Marx.

The ownership aspect of alienation has lost much of its meaning in our organized public society and now seems tinged with nineteenth century romanticism. As was stated earlier, ownership is a hardly recognizable influence on the strategy or structure of most large organizations.

The analysis of the task structure–cognitive structure dissonances should, when following the line of thought that has just been presented, define two types of *alienative* dissonance and two types where *too much thought, initiative or judgement* are demanded. These four types should be the result of the superposition of the cognitive structure–technology and the technology-task structure dissonances.

On the structural side, i.e. the vertical axis, the combination is hardly problematic. When the tasks are largely unspecified, no programs or recipes are supplied. Initiative and thought are demanded from the individual to supply the solutions to those problems which are defined as belonging to his task area. If he cannot meet the demands set by his organizational environment because he does not have the capacity to do so, he is overburdened, thus creating *ambiguity overload dissonance*. This is opposite to the description of alienation that was given above. The individual is certainly not mentally debased in this case, but rather overburdened as he cannot meet the expectations of his task environment. The inverted dissonance comes very close to Marx's description of alienation, the work is highly specified, programs or recipes are given, there is very little choice for the individual worker between alternative courses of action. Little or no demands are set on his mental abilities. He is underutilized and because the task is a highly specified part of the larger process strictly interdependent with other set parts in his task environment, he has little or no freedom to define his own work. In this sense freedom is the ability to utilize one's potential.

Problems, Domains and Tasks

The above definitions of the dissonances between the cognitive and task structures are not without problems. They arise from careless switching of levels or analysis. These problems do not yet become explicit in the description of the qualitative dissonances, but only in the quantitative ones. They become clear because it is difficult to leave out the extensiveness of the tasks or program lengths, as described in the technology variable. If we do leave this out, the assumption is made that an organization with a highly differentiated task structure has thereby created 'small' or short tasks. This is, of course, not necessarily the case. If the domain of the organization is extensive, then high differentiation does not necessarily lead to smaller tasks than low differentiation in organizations with a limited domain.

Restated, the intermediate variable problem can be presented as follows.

It seems probable that we may assume that unspecified tasks lead to the definition of problems within the tasks that are low on analysability.

The assumption that high differentiation should lead to short tasks has no theoretical backing what so ever, and it is difficult to accept.

This brings us back to the beginning of the chapter where a description was given of complexity (see p.70) and the distinction between the characteristics of the elements (the two dimensions, the number of possible relations between different elements, and the nature of these relations over time) and the characteristics of the system as a set of different elements. The characteristics of the tasks remain the same, but the size of the domain and the degree of differentiation influence each other, because they are extensive variables.

Behaviour and Technology

Technology, the intervening variable between task and cognitive structure has been treated extensively, whereas the intervening variable between personal norms and values and the control structure has escaped our attention. This variable should be the behaviour of the individual. This is based on the assumption that individual behaviour is the manifestation of personal norms and values, possibly supplemented by his estimation of the expectations of this direct environment. His behaviour is judged by his environment. An environment does not hold expectations, only individuals do. In normal usage however we equate environment with the collection of individuals that make up the social environment. Thus it is better to state that in the environment of the actor there are other individuals with expectations of the behaviour of the actor. If we call these individuals 'senders' (Kahn *et al.* 1964, p.15) there is a structural conflict when the senders are in consensus on their expectations of the actor, and these expectations are not met. If this is not the case, if the senders are not in consensus, there is an *inter-sender* conflict. Senders have incompatible expectations of the actor. These inter-sender conflicts fall outside the scope of this study, because it is a conflict of content rather than structure.

The use of the concept of control structure assumes there is a largest common factor of norms and values that is representative for the social group of which the individual wants to be a member. If that assumption is *not* made, concepts such as socialization or reference groups become meaningless.

FROM TECHNOLOGICAL IMPERATIVE TO MULTI-LEVEL EQUILIBRIUM

The theory that has been presented up to this point has been a variation on the classical theme of the relation between technology and structure. Most of the classical theory assumed a 'technological imperative', that is that the structure of the organization irrevocably follows the technological developments. The present attempt describes a multi-aspect approach that has, as yet, no preference for the direction of organizational development. It can be summarized as follows:

The nature of the problems that have to be solved in order to operate effectively in a certain domain demand appropriate reactions on both the level of the individual problem solver and of the task structure within the organization. If these reactions are not appropriate, the result is detrimental to the functioning of the organization. Because an organization is populated by social individuals, the social structure also influences the efficiency of operations in a similar manner.

Apart from being more sophisticated than the straightforward technological imperative which demands the structure to follow the technology, the theory has much wider implications. If each department were to optimize its structural characteristics through minimizing the internal dissonances the result would not necessarily be beneficial for the whole organization. Because departments interact with each other and are dependent on mutual inputs or outputs, *departmental optimization* may well lead to structural *inter-departmental conflicts*.

Intra- and Inter-level Dissonances

Both the arrays of the cognitive structure–technology–task structure and the personal norms and values–behaviour–control structure dissonances are manifestations of the individual to system orientation (anascopic, p.64).

They are the result of the analytical technique of defining levels of aggregation. A technique that is directed at analysing organized phenomena at every level. In order to show the feasibility of this technique a description will be given of intra-level dissonances. That is, dissonances between units of analysis of the same level of aggregation. The choice is made for describing interdepartmental dissonances instead of interpersonal dissonances. Interpersonal dissonances are left out, because the social–psychological approach to these problems which is dominant in *this* field of analysis is, as yet, not compatible with the presented theory.

Stated differently, the previous part of this chapter has dealt with intra-elementary and inter-level dissonances, and the next part will deal with inter-elementary or intra-level dissonances—that is, the dissonances between functionally related individuals and dissonances between functionally related departments or groups. The manner of arriving at these definitions is identical to the procedure followed up to this point.

In the first case that was presented, it was clear that there were structural conflicts between, for instance, the engineering and the development department—conflicts in the form of coordination and communication difficulties. These difficulties were quite often based on a lack of under-standing of how the other department worked or who was responsible for what. The result of these problems was that the communication and coordination was usually left to the management of both departments. The difficulties that were the origin of the problems that became manifest when analysing the activities of both departments will now be described in a more formal theoretical mode. They are presented as a consequence of the structural differences between departments.

At the departmental level there are two types of structural dissonance: those between task structures and those between the control structures.

INTERDEPARTMENTAL TASK STRUCTURE DISSONANCES

If the task structures of two different departments are compared, using the presented structural description, it should be clear that structural and quantitative dissonances are possible (see Figure 4.17).

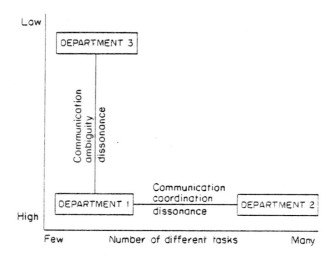

Figure 4.17   Interdepartmental task-structure dissonances

It is hypothesized that the dissonance between functionally related task structures takes the form of communication problems. Functionally related departments are mutually dependent on either the supply or the demand of materials and information that are to be processed in the departments. Their material dependence is but a variation of the information dependence when the product flow is seen as a physical manifestation of the information flow through an organization. This view is taken because of the chosen approach to treat an organization as a problem-solving system.

The communication dissonances are the consequence of the lack of clarity, for outsiders, of the availability of information inside a department. The functional nature of the organization demands appropriate information flows. The appropriateness of the information flows can be deduced from the ability of the organization to meet the information demands of the individual problems solvers or of groups of related problem solvers.

Communication coordination dissonance occurs when two departments are functionally related and the one has a highly differentiated structure and the other does not. *Communication ambiguity dissonance* occurs when the task structure of one department is highly specified and the other is not, when there is a great difference in task specificity. When both departments score high on either scale, communication is also probably difficult, although one might imagine that they are used to this type of communication problem.

These dissonances will be illustrated by applying them to the engineering and the development departments in the colour TV tube factory.

The engineering group depended heavily on the development department for information on technical specifications of the products that were to be made. These technical specifications were often in the form of tolerances around nominal measures. The understanding of the functioning and the design of the product were not such that a consistent model could be generated to show how the different tolerances were related. Slight changes in a part of the product could have devastating effects. This implied that the design of the production machinery and of the products were intimately related, demanding intense communication between the departments. In the engineering department, due to the functional task division, it was not difficult to find out who did what. The chief designer was the main spokesman of the department as regards the design of tools and machines. As soon as the design had taken its final form and had entered into a next phase, that of preparation for production, the responsibility shifted to another group within the engineering department. All the activities within the department were clearly related to the phase of the process, from design to production and testing. They were linked by a formalized planning system. If an outsider had to cooperate closely with the engineering department he had to have a clear impression of how the whole process from design to testing was organized. He had to know where every step in this process started and finished. The knowledge was easily accessible.

In the development department it was much more difficult to find out who did what. Even for the insider it would have been difficult to judge whom to contact when certain problems arose. This difficulty arose because the mutual relations between the different areas of specialization were not clear. There was no clear development process comparable to the design process in the engineering group. The composition of the different task areas could therefore not be defined by the demand for certain capacities in quantity, but rather by the necessity to cover the whole growing field of scientific and technical knowledge concerning the product.

This difference in the task structure made it difficult for individuals who had not been with the organization for a long time to find someone in the other department who could help them when certain problems had to be solved. This large difference in task structure was detrimental to the integration of the organization as a whole.

Integration can only be achieved when communication problems are minimized. (see page 53).

INTERDEPARTMENTAL CONTROL STRUCTURE DISSONANCES

The last intra-organizational dissonances that are to be treated concern the relations between the control structures of different departments. Because the contact between departments will, on the whole, take place on an individual versus individual or group level the definition of the interdepartmental control structural dissonances is identical to the dissonance between individual norms, values and the control structure. The only difference is that in the latter area of dissonance the individual refers to his social environment outside the organization. In the interdepartmental dissonance his frame of reference is the control structure of his own department. He may ask himself what the authority of his own superior is based on. In the interdepartmental control structure dissonance he will want to know the basis of the authority of the person from another department to whom he is functionally related.

In the engineering department (outside the small group of designers) there was a strong bureaucratic control structure. People knew their rights and obligations and could refer to them and depend on them in their contacts with groups outside their departments. In the development department there was no such clear-cut structure. Authority was a mixture of hierarchical status and the recognition of scientific or technical abilities. For the contacts between the two departments this led to difficulties in assessing the legality of decisions that were taken or agreements that were made. Difficulties were perceived quite differently from both sides. Because the rules on which authority was based in the engineering department were clear, and it was difficult to deviate from these rules, the developers often found the engineering department inflexible. When this was the case they found little or no satisfaction in trying to obtain other decisions higher up in the departmental hierarchy. When staying within their responsibilities, people in the engineering department were always backed by their superiors.

In the development department this was quite different. Because responsibilities were not clearly delineated, taking a decision higher in the hierarchy could have a different result because there might be a difference of opinion between the two persons or groups within the department.

As an afterthought, and it must only be seen as such, it may be interesting to show how *within* the engineering group there was a remarkable difference in control structure between the small group of designers, together with Mr Ripple, and the rest of the department. The consequence of this was that when the development department had been frustrated in their attempts to get their demands accepted, they often turned to Mr Ripple. If he took a decision in disagreement with the people in his own department, which often happened, this created conflicts within his own department—conflicts which can be described by means of an inter-group or intra-departmental dissonances.

This illustrates the idea that there is no essential difference between inter and intra-departmental dissonances. They are directly related. The distinction is one of relative difference in levels of aggregation.

THE ORGANIZATION AS AN OPEN SYSTEM

In anticipation of the reproach that the systematic analysis that has been presented takes the organization as a closed system, an attempt will be made to show that this is not necessarily so.

Despite the wide use of the concept of *system*, it is difficult to find clear definitions. They are usually of great generality. Usually the concept is taken as self-evident and the discussion is confined to the difference between 'open' and 'closed' systems.

For this study the essence of a systematic approach is that within the domain of the study, units can be *described*, to which characteristics can be attributed which *only* concern mutual relations between those units. The choice of *what* is to be earmarked as a unit is a pragmatic one. It depends on the level of analysis that is attempted. This is illustrated in Figure 2.2. The result of this manner of analysis must be made as clear as possible. This can be done for instance by the use of set theory. In this study the most elementary unit is the individual. For the individual the characteristics that are deemed relevant for this specific approach are his ability to solve problems and the ability to judge the expectations of others concerning his behaviour. These characteristics are *not* described in terms of the *inner workings* of the individual. There should be no psychologizing because that would be a break of the rule to set the boundaries sharply between different levels of analysis. At this level the individual is seen as being of one piece, within the specific characteristics that have been chosen to describe him. That does not necessarily mean that there can be no contradictions over time in these relations.

If this approach is taken, the definition of a system must necessarily be very general. It only concerns an agreement on the manner in which phenomena can (should) be described. It leads to the conclusion that the distinction between 'open' and 'closed' systems is a trivial one. A closed system is based on a *ceteris paribus* clause in the model. As long as one doesn't *know what* other things should be equal, one can only resort to defining what one *does* see as a variable. Every system is open in reality. Only for the sake of analysis can we close off a model of a system by either defining what variables we are going to assume as being of influence or by reducing the variation in certain variables to nil. Opening or closing systems is an analytical technique. Everything is (can be?) related to everything else. Our only problem is to find out how. We try to solve this overall problem by dividing it up into an indefinite number of smaller problems. In this the links between the new and smaller problems must be standardized or severed if this problem-solving technique is to work.

It is appropriate to remind the reader of the analysis that was given of complexity in the beginning of this chapter, and of the manner in which complexity may be reduced. The sytems approach, as described here, bears a strong resemblance to mathematical techniques. The division of a complex system into a number of smaller subsystems can be compared to transforming a number of higher-degree equations to a larger number of lower-degree equations. In its ultimate form this results in the linearization of the representation of phenomena.

What has been done in the construction of this theory is that the organization has been analysed as a collection of individuals or groups of individuals, as in set theory. As we have said in the beginning of this chapter, the individual is a member of a number of different sets. This diverse membership is one of the media by which the organization engages in transactions with its environment (see Figure 4.2). At every level of analysis the organization can be opened up.

The structure of the analytical framework also indicates that the technology, that is the combination of inputs–transformation–outputs is an expedient manner for describing the open nature of the organization. These 'technological' transactions describe the domain of the organization. They are what Thompson (1967, p.45) calls the core technology. However, this distinction is much more problematic than it seems. Even in a production organization where the main stream of products is quite clear, as in the colour TV tube factory, a large percentage of the personnel is not immediately concerned with the production. New products have to be developed, new machines designed, new personnel have to be attracted, people must run the canteen, there must be a guard at the gate, etc. All these tasks are interrelated in such a complex manner that it seems an over-simplification to designate one recognizable line of functions within the organization as the 'core technology'. It is like calling the intestinal tract within a human body the 'core processor'. The concept of 'core' technology presumes a certain homogeneity in a large part of the organization. If this were so the analysis of intra-organizational conflicts would hardly be interesting.

Because we have concentrated on the problem-solving aspect of organizations it seems logical to pursue this further when treating the open nature of organizations. Information should then be seen as the main medium of transactions. The organization depends on the environment for information about markets, products, techniques, etc. The environment to a large extent invokes the problems that have to be solved (the products) and also the manner in which this has to be done (the techniques). The environment can be seen as a source of information on the constraints within which solutions can be found (inputs). In Thompson's vocabulary the organization establishes boundary spanning units.

> 'The crucial problem for boundary spanning units of an organization, therefore, is not coordination (of variables under control) but adjustment to constraints and contingencies not controlled by the organization — to what the economist calls exogeneous variables'. (Thompson 1976, p.66–67).

In certain areas of organization this can be clearly recognized as in sales, marketing, purchasing, recruitment departments, etc. In most other areas there is also a boundary crossing stream of information which is necessary for the execution of the tasks within the departments, but this stream of information is less formalized, less recognizable. In the design group of the engineering department very litle direct external influence is recognizable. Professional magazines, contacts with others in the same line of work, information from competitors, etc., all influence the execution of their tasks. But the development of ideas on the desirability of more varied tasks for individuals may also be seen as influencing their work. The result of their design activities may be a change in or the creation of tasks in the production line. As is illustrated in Chapter 6, such changes are often based on the implicit assumption that unskilled labour is cheap and available. If the social and economic environment changes and this assumption becomes untenable, the designer will, somehow, have to be supplied with that information. As this does not happen through institutionalized or formalized channels of information; one has to assume that each individual, each group within the organization, is part of the information-permeable membrane that forms the analytical boundary between organizations and their environment.

Chapter 5

Towards a Theory of Organizational Structure and Change

INTRODUCTION

In this chapter a theory is presented that explains the mechanisms of structural change in organizations. The main explanatory variable in this theory is the dissonance between the structural variables from the theory as presented in Chapter 4. Because it is a theory of change it must necessarily have a dynamic character. It is hypothesized that there is an intrinsic direction in the change of the theoretical variables that can be compared to the irreversibility of thermodynamic processes. These irreversibile processes are illustrated by the technological development and the cultural diversification in our society. These two developments result in an increasing tension between structural developments inside and outside organizations. If the theory is satisfactory it should show that there are many more solutions to our problems of organizational structure than we originally anticipated.

Sociological Presuppositions

In the previous chapter a presentation has been given of a technique, a vocabulary to describe certain aspects of organizations. An attempt has been made to keep the number of assumptions on which this view is based to a minimum, and to make them explicit. The objective in Chapter 4 was to create a theoretical framework that is independent of the sociological debates concerning the problems of order and conflict. Probably the realistic approach makes the distinction as it was presented meaningless — all the more so because the conflict approach is directed at changing society. It is a normative theoretical concept. Commonsense realism only tries to describe the generative mechanisms that lead to different states of the system under study. The normative element has to be added when choosing the objectives in applying a realistic theory to a change in a real-life solution. Conflict in the context of 'sociology of radical change' is certainly a normative interpretation of the term. The basic concern of the sociology of radical change is not only to find an explanation for radical change towards man's emancipation from social structures which limit and stunt his development, but also to initiate and

138

control such changes. Development is itself a purely normative concept because it sets different values on the possible states of the system that develops.

The distinction between voluntarism and determinism can be interpreted either as factual or as normative. This is probably a question of emphasis rather than of choice.

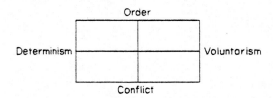

Figure 5.1   Two dimensions of sociological theory

For the presented framework no choice has been made. It can accommodate them all, as its analytical nature demands. However, when such a framework is used to present an opinion of how organizations function in reality, then one has to specify what one's assumption are on the nature of the individual and of society.

The conflict and order dimension has already been presented in the introduction and is based on Dahrendorf's (1959) analysis of sociological approaches. The distinctions between voluntarism and determinism and between order and conflict are both used by Burrell and Morgan (1979) to map the different approaches that can be recognized in the literature on organization analysis.

Strange though it may seem, it is not necessary to make a clear choice between the four alternatives. In this chapter man may be viewed as either completely autonomous and free-willed (voluntarism) or completely determined by his situation or environment in conjunction with his past. If man is seem as a completely deterministic element in an organization, then organizations cannot be designed but are the deterministic consequence of the interaction between a large number of these elementary units in a specific environment. If man however has some choice it becomes possible to direct that small amount of freedom of action he has towards the achievement of desireable outcomes. It becomes possible to describe a *technology of organizing*. In order to make such a description possible, the theory must have the total field between the four poles as its domain.

The main difficulty in presenting a theoretical approach to the problem of organizational change lies in the distinction between the different levels of analysis, the different levels of inclusiveness (see Figure 2.2), that have to be pursued at the same time. These levels range from the individual member of an organization, via the different groups in which he functions, via departments, divisons, and the whole organization in which he is an active participant, to the environment of the organization.

'PRICE' IN THEORIES OF ORGANIZATION

The engineering department, apart from the designers and experimental workshops, can best be described as having a homogeneous structure. This structure has been described as highly differentiated and specified where tasks are concerned. This also applies to its control structure. This sort of structure is dominant in most industrial production organizations. It is the result of a development aimed at minimizing loss where specific internal capacities and cost factors are concerned, and at maximizing the simplification of tasks within each capacity unit. This last aspect reduces dependence on the skills of the labour force and increases its substitutability. It is the result of 'Tayloristic' thinking: there is one best way to do a certain thing; that one best way is to simplify each task as much as possible. The problematic nature of the production process has been shifted from the actual execution of the productive tasks to the design of these tasks *and* to the coordination of a large number of such minimalized, simplified tasks. The principles behind this form of organization are simple and few; the results are easy to assess if we assume that costs can be defined under *stable* conditions.

The assumption behind the theory of organizational change, based on the presented theory of organizational dissonance, is that structural dissonances *can* be expressed as costs. The costs that are measured in practice are only those which we *wish* to quantify, using the most primitive means, which are certainly not based on a set of systematic theoretical definitions. Because the measurement of costs is easiest where the organization is concerned with 'priced' goods and services, the emphasis tends to be on the minimization of dissonances in the technological sphere and the relation between technology and task structure. This dominance of 'priced' thinking has led to the concept of the technological imperative. The organization of the production becomes a consequence of the minimization or the reduction of direct production costs. Direct production costs are those costs that are immediately attributable to the production process. If the cost price of a product or service is defined as the sum of the *necessary* costs for producing that product or service, it would be appropriate if the inevitable costs due to intra-organizational conflicts were also earmarked as necessary costs. If it is not possible to restrict or control these intra-organizational conflicts we will have to learn to live with them and work with them. The scope of the classical (theory of) production organizations is set by the economic horizon or our 'bounded rationality'. It is for this reason that a theory of organizational change should at least encompass the historical process of routinization and differentiation of labour, the *technological imperative*. Even in the technical organization it is not always easy to define which costs are functional. It depends on the manner in which they are *rationalized*. It depends on the expectations that are taken into account when judging costs. Flexibility in the production apparatus demands quantitative or qualitative over-capacity of the production machines. That implies extra costs; they are to be met by the ability to react to changing demands from the environment. Furthermore, such costs may have to be incurred in order to change the organization. That means if the costs within an organization become too high the organization has to change and if the organization changes, costs will have to be incurred.

The same can be said for the dissonances in an organization. If the dissonances become too large the organization will change. Dissonances create tensions and use up energy. They may be either productive or unproductive. Using the concept of dissonance it may be possible to discern many more types of costs than we have done in the past. The nature of the dissonance prescribes the direction of the appropriate change.

Technological Change and Markets

Evolution is the history of a system undergoing irreversible changes (Lotka 1956, p.24). In this definition evolution is *not a normative concept*. The popular conception of evolution is, however, closely associated with progress, giving the direction in which the process of change *should* take place. Moral sentiments of organizational change should be kept out of this theoretical framework. This framework should present the changes possible in an organization and if possible *how* these changes *can* be brought about. An attempt will be made to show that technological development is one of the directing forces behind organizational evolution, and that within a technical-economical system this is the basis of a process of irreversible change. The technical-economical system is mainly concerned with the operations of organizations in market systems. Market systems are viewed in the widest possible sense. This means that there is a certain amount of competition not only on the output side of the organization but also for the resources employed within the organization. A difference in emphasis on the competition for such resources may lead to more specific statements concerning profit or non-profit organizations or commercial and government organizations. All these types of organizations should fit into a general theory of organizations.

Organizations working in a market environment must be oriented towards the array of demands set by that environment. For the time being, no attention will be paid to the question of who can influence these demands. That is not of immediate importance here. As primary markets we will consider finished products and raw materials, with the transformation of raw materials into finished products as intervening variable. As yet no distinction will be made between the different elements of the transaction process, such as physical means, personnel, etc. This would be more detailed than necessary at this point.

The relation between the demands set by the markets and the nature of the product may be defined as a fit. This may be described on the level of a single product, of a whole range of products, or of a whole economy. We will concern ourselves with *one* product, for simplicity's sake. A product can be described in the context of this theory in terms of:

(a) the number of characteristics of the product that are perceived as being important to the product on the market.
(b) the manner in which these characteristics are interrelated in their contribution to the demands set by the market.
(c) the stability of the above-mentioned influences on demand, over time.

These three dimensions can be described in a three-dimensional space, as was described in Chapter 4. For practical purposes this can be reduced to two dimensions. In this case the number of characteristics of the product appears along the horizontal axis and along the vertical axis is a combination of the last two dimensions as signified by their analysability.

In order to make products that meet the demands of the market, a form of transformation must be devised that can accomplish this. Usually there are a number of constraints on the results. The most critical in a competitive environment, is the relation between the price and the number of important characteristics of the product. The price, because it is the one criteron that can be both easily recognized and easily quantified, is therefore eminently suitable for comparing alternatives.

Let us assume that we can produce a certain product, when the necessary ingredients are available, by a number of different means, by a number of different courses. These can only be compared *effectively* when the *differences* between them can be reduced to a *single dimension*. In the normal economic mode of thinking that one dimension is financial. In this theory, it is structural. The assertion is that the translation of the difference in means to achieve a specified result into a financial dimension is too dependent on culture and history to be of particular interest for a general theory of organizations. Price is based on statements of relative values of different capacities of individuals — values that are specific to individual cultures. We are concerned with a difference in *ability* to transform material, in the widest possible sense of the word, from one state into another, and the demand for that final state. Such a difference can only be handled if both the variables are described in the same dimensions. Ashby uses the term *variety* for this. He states that the variety of the transformation process will have to be at least as large as the variety of the product. If the variety of the production method is much larger than that of the product, it will be attractive for the producer to utilize this surplus capacity and create products that have a closer fit with the means of production. A financial comparison reduces all the variables that can influence our choice to one, and that one has acquired a cultural content that is very difficult to specify. A structural comparison is as yet devoid of content and values and can furthermore employ three dimensions. These dimensions must then be weighed against each other in a manner that makes value judgements possible.

DISSONANCE AND CHANGE

The ability to change organizations and the manner in which demands for specific results can be met may be described in a dynamic system. Such an (evolutionary) dynamism can best be formally described in the structural framework.

The influence on structural change is proportional to the extent of the dissonance between two related structural variables.

For example, if in a production plant a highly sophisticated machine is in operation when there is little or no work that demands such a sophisticated machine, work will be sought to utilize its capacities. The greater the discrepancy between the capacities of the machine and the demands set by the existing work, the greater the influence towards a change in work will be. This becomes all the more plausible when the sophistication or the technical capabilities of the machine are expressed in a hourly tariff that is much higher than that of less sophisticated machines. Also the price of more complex products is higher. The lack of fit then becomes calculable and is therefore easy to identify.

If we state that the extent of the structural dissonance is proportional to its influence on structural change the question remains: *which* structural variables will shift to decrease the dissonance? There are two distinctly different but complementary approaches to this question.

These two approaches are inherent to the structural analysis. As was stated in Chapter 4, we can distinguish between the characteristics of the elements and between the characteristics of the system of which they are a part. The first approach also concerns the changes in the characteristics of the elements.

The result of the *first* approach is that *the structural rigidity increases when the structural complexity decreases.* In the diagrammatic representation it means that the structural variable is situated closer to the horizontal axis.

This implies that structural change will be *predominantly oriented towards the horizontal axis*, under the influence of *competition* from similar organizations. This approach is reflected in the ever-increasing routinization of work and the formalization of structures. It indicates the irreversible nature in overall perspective, of the evolution in organizations, under circumstances of direct economical competition from organizations supplying the same goods or services.

The whole socio-economic development of our industrial society is a reflection of this tendency as is described by Lasch (1979, p.168)

'. . . industrialization reduced artisan or peasant to a proletarian, stripped him of his land and tools, and stranded him in the market place with nothing to sell but his laborpower. In our time, the elimination of skills not only from manual work but from white collar jobs as well has created conditions in which labor power takes the form of personality rather than strength and intelligence. Men and women alike have to project an attractive image and to become simultaneously role players and connoisseurs of their own performance.'

This signifies that not only in the 'functional' aspect of organization, the shift towards the formalized specified task structure dominates, but also that social emphasis is directed towards recognizable 'role patterns'. It results in the emphasis on the 'organization man'.

The second approach is that the organization is seen as a network of interrelated structural units with different levels of inclusiveness (see Figure 2.2). In this view, the structure of the network and the total result of all the possible dissonances indicates the direction of structural change. This will be treated later on in this chapter.

The Irreversible Process of Technological Change

If technology is seen as the knowledge of getting things done, as was suggested on p.81, then there are a couple of irrefutable statements that can be made to show that there is an irreversible development in this knowledge. When solutions to specific problems can be communicated, and thus disseminated over a wider audience, this furthers the quest to solve the next problem that arises, which is more difficult. Our increase in knowledge, under the assumption that its acquisition is cumulative, results in a decrease in the necessary effort to execute the solution of similar problems. If an algorithm can be constructed for the solution of a problem or a class of problems, then the application of such an algorithm to appropriate consecutive problems sets lower demands on the problem-solving capacity of the individual. It can contribute to the routinization of the problem-solving activity of individuals concerned with such problems. Solutions in a sense become programmable. A technique can be constructed that changes the demand for analysis into a demand for systematic application of specific operations. Thus it is not only the process of industrialization that stripped the artisan or craftsman of his tools and unique craftsmanship. More basic is the increase in the understanding of the transformation process of raw materials into finished products. This increase in understanding is found in the nature of the materials used, as exemplified by the growth of knowledge concerning physics, chemistry, metallurgy, etc., and also in the nature of the possibilities of changing their characteristics or form, as exemplified by the increase in technical know-how, the mechanics of distorting metals, the knowledge of thermal engines, hydraulics etc. Thus, as the total body of knowledge grows, we can keep our attention fixed on the widening frontiers and leave the replication of earlier solutions to formalized problem-solving 'mechanisms'. This means that we can pursue problems of increasing complexity, taking more variables into account and constructing more complex networks of assumed interrelations between these variables. In the two-dimensional description we are moving away from the origin in our ability to solve problems. Problems are becoming more analysable because our analysis can be based on our previous achievements and experience. We learn much and hopefully forget little. More—we learn to analyse. We learn to create mechanisms which can do the tedious jobs that are part of the information processing that is necessary for problem-solving.

We have created mechanisms that shift the complexity from the structural dimension into the quantitative dimension, which then allows us to attack it with 'mechanical and systematic' means such as simulation programs in computers. Technological development, combined with a Tayloristic approach to the organization of production, has led to what some call inhuman work situations. There are two important aspects to this problem of dehumanization of work. The first is when operating in a competitive system, prices tend to be under pressure, which forces organizations to keep their production costs as low as possible. The second is that workers are also consumers. They will choose products with a relatively low price, independent of the fact that these products may be the result of a highly unpleasant work. Because income is expressed in money, i.e. the ability to acquire goods and services, and not in the pleasure one derives from one's job, cheap products and unpleasant work may be a necessary combination. On the one hand there may be cause for optimism, based on our increased technological abilities. The solution of many serious problems in the past century has created a tremendous increase in material and physical welfare in the western world. The health situation can hardly be compared with that of a hundred years ago. On the other hand, many of the solutions that have been found may only be *partial* solutions. When liberally applied, such solutions can create worse secondary effects in the long run than the initially expected beneficial results. These negative effects may be the consequence of the methodical dilemma which was mentioned in Chapter 3: the generalization of specific statements without first analysing the circumstances under which this generalization is permissible. This is certainly the case when the generalization draws conclusions about variables which were originally not an explicit part of the theoretical framework.

In economics, a convenient solution to this dilemma has been sought in the definition of external effects or external economies and diseconomies as made famous by Marshall and Pigou. Widespread polution, resulting in the extinction of biological species, is an unwanted side effect of our economic affluence, as is the decrease in the power of the individual to determine his own possibilities and needs.

Complexity and Alternatives

The structural approach would indicate how such complex interrelated problems can be *described*. The systematic analysis and its representation does not necessarily lead to viable solutions, just as complex mathematical equations do not necessarily have *one* good solution but may have many *equivalent* solutions. The increase in our ability to handle complexity *may* result in the presentation of more possible courses. This is probable because less attention needs to be paid to the solution of problems that can be routinized (i.e. assuming that these routine solutions do not present us with unwanted, negative side effects that initially escaped our attention).

The development of products in an industrial organization evolves away from low complexity and results in the increase in the features of a product important to its quality or attractiveness to the market. The colour TV tube initially only had one important quality, the quality of the projected image, especially the clarity of its colours. The original TV sets could not be moved around because the earth's magnetic field influenced the deflection of the electron beam. At that time, that was not really a problem. Nowadays, such a set would be nearly impossible to sell. The size of the screen, the depth of the set, the time it takes for the set to warm up, the rigidity of the construction so that it can be used in a portable set; these factors are now of nearly equal importance. They have, in one way or another, all become part of the feasible solutions and we can shift our attention to new features that again take on an important time aspect in the sense of fashionability. The essence of fashion is its restricted life span, its change.

Just as technological development irreversibly changes the nature of the product, it also influences production methods. It boils down to *not having to* discover the wheel time and time again. Technological development implies the formalization of transformation processes, implies the substitutability of production means because the problem solution is incorporated in the design rather than in the execution of the necessary operations. Because the process of technological development is presented as irreversible, it is appropriate to compare this process to thermodynamic processes. In thermodynamics the irreversibility is represented by the ever-increasing entropy of a closed system. The entropy of a subsystem may decrease, but that can only happen if the entropy of the total system at least remains the same or else increases. In this metaphor entropy can be compared to knowledge. In the process of looking for new solutions to our problems we may backtrack along our course of the development of known solutions in order to see if somewhere down the line we can find an opening for new solutions. If we succeed, new knowledge has been gained. If we do not succeed, we have only expended unnecessary energy.

Summarizing, it can be said that technological development implies the routinization of transformations, opening wider perspectives for attention to further development.

The Irreversible Process of Cognitive Change

It has just been hypothesized that knowledge is additive, resulting in an irreversible process of technological development. Now we have to switch to a next higher level. The development of cognitive structures, which are the origin of technological problem solving. This results in a second-order effect: the ability to influence the rate of technological development.

Apart from the rather dubious possibility of intelligence being genetically conditioned, it may be asserted that the ability of individuals to solve problems is to a large extent determined by their learning experience. This experience may be informally gained in the environment of the family and their social relations. More formally it is gained in educational institutions and later on in life through working experience. It is without doubt that the general level of education in western Europe has risen sharply in the last hundred years. It also seems that the level of education of the parents is reflected in the learning experience of the children in their family environment. This leads to a compound effect on the growth of learning. It results in the double-barrelled effect that an increasing number of individuals are capable of handling increasingly complex problems.

It means that the cognitive structure of the population is developing away from the origin of the two-dimensional representation of that structure. It means that not only more complex problems can be handled, but that they will also be sought.

The Irreversible Process of the Reduction of Complexity

When describing technological change it was hypothesized that technological change led to routinization of labour. This issue will now be dealt with, in combination with the increase in complexity of the cognitive structure.

When a transformation is well understood, it may be defined in such a manner that the solutions to the original problems are incorporated in the design of the operations of the execution of the transformation. This can be called the routinization of the transformation.

The next step is that the understanding of the operations is so complete and so well ordered that the solutions to the problems concerning the execution of these operations can be designed into a machine which can perform these operations. This is the step of mechanization. The physical components of problem solving are shifted to physical mechanisms, as can be seen clearly in the era of industrialization. This necessitates the use of external sources of mechanical energy such as steam engines and electric motors. Mechanization is not restricted to this shift in physical work. It also concerns *mental mechanisms* when, for instance, we consider calculators. The essence of mechanization is the analysis of the processes and operations to such a degree of accuracy and precision, that specifications for each part of the operations can be defined. The result of mechanization is a rigid sequence of operations. The adjustment of the operations either in sequence or in internal programming demands the direction or guidance of an individual. The operations and their execution are seen as rigid, deterministic sequences.

The next step in the transfer of human activity to an external device is based on a further command of complexity. With mechanization, the rigid sequence of operations, high standardization of materials and operations are presupposed. Every deviation from a standard results in a deviation in the finished product. In the next step towards automation, the problem solving that lies at the basis of the adjustment of the operations to nascent deviations is so well understood that it can be formalized. This necessitates *feed-back loops that react to deviations that occur during the process.* If the previous stage could be described, in a mathematical mode, as a number of second-order differential equations, this stage must be described in at least a number of third-order differential equations. The previous stage assumed static values for the characteristic variables of both the materials and the operations. In this stage, these values can vary and mutual adjustments can be defined beforehand. Such feedback control may be found in numerically controlled machining centres, but are even more widespread in chemical-processing control. Information *processing* is an intrinsic part of the design of the operation, while in the first step of mechanization there was only information storage.

We have thus outlined the beginning of an unending sequence of *complexification* of problem solutions. When our insight into the manner in which we have achieved the solutions on the previous level has become clear enough for us to formalize the findings of such solutions, and we have been able to generalize specific solutions so that they can be applied in widely varying circumstances, then we have made the first step towards the next level of automation. Admittedly at every step along this hierarchy of the automation of problem solving, the *chance* increases that the application of the acquired techniques *can* have detrimental results. This is so because, when we describe the problems, in a mathematical mode, as sets of differential equations, the number of coefficients and constants that have to be filled in grows exponentially at every higher level of the model. Each faulty coefficient or constant results in a faulty specific solution. As stated earlier, the change of making mistakes is also increased by the possibility of mistaking a specific solution for a general one, and then applying such a specific solution to an inappropriate problem.

This increase in understanding of the different levels of problem solution and its application in an organized context can only be based on an increase in analytic and diagnostic capacities of individuals within the organization. Initially this increase can only be arrived at through collaboration between intuitive and systematic thinkers, because the intuitive thinker tends to look for new ways of solving problems which can be formalized by more systematic thinkers. However, by using a computer to process information, part of the intuitive search can be substituted by executing a large number of systematic operations. Our ability to translate structural complexity into quantitative complexity while retaining a high congruence to our initial representation, supplies us with a technique that makes 'mechanization' of problem-solving feasible. The result of this is that the repetition of solving specific problems or even specific classes of problems becomes unnecessary. We can concentrate on defining and solving an ever-widening range of new problems. *Let us hope that most of these problems are not the result of our own interference with our environment.*

THE MULTI-LEVEL INTERRELATION OF ORGANIZATIONAL ASPECTS AND CHANGE

As was briefly described, an organization can be viewed as a network of structural units with different levels of inclusiveness (see Figure 2.2). At each point in the network, one can analyse the nature of the dissonances the focal unit experiences with units in its environment. The composition of these dissonances influences the internal structure of the unit. If a purely mechanistic, deterministic approach is taken, one could hypothesize that the internal structure of an organizational unit would be such that the total dissonance experienced by that unit would be minimized. The unit would evolve towards a position of equilibrium as far as the dissonances are concerned. This view leads to a theory of organizational dynamics where the structure of (units of) organizations are determined by autonomous developments in the environment of the organization or within the organization. This manner of thought shows a marked likeness to the evolution of a species as a consequence of changing environments and genetic mutations. In order to clarify this somewhat cryptic argument, the engineering department from the first case, the colour TV tube factory, will be described using a network analysis.

Transformation-task Structure

The domain of the engineering department is such that it poses problems to which certain types of solution techniques are appropriate. These techniques have been developed over the last 150 years and have been incorporated in the profession of mechanical engineer and the whole engineering craft. These techniques concern the division of a transformation process into definable discrete operations, and the definition of an object in dimensions with appropriate tolerances. They concern standardization of materials, objects, movement, and interactions between them. As is described in the last chapter, the mastering of these techniques and the application of them to their own work has resulted in a highly differentiated and specified task structure within engineering departments. That is the situation with which we are confronted in the engineering department of the colour TV tube factory. It is the result of the fit between the state of the art of transforming material from one state into another and the manner in which this is achieved in an organizational context.

To show how developments in one of the aspects can influence another, a description will be given of the possible change in task structure due to the introduction of numerically controlled machining centres.

The present design process is such that from the definition of the specifications for the machine a design is made which can answer to those specifications. The machine is usually made up of discrete parts which have to interact such that all the necessary operations can be executed. The necessary precision of the operation defines the precision of the dimensions of the parts. The precision of these dimensions defines the manner in which the parts have to be made.

The design process is organized so that the chief designer defines the broad principles of the design and determines what are the crucial parts, in order to meet the set specifications. The designer is then responsible for designing the parts of the machine and establishing the different dimensions and their tolerances. The actual making of the drawings for the blueprints is left to the draughtsmen. When the design is completed and the manufacture of the parts can begin, the designed parts are analysed to establish the necessary operations which must be executed on the different machines in the workshop. This preparation results in a set of instructions for the machine operators and the different operations are scheduled. When the materials and the tools are available, the machine operators only have to follow the prepared instructions.

In this design sequence the problem solving is split up into many small parts of increasing routinization. An alternative sequence, made possible by the development of computers and numerically controlled machines, can short circuit this process.

The design activity is brought back to its most essential characteristics. A machine has to meet certain specifications, defined by mechanical boundaries and physical properties. The mechanical components of the machine are characterized by their 'shape' and their interaction. This 'shape' is fixed geometrically and can be translated into programs to be executed on production machines. Instead of following the whole sequence of design activities the designer could write these programs straight away. However it is rather tedious work, because it demands a high degree of conscientiousness and accuracy in executing repetitive tasks. These tasks can be taken over by computers using programs that translate the geometry of both the design and the raw materials into an optimal sequence of operations, using the right tools under the right circumstances and eventually producing the paper or magnetic tape that provides the information to the numerically controlled machine. This makes it possible for the designer to incorporate considerations of both the functional aspects of the part in the machine and the economic and technical aspects of producing those parts. Furthermore, it makes the more routine jobs that originally had to be done redundant. In other words, it can create a shift towards more complex and complete problem solving in the higher echelons of the design team while phasing out the routine jobs.

In reality, we find that these new means of design and production have only been accepted reluctantly. Only in those sectors of industry where very high demands are set on the accuracy of very complex components, such as the aircraft and microelectronic industry, do we find widespread acceptance of these new techniques. It is even questionable if these complex parts, as used in aircraft or in microelectronics, could have been made using classical techniques.

Concluding, it may be said that the rigid hierarchical organization in the engineering department was a historical consequence of the techniques employed in the design and production of machines. When new techniques are developed this should lead to new task structures which reflect the transformation process. However, the existing task structure may be so rigid that the new techniques cannot result in the appropriate changes. This may result in *not* employing those new techniques or not employing them *appropriately*. Having the design made along the classical lines in the design department and letting the functionary who used to prepare the work for the workshop do the programming for the new machine is an example of this. Inefficiency is then expressed not only by higher costs but also by a lack of fit between technology and task structure.

In the engineering department, these new techniques were not available, neither were they sought. The hierarchical organization dominated all activities through the 'logic of calculable costs' derived from the fit between the transformation and task structure. This resulted in an inflexible attitude towards the environment; not only the environment that supplied them with *work*, with orders for new machines, but also the environment that supplied them with *workers*.

It may hardly be assumed that the educational facilities in a country supply the graduates that its society demands. Supply and demand in this area are not linked in any teleological manner. In the field of craftsmen for the mechanical engineering profession we see a strong trend towards an increase in the level of education and training. Apart from the experimental workshop and the repair and maintainance teams, little high level work was demanded within the engineering department. Nor could the management of the engineering department be influenced to analyse which organizational forms might make the 'fit' between available workers and the tasks within the organization more suitable.

An experiment was tried where a group of workers in the machine shop was allowed to make a machine from the design stage without the supervision and coordination of the planning department. The workers could contact the design department if problems arose. The experiment was quite successful. Both the design department and the workshop agreed that in the future it would be helpful if a more intensive communication about the designed apparatus occured earlier in the design and production process. The experiment was dropped because the planning of such groups was problematic and the interference with the existing manner of working had a detrimental influence on the planning process in the workshop. A further motivation for not repeating the experiment was that the calculable costs concerning the degree of utilization of the more expensive machines were higher than in the highly differentiated normal way of operating. The workers in the workshop enjoyed the experiment. They were confronted with more interesting work and they had to solve a larger variety of problems. Furthermore, they could try to influence the designers to take production techniques into account when designing their apparatus.

Summarizing, the development in the relation between the technology and the task structure can be presented as follows. The technology of design and production of machines is well established and increasingly well understood. This has resulted in a highly differentiated and specified task structure and control structure. Opposed to this is the social development in the environment of the organization. Individual workers receive more education leading to greater problem-solving abilities. The social structure in the environment has changed dramatically over the last 50 years. Rural societies have largely disappeared in Europe and our culture has become more cosmopolitan. These last two changes are perpendicular to the changes within the organization with an interface at the level of the individual and his reaction to his organizational environment. The evidence in the engineering department is that the individual loses out to the principles of autonomous differentiation. Even the demands of the technical environment (on the one hand from the development department asking for a more flexible pattern of reactions and on the other hand, new design and production techniques) are not able to counter the gravity of the *coordination through conformity.*

DESIGNS FOR CHANGE

Let us return to the second case that was presented in the first chapter. This concerned the design of a complex integrated information system controlling the purchase of raw materials, the planning of production and the registration of orders, together with many other administrative and information functions within a plant producing lighting fixtures. The system was based on a theoretical, cybernetic model of a production organization. Such models imply that organization are teleological transformation mechanisms which can be represented by a number of interacting quantitative models. The technology of decision making based on quantitative models is accepted as peremptory. On the basis of such a model of an organization, a design can be made for a controlling system that processes all the information relevant in the formalized model. This presupposes that the individuals within the organization will suit their activities to the controlling system. Such an approach is often called a top-down approach.

The Top-down Approach

The essence of the top-down approach is that the organization is seen as a decision-making mechanism. Each individual decision is oriented towards contributing to an ultimate objective or goal. The decisions are made according to rules which represent all the variables seen as influential for the actual production process within the organization, and according to criteria which not only make alternatives comparable but distinguish the desirability of these alternatives. The problem of running an organization is seen as one of building the appropriate quantitative model of the production process and defining the criteria that will lead to an optimal solution. The actual organization should be made in the image of its quantitative model. From a structural point of view this means that the problem of coordination has been solved. It has become analyzable. This demands, according to the prevailing manner of thinking, that the task structure follows suit. It most certainly has to become more specified if it is to reflect the quantitative model. The organization has to be twisted and teased into the *technostructure.*

The optimal solution is defined by the minimization of costs. That means that a cost aspect will have to attributed to each variable. As was said earlier, in the technological aspect of an organization such *costing* is easier than elsewhere.

In the second case the expected savings due to the system that was designed were so attractive that the management of the organization was initially willing to attempt such an organizational wrestling match between the technical rationality and the social rigidity within the plant. Eventually the system was only partly implemented. The remaining parts proved to have unacceptable consequences for certain groups of individuals within the organization and they succeeded in torpedoing the changes that were demanded.

The top-down approach is based on the assumption that within organizations information is received, processed and decisions are taken and information is produced which is again processed, etc. If the objectives of the organization can be specified and the technique of production is well understood, then the making of a blueprint for an optimal information and production system becomes feasible. Within such a blueprint there are different analytical units which either process information or take decisions. The structure of the organization can be designed to minimize information transmission costs and coordination costs between information processes. This leads to an ideal construction where specific processes and decision mechanisms are combined into one organizational unit in order to minimize costs and to minimize the chances of faulty coordination of activities. Whether in this top-down approach these ideal organizational units by any chance coincide with the real task divisions within the organization is not a point of concern. The actual organization is viewed as a flexible pattern of interaction between individuals which can be moulded to the demands set by the technical processes. Because of the goal orientation and the unidimensional decision criteria, the result is usually a strictly hierarchical decision structure where the

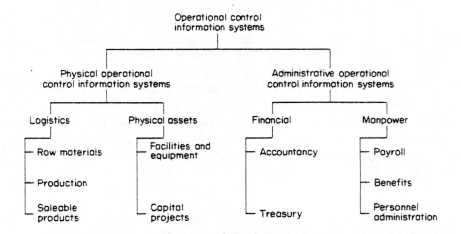

Figure 5.2   Partial classification of operational control system

next higher level can compare and coordinate decisions at lower levels. There may be information flows within a hierarchical level in order to supply other units with the necessary information, but decisions at the same level do not influence each other. This can only happen through combination or coordination at a higher level. Figure 5.2 gives an example of systematic subdivision of an operational control information system (Blumenthal 1969, p.52).

Because the ideal organization decision units do not coincide with the existing task structure, important changes are usually necessary when implementing automated control systems. These changes are often difficult to bring about. The individual members of the organization prove to be recalcitrant and jeopardize the functioning of the system. This led the writers of the ARDI system design handbook to advise their readers that in such circumstances there were two courses open to the systems manager:

(a) move the recalcitrant person to another department;
(b) fire him.

These alternatives are no longer viewed as attractive. This has made system designers think about the problems of implementation. How can one sugar the bitter pill of compulsory change? Strange though it may seem, these difficulties in implementing control systems have hardly led to any coherent analysis of the relations between such systems and the human social organizations in which they should function. Most of the work in this area concerns the help that could be given to automation teams when they try to implement their system. How can people be brought to change their behaviour or their wishes towards the work they are to do? The answers are supplied by psychologists, sociologists and other *agents of change*. By involving the future users of the system in the design phase of the automation process they can get an early introduction into how they will have to change. Possibly their resistance against change will be weakened if they are inundated with preparatory activities and left to steep in the jargon and paraphernalia of the wonder boys of systems analysis and computer science.

The rather sombre presentation given above can be summarized as follows: the organization as a decision-making system can be modelled in such a manner that it becomes analysable. This means that the *technology of control* moves closer to the horizontal axis in terms of the model as presented in Chapter 4. In order to lower the tension between the new-found technological solutions and the more human aspect of the organization, the task and control structures will have to change in a similar direction. This is in line with the *irreversible process of technological change* as presented earlier in this chapter. It leads to a further routinization of the task structure and a formalization of the control structure.

Bottom-up Approach

The essence of the bottom-up approach is that the organization is seen as a human social system in which the main characteristic of the activities is the

154

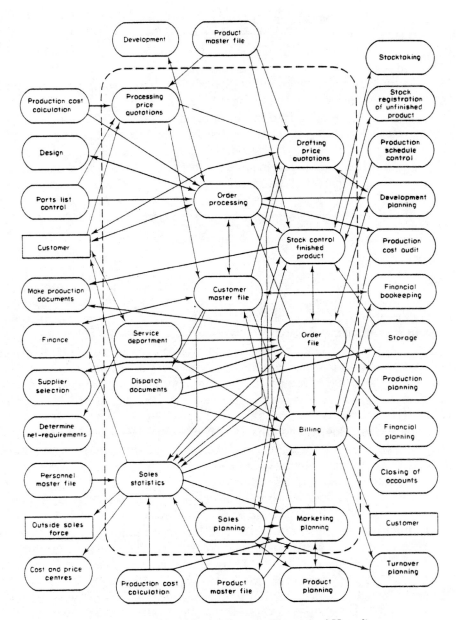

Figure 5.3   Plan of sales domain (Köster and Hetzel)

treatment and exchange of information on which decisions concerning each other's activities are made. The existing organization is taken as a point of reference and not an ideal type of a control system. The existing condition is analysed exhaustively. All information flows are traced. Documents are inventoried, their trajectories through the organizations established. Tasks of individuals are analysed from a point of view which focusses on the processing of information and the taking of decisions. The manner in which the actual decisions come about is not taken into account; that would invade the discretion of the individual member of the organization. In other words, a detailed map is made of the information flows within the organization. The context of the information can be characterized by a number of domains. In the AEG-Telefunken approach (Köster and Hetzel 1971) ten of these domains are defined.

(1) sales;
(2) corporate planning;
(3) development and design;
(4) raw material supply;
(5) production control and production;
(6) personnel;
(7) cost accounting;
(8) finance;
(9) organization and data processing;
(10) general scientific principles (such as O.R. models, etc.)

A detailed plan of each domain is made (see Figure 5.3) in which all the operations can be traced to either departments or individuals. The next step is to help these individuals or departments get a better grip on their own activities, to help them with their 'private' technological problems. In order to explain why this is a feasible step, a theoretical detour will have to be made.

Power and Conflict

An attempt has been made to keep our discussion as short and clear as possible. This theoretical detour concerns the aspect of power as one of the influences on the behaviour of individuals or groups of individuals within organizations. The use of *power* as *one* of the explanatory variables of organization structure or behaviour is very unpopular within most organizations. In the research department which was responsible for the design of the automated control system for the lighting fixtures plant, the mere mention of the viewpoint that a difference in power between departments might be an important influence in the acceptance of certain proposed changes, made people aggressive. They strictly adhered to a harmony model of organizations in which there was no place for such a *conflict-prone concept as power*. This brings us back to the basic assumptions that were presented at the beginning of this chapter: order versus conflict and deterministic versus voluntaristic. The introduction of the power approaches places the theory squarely in the voluntaristic-conflict quadrant.

Intra-organizational Power and Change

The observation that some individuals have greater influence on the functioning of an organization than others is difficult to dispute. Hickson (*et al.* (1971) have presented 'A Strategic Contingencies' Theory of Intra-organizational Power', which gives an explanation for this difference in power between individuals or groups. The essence of this theory will be reproduced here. Their main proposition is that power is based on the control of strategic contingencies. The *strategic quality* is mainly defined by two variables:

(1) 'Given a view of organizations as systems of interdependent roles and activities, then the centrality of a subunit is the degree to which its activities are interlinked into the system.' This is also termed workflow pervasiveness.

(2) 'Secondly, the activities of a subunit are central if they are essential in the sense that their cessation would quickly and substantially impede the workflow of the organization. This workflow immediacy is defined as the speed and severity with which the workflows of a subunit affect final outputs of an organization.'

These two variables depend on the contents of the tasks of different subunits and are not necessarily structurally defined.

The next influence is also a consequence of the nature of the tasks performed.

> 'Concepts relating to the availability of alternatives pervade the literature on power. In economics theory the degree of competition is taken as a measure of the extent to which alternatives are available from other organizations, it being implied that the power of an organization over other organizations and customers is a function of the amount of competition present' (p.220).

Hickson *et al.* define substitutability as 'the ability of organizations to obtain alternative performance for the activities of a subunit'.

This substitutability is influenced by a special type of routinization, one of two as described by Hickson *et al.* (p.224): 'Routinization may be (a) of coping by information or absorption which defines how the uncertainty which occurs shall be coped with; and (b) of coping by prevention, which prevents the occurance of uncertainty'. The first type is embodied in job descriptions and task instructions prescribing how to obtain information and to respond to uncertainty. For maintenance personnel, it lays down how to repair the machine; for physicans, it lays down a standard procedure for examining patients and sequences of remedies for each diagnosis. This description can be translated to the structural definitions that were given in Chapter 4.

(a) Coping by information or absorption can be described as creating highly specified tasks. As was said on p.110 this creates the possibility of inter-dependence dissonance.

In effect Hickson *et al.* illustrate the technological imperative:

Formalize a specific procedure for finding solutions to prevailing problems.

The danger that the performance of these procedures becomes the objective of those individuals who have made it their tasks, leads to the bureacratization of the organization.

Hickson *et al.* say 'it increases substitutability. The means of coping become more visible and possible substitutes are unskilled personnel from another subunit who can follow a standard procedure but could not have acquired the previously unexpressed skills.'

(b) This form of routinization says something about the formalization of previous problem solving activities. If this has not been done in an appropriate manner then inter-dependence dissonances are hypothesized to arise. This brings us to the definition of contingencies as given by Hickson *et al.* (p.222). 'A contingency is a requirement of the activities of one subunit which is affected by activities of other subunits.' Such contingencies are influenced by the uncertainty of these activities.

'Uncertainty may be defined as a lack of information about future events, so that alternatives and their outcomes are unpredictable. Organizations deal with environmentally derived uncertainties in the sources and composition of inputs, with uncertainties in processing of throughputs, and again with environmental uncertainties in the disposal of outputs.

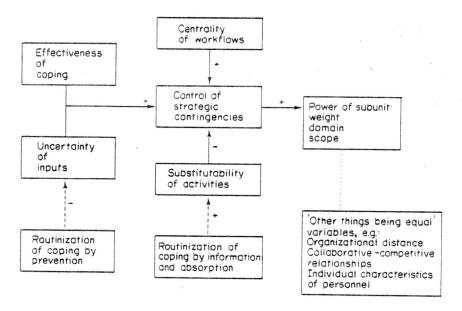

---------- Direct relationship with power
- - - - Indirect relationship with power
·········· Relationship with power other than by control of contingencies

Figure 5.4   Hickson's strategic contingencies theory of intraorganizational power

They must have means to deal with these uncertainties for adequate task performance. Such ability is here called coping' (p.215).

The above mentioned concepts are related to the power of a subunit within an organization by the following hypotheses:

(I)   The more a subunit copes with uncertainty the greater its power within the organization.
(II)   The lower the substitutability of the activities of a subunit, the greater its power within the organization.
(IIIa)   The higher the pervasiveness of the work flows of a subunit, the greater its power within the organization.
(IIIb)   The higher the immediacy of the work flows of a subunit, the greater its power within the organization.
(IV)   The more contingencies are controlled by a subunit, the greater its power within the organization.

This is all summarized in Figure 5.4.

Dissonance and Power

The approach as described above will now be translated to the structural dissonance theory. The organization is viewed as a problem-solving construction where certain subunits concern themselves with specific types of problems or specific problem-solving techniques. The analysis of workflow pervasiveness and immediacy remain the same as in Hickson's theory. The other variables are to be seen in a different light, from at least two angles.

The first is the ability to define problems and solve them; the second is the availability of data or information. These two angles are highly related; the solutions to a number of problems may be the necessary information for the next steps in the problem-solving process.

The first angle is technological in the sense of Thompson (1967, p.14):

> 'Instrumental action is rooted on the one hand in *desired* outcomes and on the other hand in beliefs about *cause/effect relationships*. Given a desire, the state of a man's knowledge at any point in time dictates the kinds of variables required and the manner of their manipulation to bring that desire to fruition.'

Most knowledge is not complete and does not give us a 100% certainty of achieving the desired results. The more complete our model of the whole system of cause/effect relationships, the greater our chance of success. This may be stated as: knowledge is power. The more complete one's knowledge is of the process that can fulfil the desires of others, the more power one has. Such power may be indicated, instead of really existing. By suggesting that there are more variables required than used, and suggesting that you know which those variables are and how they are related to those already employed, one may gain a basis of power. This may also be done by suggesting that one has information available that can influence the success of achieving certain desired outcomes, information which has hitherto not been taken into account. This means that one implies that one has a more complete model of the problem situation than one's opponent. The *effect* is the same as withholding information which one's opponent deems necessary for solving his problems.

The nature of the model to solve the posed problems is itself of influence on the intra-organizational power relations. If that model is formalized, highly specified and therefore accessible for others, it loses its power base. It becomes substitutable. It is just for this reason that the introduction of automated information systems has such a strong influence on the power relations within organizations. Information systems can only work with formalized quantitative models. Such models are usually made by experts from outside the organizational unit that uses them. These experts usually do not have the expertise in the specific area of which the model is to be made, but rather on the manner in which existing models can be formalized. Such formalization makes the model more analysable, and by virtue of this, also more open to critical scrutiny. Where in the past the unit could hide behind vague descriptions of its own expertise and often a certain mysticism of craftsmenlike abilities, they are not presented with a blueprint of their own activities. Their superiors can also, without spending too much time or effort, read such blueprints. They can find out how decisions *should* be taken and what the most *critical* variables are. This means that the functioning of the subunits becomes easier to check.

In other words, an increase in knowledge leading to *formalized* procedures for problems solution shift the transformation variable towards the horizontal axis. This leads to increased substitutability of the subunit, and to a decrease in relative power.

The approach as given above is summarized in Figure 5.4. It should be seen as a translation of the diagram of Hickson *et al*.

The *immediacy* (1) and the *pervasiveness* (2) of the work are parallel variables. They influence relative power independently. They are both intervening variables between the ability to cope with uncertainty and the ultimate power of the unit of analysis. The coping with uncertainty is influenced by two main variables.

The first variable is the *completeness of the model used* (3) to solve the problems. The more complete the model, the more variables or influences can be taken into account.

The second variable, the level of *formalization of models available* (4), influences the ability of other subunits to gain access to the models that are used. Furthermore, formalization stimulates routinization.

160

The influence of the models used to solve problems is dependent on the control of vital information flows within the organization and across its boundary (5). If a subunit *generates* information and it can *restrict* the use of that information to itself, it can gain power from that restriction. The opposite may be hypothesized too. The control of information flows by other departments may be detrimental to the relative power position of the subunit (6) (see Figure 5.5).

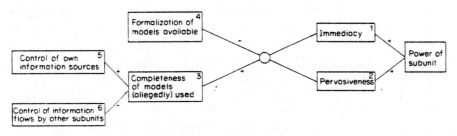

Figure 5.5   Intraorganizational power based on the availability of information and models

TECHNOLOGICAL VERSUS SOCIAL CONTINGENCIES

The requirements of the activities of a subunit are not only of a technical nature, but also of a social nature. These requirements can best be met when the internal functioning of the subunit is relatively carefree. All the attention of a unit can be given to its external relations. This means that the fits between technology, task structure and control stucture should be close, as also the fit between the individuals working in the subunit and the subunit itself.

The analysis that was presented at the technological level, where the interrelations between the functional tasks were taken as the powerbearing medium is the least difficult to perform. The analysis on the control-structure level is at least as important but much more difficult to perform. Here, we are not concerned with the solving of problems, but rather with the taking of decisions. We are not concerned only with information but also with physical attributes and coercive means. Who has the *authority* to eject a member from the organization? Who has the authority to veto projects or investments? Who has the authority to merge one organization with another? Such decisions *may* be independent of the prevailing flows of information and models used for problem solving within the organization. It is hypothesized that parallel to the technically or functionally based power network there are *other* networks of which the authority relations are the most important for the analysis of formalized organizations.

Another power base may be the ability of an individual or group within or from outside the organization to *inflict damage* on that organization or its functioning. Here we can think of personnel having access to a vital part of the organization's machinery. In this sense even minor functionaries can be very powerful. The night porter may let in saboteurs, the system designers may destroy information systems and technicians in a nuclear power plant may block safety devices designed to make the installation fail-safe. This last category does not fall within the scope of this study, even though both the immediacy and pervasiveness of the consequences of such activities are part of a possible analysis. Also the use of this kind of power may be an important instrument in negotiating at other levels, as is the case with the organizing of strikes and picketing.

We return to the power based on the social framework of the organization. Such relations as described within the control structure are based on mutual recognition of the difference in authority by the leader and those he leads. The leader's authority is based on his certainty that his orders will be executed by others. The existence of social authority is based on organizing abilities and is an attribute of every social system. The original basis may be the ability to personally reward or punish other members of a social group, but as soon as the group becomes larger and more structured, such personal interference becomes impossible. Power can then only be exerted through an intermediate organized group which recognizes the authority of the leader.

In our structural analysis, those control structures which are highly explicit are the most tenacious because every *change* demands a *conscious shift* in norms, and a recognizable shift in power relationships. An example of this difference in control-structure rigidity has been described for the engineering and the product development department in the colour TV tube case study. The decisions in the engineering department were always backed by its management, whereas in the development department it all depended on the opinion of each specific member of its management. This may be formulated as *the irreversible tendency towards formalization of authority structures in organizations in a stable environment.*

The combination of the technical and the social basis of power relations becomes plausible when we refer to the design and implementation of automated information systems.

In the original non-automated situation, functionaries within the organization could retain a certain amount of autonomy. This was based on their ability to cope with the uncertainties of others; also their tasks were not substituteable because the models they used to process their information were implicit and non-formalized. Superiors could hardly contradict them with rational arguments because they did not have access to all the necessary information. Nor could they evaluate or handle such information. They could only contradict them on the basis of authority and the explanation that there were other important implicit factors outside the scope of the functionary that influenced the decision. In the automated situation as a result of the top-down approach, the superior could have access to all the necessary information and the formalized model as used by the lower level functionary. That functionary still could not have access to the information on which his superior based his authoritarian decision. One weight has been lifted from the power scale and it has therefore tipped even more precariously.

Power as the Mediating Variable between Top-down and Bottom-up approaches

As was explained at the end of the previous section, in the top-down approach to information control systems the technical and social power relations coincide. The hierarchical authority structure is superimposed upon the information system. Every responsibility is clearly outlined and results in the disappearance of lower management functions because the basic planning decisions taken at that level are now taken by the automated planning system on the basis of decision rules that have been deduced from quantitative cybernetic models; such models are oriented towards the minimization of coordination costs from a technological point of view. The implementation of such a top-down designed information control system demands far-reaching social changes within the organization because the design does not take the existing (social) organization into account, nor does it reflect societal developments outside the organization.

An approach is proposed that does not take a lopsided view of the influence of one of the organizational aspects.

The anlysis of the organization as a problem-solving and decision-making system, combined with our knowledge of cybernetics, makes it possible to design more efficient control systems. However, due to the fact that organizations are human social constructions, we must also consider the costs that are derived from the inefficient use of the human potential within the organization. The bottom-up analysis of the information flows gives an indication of the manner in which the existing organization is run. Usually the discrepency between the present state and the cybernetic ideal is large. By using the bottom-up analysis as a starting point, it is possible to help functionaries execute their present tasks more efficiently by helping them understand the more systematic side of their work. This understanding can eventually be made to fit the idealized cybernetic model. Every change that is made within the existing system can be compared to the cybernetic model to ensure that no developments occur that will be detrimental to the end result. Subsystems can be designed to fit the needs of the different task groups within the organization. The constraints on the design of these subsystems can be based on the analysis of the power relations as sketched in the previous section of this chapter. The responsibility for the design rests with the (sub)department that is to use it without necessarily divulging to their environment the manner by which they solve their problems. If the existence of power relations is accepted as an important factor for the functioning of individuals and groups within an organization, these relations can be used to stimulate change. *Changes in power need not necessarily be a zero sum game.* It is quite possible to raise the total ability to cope with uncertainty without drastically changing the relative power structure. The design of subsystems, within a total framework, oriented at the existing relative power relations makes such an increase in ability to cope with uncertainty viable. The responsibility of the functioning of the total information control system remains with the higher levels within the hierarchy. The important difference in approach is that they do not concern themselves with the internal design of the subsystems within their area of responsibility, but rather with the compatibility of interfaces between subsystems. In Figure 5.3 they concern themselves with the control of information flows between departments. They can specify which information must be made available and in what form. This means that the higher management levels make it their responsibility that the communication between departments (also subsystems in the total information system) functions well. The knowledge of which information is necessary can be derived from the overall cybernetic model together with a negotiating process between departments and between management and different departments. The higher level of management does not have to fully understand or master the intricacies of local planning systems. If this were the case, the local planning departments would be deprived of their relative power base, and therefore of their organizational identity.

In the second case history, as presented in the first chapter, such an approach would have led to a completely different scenario for the design and implementation of a sophisticated information system. The inventory for the bottom-up method could be started immediately. The top-down study for an ideal cybernetic control system could, to a large extent, be done relatively independently of the functioning of the present planning and information. The main characteristics of the production process, the supply of materials and the nature of the demand on the scales side could be acquired from the higher levels of the management of the organization. From this top-down analysis, the most important information flows could be defined and used as *constraints* in the process of helping the different subdepartments within the organization to function more effectively. The result would have been a less optimal functioning of the information control system as compared to the ideal cybernetic model but a more acceptable form of social interference. No longer directed at making the individuals and groups perform the programs specified from a technologically imperative blueprint, but directed at strengthening, or at least maintaining, the social identity of the existing groups within the organization. Eventually this may lead to the forming of coalitions that come closer to the blueprint of the technologically derived ideal model. Such coalitions should not be the result of a suggestion with no room for alternatives.

In the lighting fixtures factory the expected savings were so attractive that the top-management was initially willing to implement the system as designed. Eventually resistance to the changes demanded by the sysem proved too large and only the most important parts were implemented successfully, thereby achieving the greatest part of the expected savings. Such disappointments have been quite common in the design and introduction of information systems. Strange though this may seem, it has hardly led to a coherent analysis of the relations between such information systems and the human social organizations whose operations they have to control. Most of the work in this area concerns the aid that can be given to the automation teams when implementing their systems, the support they can get from sociologists or (socio)psychologists in getting their clients to accept the necessary changes in their social relations and positions within their organizational environment. Instead, the *real* clients in the organization should demand support in their battle against the infringement of their tasks by incomprehensible data specialists by more clearly specifying their demands and the constraints within which they have to be met. Agreed, this would demand a Copernican turnabout in thinking about organizations. If such a turnabout could be achieved; more realistic automation policies could be defined. Technically, the development within the information processing machinery makes such a *differentiated system approach* more viable. This increase in viability is based on the following assumptions.

(a) The cost of hardware, where it concerns intelligence (i.e., electronics), is rapidly decreasing, certainly when compared to the cost of labour. From a hardware point of view, economies of scale are inconsequential compared to the costs of labour.

(b) Data transmission costs may decrease through the utilization of transmission techniques capable of employing higher information densities. This decrease seems to be nowhere of the same order as that in intelligent hardware.

(c) The flexibility of both the technological system and the social system need to increase because market fluctuations and product changes are following each other with increasing frequency. On the social side there are important shifts in the problem-solving abilities of individuals and their social attitudes and morals.

(d) Certainly in the financial, technical and social service sectors of the economy (in the developed countries by far the largest part of the working population) the productivity of the individual is much more important than the productivity of the appliance he uses to accomplish his tasks.

(e) The 'alienation' due to the absence of identification with his work, influence the worker's productivity. This identification is not seen as the result of an ownership relation with the means of production. Who owns a government organization, a large bank or a hospital? The identification is primarily the result of the social identity he derives from his ability to interact with and influence other people in his direct environment (power) through his work. Secondarily it is the result of the satisfaction he derives from utilizing his capacities during his organizational activities.

It is assumed that it is not at all necessary to maximize this utilization of the individual's capacities during the *whole* work period. It seems probable that a certain percentage of routine activity within the task is even desirable. This *could* result in a more even distribution of routine tasks over a working population. Where in the past unskilled labour was abundant, there is now an over-supply of semi-skilled and skilled labour. Where in the past this scarcity of skill led to a necessary routinization, pressure can now build up towards the spreading of routine work over larger proportions of the working population. As has been said before in this study, the increase in relative scarcity of unskilled labour and the artificial maintenance of low wages in this area are the result of an undue conservatism in the theories of organization and management. These low wages are maintained, on the one hand, by means of the import of foreign labour or by restricting the entry into higher-paid jobs. On the other hand we export our routinized form of production to countries where unskilled labour is still abundantly available.

The organization operates within an environment that sets constraints on the direct attributable costs to the products and services it provides to its clients. In commercial organizations this assumption is evident; in government organizations possibly less so. However, such costs are usually not viewed as constraints, but the *minimizing* of costs is seen as an objective.

Schematization of the Theory of Change

Within a society there are a number of relatively independent developments that influence the functioning of organizations and individuals in organizations. In a previous section the irreversible trend of technological development has been illustrated in the structural theory. This trend inexorably shifts existing problems towards the horizontal axis in the direction of greater analysability. On the one hand, this movement makes existing tasks increasingly susceptible to routinization and automation. On the other hand, it provides organizations with the scope to widen the boundaries of their problem definition and take more variables into account.

The trends in technological development and the subsequent pressures on the task structure are opposed by a number of societal developments. In the first place, the increase in the level of education and in the second place, the change in society itself. This change in the structure of society is away from rural agricultural communities towards the urban industrial or rather service communities that are no longer homogeneous in such characteristics as race, religion or cultural background. The structure of government demands emancipated citizens willing to take part in the activities that are necessary to run the country. Such emancipation demands an increase in scope of decision-making activities outside the employer–employee relation. Choices in all areas are widening: from the possibilities for choosing a place to live, the possibilities for spending one's income, the possibilities for educating one's children and the astounding variety for spending one's vacation. (Outside the defence industry, the tourist industry is the largest in the world.) This emancipation is depicted in the shift of personal norms and values away from the origin, both in a quantitative as in a qualitative sense, or along the specificity dimension. Obedience to authority is seen as a danger to mankind (Milgram 1974), certainly after the intense confrontations with excesses in that direction after the Second World War and the war in Vietnam. The development of standards of social morality which are partly reflected in the general emphasis on democratic forms of government, is away from simple clear-cut *conventions* towards norms which are related to the relative social positions of actors. The norms demand a weighing of one's activities with regard to the consequences they might have for others (Kohlberg 1969, p.376). They should be oriened towards conscience and mutual respect and trust as a directing agent instead of towards accepted conventions. This shift in social norms is not reflected in the structure of the control system of most organizations. Certainly not in the technically oriented literature based on quantitative techniques or the literature oriented towards automated information systems (Van Aken 1978). There seems to be an implicit assumption that the goal-oriented nature that is attributed to organizations is sufficient motivation to demand obedience to authority from its employees or members.

This difference in direction of the evolution of the structure within the organization and that of society, as transmitted by individual members, leads to an increasing gap between the demands set by the organization on the individual and the capacities of the individual. This results in an increasing tension between the roles of individuals inside and outside organizations. Assuming that the developments in our society are not on the brink of changing direction towards a lower complexity and more explicit norms, that we are not about to regress to our cultural past, then we will have to adjust our organizational structures in order to decrease this tension. These changed structures may seem to lead to higher costs, but that is only so because in the past we have neglected to take those costs into account that are difficult to quantify. If wages are used to provide the individual with goods, services or circumstances that give satisfaction to the worker, then satisfaction in the working situation may be seen as income too, and calculated as such.

DESIGNING ORGANIZATIONS, AND CONSULTANTS

The methodological characterization, given at the beginning of this chapter contains an important distinction for the ability to use theories in organizational practice. The opposite of practical is impractical and not theoretical. The difference between voluntarism and determinism should have inevitable consequences for the scope of changing organizations. When a deterministic view is taken there is little or no margin for influencing organizations towards a new or different position. When a voluntaristic view is taken, choices are open, and each choice has its specific consequences and problems. It may be for this reason that the deterministic nature of many theories of organization has precluded a (sound?) theoretical base for organization or management consultancy. The distinction between the consultants lies in the difference of their respective standard prescriptions instead of in the use of different explicit theories of organization or in the different interpretations of similar theories.

This view begs the question of whether the theory, as presented, supplies us with a tool for designing or changing organizations. If this is to be answered positively, then the first demand that has to be met is that the theory itself describes the scope of the choices that are open. The second demand could be the prediction of the consequences of the choices that are alleged to be open. An attempt has been made to meet both these demands. They have been formulated in a non-normative manner.

The distinction between a normative theory, telling us what the world should be like, and a positive theory telling us what the world is like, as described by Blaug (1980, pp.129–56) seems a bit beside the point. A non-normative theory does not say what the world should be like, and a non-normative voluntaristic theory states what the world can be like. Positivism is not a distinction with one variable; it specifies both a non-normative characteristic and the existence of empirically falsifiable relationships between variables. The possibility to falsify statements empirically sets extremely heavy demands on the soundness of subsequent measuring theories.

The values that can be attributed to the consequences of the choices that are open can be filled in by each user of the theory. Adherents to radical change ideologies will emphasize certain dissonances and can use these to pressure the organization or individuals in it towards appropriate changes. On the other hand, the adherents to ideals of regulation can use the theory as an analytic tool to find out which structural shifts lead to the most effective forms of regulation within the organization, given the environmental conditions or restrictions.

The consequence of a non-normative voluntaristic theory should be its efficiency in analysing existing situations and in defining possible alternatives. It should also give an indication of the changes that should be made in order to achieve the demanded results. In the hands of a management consultant, it should be both an analytical and instrumental aid which also helps him to give motivations for the advice which he gives to his clients.

CHANGING ORGANIZATIONS, AND CONSULTANTS

The manner in which the changes that are demanded can be achieved falls outside the scope of this study, and certainly outside the competence of this author. The description of part of the mechanism of organizational change does not imply the ability to control change processes. Certainly when a theoretical framework has been formulated, showing that these change processes may take place on different levels within the organization from within the individual to the structure of the whole organization and its relations with its environment, it can hardly be expected that a pat solution can be given.

If a scientific approach can be found to our ability to change individual behaviour and to influence interaction patterns between individuals and/or groups, then such an approach could well be combined with the presented theory.

If there are a number of different approaches to changing individuals or organizations, theories such as this can only be used to choose between them on the basis of the direction of the demanded change that is required and of the circumstances that prevail.

The most important methodological point that should be kept in mind is that a theory should only be used to explain phenomena in its intended domain. One must be modest enough not to try to explain everything, but only those things for which one has a consistent system of explanations. In this case, this results in a lack of prescriptions for processes of change. It can only generate proposals for alternative structural solutions.

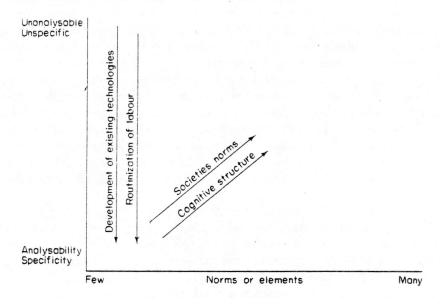

Figure 5.6   The opposing trends in the development of society
as a whole and organization

Chapter 6

Interdepartmental Conflicts Analysed

INTRODUCTION

My remarkably silent departure at the end of the case concerning the planning of the development and the engineering department of a colour TV tube factory may be seen as a proof of the pessimistic opinion expressed by my superior at the beginning of that assignment. He had told me that there was no simple solution to the problems that were described, therefore he feared it would be a waste of time. I hope this has not been so, but that it has led to the development of a mode of analysis that can give us a greater understanding of such problems in organizations—an understanding that strengthens the doubt of my superior that there are no 'techniques applicable' to such situations, because there are no simple, feasible solutions.

This study still doesn't supply ready made solutions in the manner that was originally required. It should show that interdepartmental tensions and conflicts are an essential part of the phenomenon of organizing and that they are part of the mechanism of organizational dynamics. Only when certain types of conflict are inordinately strong can a solution be sought by either restructuring the division of labour, the tasks, in the related departments or the manner in which they are controlled. Undoubtedly this will have side-effects on the relations with other interacting departments and these side-effects will more likely than not, be negative. The structures of the different departments have probably developed as a result of a tendency towards equilibrium in the field of intra-organizational dissonances and forces from outside the organizations.

I went back a number of years later to find out how the situation had developed in the organization. The engineering department had changed, necessitating the departure of Mr Ripple. The manner in which the tasks were coordinated within the department had been changed drastically, which had not been without effect on the creativity of the design group.

Retrospectively it was doubtful if Mr Thrasher had really been inclined to change anything in the organization. He was nearing his retirement and could well sit out the interdepartmental squabbles which everyone found so irritating. Futhermore, he was situated in a focal point of intraorganizational forces; the commercial department tried to pull him one way, the development department the other way. Each department under his supervision tried to influence him in their own manner and direction. It was only necessary for him to show his good will by proving that attention was being paid to these conflicts, thereby absolving himself from further endeavours to really influence the situation. This would leave him enough leeway to push through his own choices based on either a strong intuition gained from experience or on shifting personal alliances. This also seems likely from a theoretical point of view. If the existing structures are the consequence of a historical development, based on a tendency towards equilibrium of intraorganizational dissonances and external forces, why would this not apply to individual functionaries? A strong indication that the problems were not really to be solved but that Mr Thrasher needed a tactical instrument to defend his position with, may be found in the ambivalent nature of our sporadic meetings.

These meetings were of two kinds. Once in a while I would make an appointment with him when there were specific points which I thought needed his attention rather than that of the heads of the departments, or when I wanted to present certain findings. More often than not these meetings were cancelled or shifted because something more urgent intervened on his side. The other kind of meeting usually took place at the end of the day — most often on Fridays when he had some time to spare. Either he would saunter through the development department chatting with the product developers, or he would call me up to his office. We would not discuss the problems which I thought I had to solve, but rather all sorts of organizational problems as he saw them around him. He always did this in a very fatherly fashion, often alluding to his son-in-law who was studying the same type of problems in an academic surrounding, thereby indicating that he was also interested in more theoretical answers apart from the direct consequence of my advice for the organization.

Roles People Play

These last discussions were always so stereotyped that once, just before he was to retire, I decided to try to convince him of the unchanging pattern of our meetings. When I arrived at his office, after he had summoned me by telephone, he was standing in his secretary's room finishing off some last minute instructions. I went into his room. Instead of remaining standing until he returned, I seated myself behind his desk. As he entered, I did my best to imitate his voice and said:

'Well, young man, how is the science of organizations helping us to get our problems solved?'

I immediately got up, walked to the other side of the desk, sat down and answered in my own voice:

'As you have often told me there seems to be no science concerning organizations. And what our problem is hasn't altogether become too clear either.'

Again I got up from my chair and sat behind the desk.

'Oh! You try to evade me. This is a commercial business, profits must be made, decisions taken. We must have an industrial machine that runs smoothly. You are here to reduce the friction between the parts of the machine.'

Again I got up from his chair to step over to my own side. Mr Thrasher was rather taken aback, but not enough to stop the show.

'Friction can not always be reduced by adding a lubricant. Usually it also has something to do with the functioning or the design of the interacting parts. That is an aspect which is often left out in our discussion. Usually it boils down to just a drop of oil here and there or a little more planning here or there.'

I got up from my chair, sat down in his and laid my hands on the edge of the desk. With repressed irritation lightly tapped the desk top—a gesture so typical of him.

'You talk as if such things can be changed overnight, as if these departments haven't grown into the way they are, over the years. If the people heading the departments are not the most capable inside, and probably outside, this organization.'

Mr Thrasher interrupted me.

'Enough, enough! Do you think you can get away with this kind of joking?'

I was by now standing beside his desk and he stood between me and the door, looking perturbed, but as far as I could judge, not really angry.

'To be quite honest; I think I can,' I said. 'If I can't then there doesn't seem much to lose. The conversations we've had are usually a rehash of the previous ones. Your reaction to my review of the consequences of employing more formal planning systems was so strongly coloured by your own experience in product development, therefore by the fear that planning would disrupt the creative impulses necessary for developing new ideas, that I have come to the conclusion that whatever planning systems can be devised, they can never succeed on their own merit in this environment. Because I have stated my opinion that in reality we are not being confronted with a planning problem, which is opposed to your opinion, a deadlock has been created—a deadlock that is only strengthened by your telling me that the existing planning problem cannot be solved by introducing a formal planning system. By restricting the possible solutions, a solution-oriented analysis of the problem becomes impossible. A general analysis of the problem directed only at achieving a greater understanding of what is the matter has been unlikely from the beginning.'

'It is, indeed, best to fit your analysis to the solutions you have available. Then there is a reasonable chance of success. I doubt if we've covered all the possible planning sysems to fit our problem,' he answered.

We were back to where we had started.

Mr Thrasher soon left the organization and his successor decided that possible solutions should be sought in quite a different direction—a direction that demanded a shift in personnel, of which I was most certainly to be a part.

Thus I also left the organization and entered into the field of automated information systems.

Six years after my departure I tried to find out how, in the mean time, the situation in the colour TV tube factory had developed. Although outside the organization the market situation had changed considerably, as had also the social climate, certainly where it concerned labour relations, inside the organization things were still much the same. The same problems still existed. Certain people had been shifted — most of them within the organization — but that had not really changed the situation.

My analysis of the situation has changed considerably. Through the development of a theory of multilevel analysis of organizational dissonance, at least a mode of representation has been constructed with which some of the underlying principles leading to intra-organizational conflicts can be described. If the chance had occurred I would have represented my views to Mr Thrasher in the following manner instead of putting up the show that I have just described.

An Imaginary Conversation

Waiting for Mr Thrasher to finish his last minute directions for his secretary, I looked out the windows at the laboratory building opposite. The rain slanted through the courtyard, eddying under the air-bridge between the two buildings. The cars in the courtyard gleamed in the orange light of the sodium lamps. The building was brightly lit, people were busy clearing their rooms making ready for the weekend — a typical sight for Friday afternoon. Mr Thrasher came into the room and without greeting me said:

'Well young man, how is the science of organizations helping us to get our problems solved?'

'As you have often told me, there seems to be no science concerning organizations. As for our problems, I sometimes wonder if they are really problems which are different from those in any other organization. Even though we think we have problems, it may well be that they should be quite acceptable, may be even healthy for the organization.'

'According to you they may be healthy for the organization, which I can hardly imagine, but they are most certainly not healthy for me. I feel most uncomfortable — no, sincerely dislike — such situations as our meeting with the commercial, the engineering and the development departments some weeks ago.' Mr Thrasher said.

'I can well imagine. I doubt though, whether an easy solution to such situations can be found. We can try to present a clearer picture of how such situations arise — what the necessary circumstances are for such structural conflicts to surface. When we have achieved that, we can start looking for feasible solutions.'

'This is a commerical business, profits must be made, problems solved, decisions taken. The industrial machine must run smoothly. You are here to reduce the friction between the parts,' Mr Thrasher said jocularly.

'Friction cannot always be reduced by adding a drop of oil here or there. Furthermore, you need different kinds of oil for different kinds of interacting materials. Therefore you must know what to use and when. Otherwise you might try to use water as a lubricant for steel cogwheels, which doesn't work, whereas it does for plastic.'

'You have the freedom to choose from all types of planning systems, don't you? Mr Thrasher asked.

'As I said earlier, that depends on the question of whether it is actually a planning problem.'

'That should be clear by now,' he said, rather testily.

'Before we go into the prerequisites for planning again, I would like to try to paint you a picture of the situation as I see it. We have come to the agreement that a problem exists on the interface between the development department and the engineering department. This problem, according to you, can be solved by supplying the two departments with better planning systems. Before we decide what the requirements are for such planning systems, let us decide on what forms these problems between the departments take.'

'You know quite well what form they take,' he answered in a rather piqued tone. 'The engineering group find it hard, to put it mildly, to meet the deadlines they have accepted.'

'That is only partly the case. If they are allowed to fulfil their orders without being interfered with, by having to modify their designs, they can usually meet their deadlines quite well. But constant interference and changes in priority wreak havoc with the unflexible manner in which their production is organized.'

'Well, then we must do something about that inflexibility. Supply them with planning techniques which enables them to adjust more quickly to changed situations.' Mr Thrasher exclaimed.

'But why has that technique and their organization developed in the way it has?' I asked.

'Probably because in the past, when we were still a relatively small organization, it was appropriate.'

'That may be true. On the other hand, we find that most engineering groups are similar; both in structure and in the planning systems they use. Most of them are inflexible and have long throughput times. The larger the organizations become, the graver these problems turn out to be.'

'Nowadays there are automated planning systems, aren't there?' he interrupted.

'There are. I know from experience that the introduction of such planning systems turns out to be extremely hazardous. The changes which are necessary to get the organization to react in a fitting manner to the automated planning system are extremely difficult to effect.'

'They solve the problem, don't they?'

'Only partly. Theoretically they give very attractive solutions to planning problems. In practice, old habits often prevail in the organization, making the new systems ineffective.'

'That indicates there is a lack of discipline in the organization. People should put the decisions that have been made into effect,' he said.

'I always remember your stories about one of your colleagues, how he diverted funds from projects that had been accepted, to projects that had been rejected, and how his disobedience payed off in the form of some very successful developments. A mentality of strict discipline may be appropriate in an industrial production plant, although I doubt it, but in an organization with many professionals who often know more about their work than their superiors do, such a mentality would be quite inappropriate, as your own stories show.'

'Maybe I did not say it subtly enough,' he interrupted.

'Oh, I don't know. I think it is indicative of the diagnosis of the problem on hand. We are concerned with two highly professional areas of work. The engineering department is a classical example of a functionally differentiated task structure. It has clearly delineated tasks in a hierarchical sense, from chief designer to draughtsman. The whole structure is based on a long history, dating back to the industrial revolution, and it is also based on a strong urge for efficiency. This urge for efficiency has led to a fine pattern in the division of labour.'

'But even in such an organization, flexibility should still be possible, shouldn't it?'

'It should be possible, but it isn't probable. The coordination between all those different tasks takes time and effort. The effort has been minimized by means of standardization of communication channels. Flexibility demands a more adaptive mode of coordination than that built into the task structure. In my opinion one must necessarily change the whole structure of the organization, when introducing new modes of coordination. That is no mean measure. A very difficult task to accomplish.'

'So you suggest we leave it as it is, I suppose.'

'I didn't say so. I'm not trying to present solutions. First I want to present a relatively clear picture of the problems we've encountered. Then I want to discuss with you the pros and cons of possible alternative solutions.'

'All right. I understand.'

'Well. The structure of the engineering department is oriented towards an optimal use of specialized resources. The main area of coordination is the balancing of the capacities of the different specialities. Without very sophisticated planning systems and strict discipline in adhering to the plans, this leads to long throughput times. The variables in the classical optimizing function are the degree of occupancy of the different specialized units related to its cost per unit of time.'

'That seems to be a sound economic procedure,' Mr Thrasher said.

'Maybe it is. But it is too limited in scope. Costs related to a lack of flexibility are ignored because they are difficult to express, or rather, to quantify, even though the consequences of such a lack of flexibility may be quite clear within the organization.'

I remained silent for a while, waiting for a reaction from Mr Thrasher. As it was not forthcoming, I went on:

'So on the one hand there is a form of organization that is based on sound economic reasoning, on the other hand, there is a demand for more flexibility and fluent interaction of which the results cannot be readily translated into quantified profits but of which the costs can be calculated. This leads to a strong prejudice in the basis for decisions.'

'I understand what you mean to say. In the past we used to have an independent subdepartment in the engineering department, situated in the development building. This turned out to be too expensive because it was difficult to keep the different specialists fully employed,' Mr Thrasher said.

'Quite right. In other words, the economic rationale was stronger than the organizational rationale. Or to put it more precisely, the rationale of the calculable rather than the economic in general.'

'You mean that there are solutions possible which might be more economic, but they are difficult to assess because the costs . . . no not the costs but rather the benefits are difficult to describe in terms of money.'

'That's it. This sort of situation can be found in most areas of organization. For example: automation or mechanization projects are attractive where machines can substitute expensive labour. Usually the well-paid jobs are not the most boring or physically the heaviest. Boredom and/or high physical strain may produce absenteeism and medical costs. I can show you places in the production line which should be very attractive to mechanize because the physical loads are too high or because the work is very boring. These mechanization projects are impossible to get started because the manner in which the benefits of such projects are calculated do not take these consequences into account. The same can be said about changes that may lead to a more flexible organization at the same or a higher cost. The economies of scale lead to a decrease in organizational flexibility with its related costs.'

'The economies of scale part is not quite clear,' said Mr Thrasher. 'Bigger plants are usually cheaper per unit of production. There is extensive literature on the manner in which this reduction of costs comes about.'

'Quite so, but there is hardly any literature on the loss of ability to react to changes in demand or to differentiated demands. In the automobile assembly, a good example of the economies of scale, the reaction to a differentiated demand is being solved by using extremely sophisticated techniques of production scheduling. These techniques synchronize the flow of the necessary parts in such a manner that specific though different combinations can be made within one programme. If one of the branches of the synchronized production stream is interrupted, then the whole production is held up. Changes in the process are very expensive and difficult to introduce.'

'You mean cars with different colours can be made, each having the appropriate interior colouring or additional features. However, it is expensive to introduce a new model on the production line.'

'Absolutely. This is also the origin of the distinction between, on the one hand, consumer goods such as cars, which are highly standardized and can be produced on automated assembly lines, and on the other hand, professional goods, such as for instance mobile cranes, which are usually produced to the specification of individual customers and in much smaller numbers. But also in the professional goods we see that standardization is bearing fruits because of the lower prices and the greater reliability of such goods.'

'So there too, the economic logic prevails,' Mr Thrasher interrupted.

'On the other hand: yes. However, even though it is evident that from a point of view of costs, standardization and the economies of scale are attractive, it seems worthwhile to find out why the professional users originally demanded equipment to their own specifications.'

'What kind of professional users have you in mind?' Mr Thrasher asked.

'Well. For instance our own organization. We could use enameling machines which are available on the market.'

'To answer that is quite simple. We make unique products, certainly as far as quality is concerned, and on the whole those standard machines cannot meet our specifications,' Mr Thrasher said.

'Similar arguments are used by shipowners and truckers. They also provide unique services, demanding unique equipment, even though they realize they are incurring higher costs. The use of standard ships is hardly ever taken into account, not even in the transport of such a standard product as crude oil. During the Second World War the production of Victory and Liberty freighters proved highly effective for both the builders and the users.'

'I don't see what you are getting at,' Mr Thrasher interjected.

'What I am trying to illustrate is that most organizations are convinced that they are pursuing economic ends by efficient means, but in their selection of means they do not employ the same clear-cut economic rationale as they do when rationalizing their decisions retrospectively. Their choices are often based on the implicit opinion that their products and the processes by which they are made demand unique solutions, which certainly lead to technological development, but not necessarily to low costs.'

'That's all quite fine. But when you want to be at the forefront of your industry you will have to supply your own technology. And that is what we are doing.' Mr Thrasher looked quite irked and seemed to take my remarks as unfair criticism on the policy within the organization for taking decisions on mechanization projects.

'You're quite right, of course. However, that does not necessarily mean that you have to supply your own technology along the whole line. As a decisive factor one could take the direct influence on the quality of the product.'

'That seems sensible.'

'In our case that would mean that the engineering department could concentrate on a smaller field of development and probably scrap a lot of projects they are working on.'

'Who would decide which projects to scrap and which to pursue? he asked.

'Don't ask me. That's part of your job. At this point I'm not concerned with the authority of certain individuals or groups to decide such issues. I am concerned with exploring how an organization can be brought to ask the most relevant questions before it starts to generate answers.'

'What questions have you in mind?'

'Let's take the projects in the development department. We can agree that it is necessary to develop new products in order to remain competitive. Competition is influenced by two main factors: (a) price, and (b) quality. Because the level of our wages is high, it is unlikely that we can compete with cheaper countries when using similar production techniques. Thus we find an exodus of production facilities to cheaper countries.'

'We have remained competitive by mechanizing and automating our production,' Mr Thrasher said.

'You're absolutely right here. On the other hand, why shouldn't the countries where the labour is cheap also mechanize and automate?'

'Usually they don't have the know-how.'

'We give them the know-how or we sell it to them. In the case of selling it is a rational calculation they can make. In the case of giving it away, as we do when we bring our production to other cheaper countries, we say that the profits remain within the company, but we do create a form of hidden unemployment in our own country. Furthermore, we can conclude that mechanization is a process of diminishing advantages — a process with its own specific problems.'

'Such as?'

'In our own factory there are departments where not a word of Dutch is spoken. We have imported labour to do the jobs we ourselves are no longer willing to do. We have created jobs that are so uninteresting and unattractive that we cannot find individuals to fill them.'

'You know what I think about the decrease in work ethic, high absenteeism and shoddy work. I don't think it is necessary to go into that again,' Mr Thrasher exclaimed.

'There may have been a change in the work ethic, but I wonder if that is the crucial difference. I think there are more important, more fundamental developments.'

'You must agree with me that staying away from work while being paid can hardly be called ethical. More likely it is theft.'

'I wonder if you had to do boring and heavy work in an unpleasant environment, to put it mildly, for a relatively low pay. Would you be so scrupulous about staying away?'

'Of course I would. I am well aware of my responsibilites,' he said indignantly.

'Of course you are right. On the other hand we are also confronted with a working population with an increasing level of education. Maybe it is also the responsibility of those groups who design products, production means or organizations to match supply and demand. If the average person has been to school for twelve years, has learned to solve all kinds of problems, has many social responsibilities, can be active in the labour union, political party or for instance a local sports club, shouldn't most of these facilities also find some reflection in his working environment?' I asked.

'You talk as if we are some kind of charitable social institution instead of an economic production unit,' Mr Thrasher exclaimed.

'If one views a worker as a production unit, then he becomes comparable to other production units, to machines. Would you want a production machine to be working below its optimal capacity? Would you make simple cheap products, that do not demand great precision, on a sophisticated high-precision machining centre, that is very expensive to run?'

'Of course not. That would be uneconomical.'

'In my opinion it is just as uneconomical to under-utilize human potential, particularly if this under-utilization has negative side-effects such as boredom and a decrease in motivation.'

'I think you're wrong there. It is more a question of supply and demand. Industry demands unskilled labour and society doesn't supply it anymore. Certainly not for an acceptable price. Because that is the case, industry necessarily has to look elsewhere for new sources of unskilled labour.'

I got up from my chair and walked to the blackboard, which hung next to the door, in order to illustrate the point I was trying to make. Chalk in hand, I tried to explain:

'If we take the development of society as an autonomous process (probably made possible by increasing welfare and income supplied in part by industrial production) and if we find it laudable that the individual in society is supplied with the intellectual luggage necessary to bear his social and political responsibilities, then why should we demand, in his work situation, that these capacities should be left under-utilized?'

'I think you take a wrong approach. A person is paid to do certain work. He is not paid to enjoy himself. For the discomfort, the displeasures of work he is given financial compensation,' Mr Thrasher told me in a rather bored manner.

I knew I was being sidetracked, but could not withstand the impulse to oppose this point of view.

'The logical conclusion is then that the more uncomfortable the individual is in his work, the more he is to be paid, whereas in reality it seems to be quite the opposite. Public esteem and self esteem are not the result of unpleasant or dirty and boring work, but are combined with interesting and responsible jobs which are nicely matched with material gains.'

'As can be concluded from what you yourself say, there is a second important influence on the compensation. And that is the responsibility of the job, and the stress this places on the manager.'

'That may be so', I admitted, although I disagreed wholeheartedly. Not wanting to fall into the same dispute over and over again, it was necessary to try it over another tack.

'However, we can agree to the fact that absenteeism is high, that it is politically infeasible to change the labour laws in such a manner that the people are pressured into working harder and that we don't know how to influence the work ethic.'

'As far as the work ethic is concerned, I think a lot of harm is done in our school system and in the mass media. A lot of youngsters are inundated in so-called progressive tripe instead of being presented a clear picture of how the world really works,' he said.

'I won't agree or disagree with you. Here too, we don't know how to influence this. What we can influence, at least partially, is the way things are organized within our own organization and the manner in which we manufacture our products. If we accept that the level of education is rising and cannot be influenced by our own organization, except in a direction of an even higher level or towards more specialization; then it may be worthwhile to see how we can adapt our work so that we can take advantage of these growing resources, or reservoirs of intellect.'

'Probably that will not be economically feasible,' Mr Thrasher interrupted. 'In a commercial organization there is very little space for idealism.'

'There seems to be very much space for absenteeism at this moment, so why not see if these two cannot compensate each other?' I said. He was silent for a while and looked at me critically.

'I agree that one could calculate the costs of absenteeism and of high reject rates. It is however difficult to make comparisons,' he said.

'There are more ways than one to look at such problems, even from a point of view of economics. It depends on which variables we are willing to take up in our calculations. If we take up different variables from those we have considered up to the present moment it will possibly prove to be worthwhile to mechanize or automate many of the jobs that are now filled by unskilled workers.'

I was still standing in front of the blackboard, chalk in hand. My fingers were white and dry from playing with the stump of chalk.

'And what do we do with the people whose jobs we have automated? Throw them out? It's good to hear that from such a progressive young man,' Mr Thrasher interjected sarcastically.

'If I have my information right, there is a great shortage of unskilled labour in our organization so I don't see the necessity to kick them out. Furthermore, if you really want to be progressive, as I am certain you wish to be, then unskilled labour can always become skilled if you are willing to pay enough attention to the educational aspect.'

'I still don't see where we can get the money from to achieve this.'

'Before I can start to answer that question, I am certain you are ready with another realistic deterrent against change. Therefore I won't answer your question but will illustrate my point further.'

'A weak reply.'

I ignored his interruptions and went on: 'If we see the development in the distribution of education expressed in percentages of the labour force with a specific number of years of schooling, it can be represented as follows: We see that in the beginning of the twentieth century our population mainly had very little schooling. Higher education was for the select few. Now we can see that the average level of education is rising quickly, moving the centre of gravity to the right. Those are the two lines in this figure (6.1.a). If we then sketch the demand for certain kinds of labour, the type of labour specified by the number of years of education necessary in order to fulfil the job, then we can see the following development (Figure 6.1.b). In the beginning of this century there

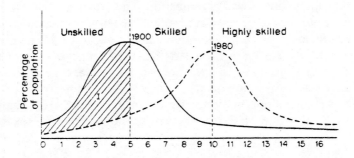

Area I: decrease in supply of unskilled labour

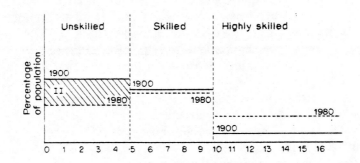

Area II: decrease in demand of unskilled labour

Figure 6.1   The relation between the supply of and the demand for different types of labour in the twentieth century

was a high demand for unskilled labour, and a growing demand for highly skilled labour. This last category was partly responsible for the development of mechanized, and later, automated production processes, product development but also for such developments as the changes of methods of production in agriculture. If we superimpose the present trend as I have tried to illustrate it, we see the following. The availability of highly educated personnel makes it possible that great advances can be made in understanding means of production. This leads to the possibility of mechanization and automation. This increase in understanding leads on the one side to a decrease in the demand for craftsmanship based mainly on experience acquired by trial and error and apprenticeship as opposed to understanding of the way things work or scientific knowledge. And thus on the other hand to an increase in unskilled routinized labour, relative to the availability of such workers. This can be seen from the combination of the two figures. The two shaded parts of each figure have a quite different area. I is the decrease of the supply of unskilled workers. II is the decrease in demand for unskilled workers. Because I is larger than II we see the relative scarcity become larger.'

Mr Thrasher watched me without much interest when he said:

'Maybe it is quite interesting what you have shown me, but I don't quite see why we should concern ourselves with these problems.'

'Our concern should be based on the hypothesis that the individual, when performing a job, does not want to do work which is far below his ability. If this is the case, it will result in side-effects which lower his efficiency. The second hypothesis is that these side-effects cannot be completely compensated by for instance higher pay.'

'I still don't see why I have to concern myself with this,' he interrupted impatiently.

'Maybe I'm a bit long winded. What I am trying to say is that it may be more economic to decrease the number of unskilled jobs at a much higher rate than we are doing at present, because the benefits of such a change may be much bigger than we have realized in the past. This difference in our appreciation of the changes is due to the prejudiced manner in which we calculate costs and benefits. Two possible positive results of such a policy would be:

(a) a more dependable production process, with lower reject rates and less organizational dilemmas; and
(b) possibly, cheaper products.'

'If it were all so straightforward, why haven't we done so in the past?' he asked.

'The reasoning behind it may be straighforward, but the manner in which it can be achieved is not.'

'I don't see why that should be difficult. If what you say were true, which, as yet, I don't believe; then it should be quite easy to change our policy towards mechanization of our production,' he said.

'These last years I have studied the manner in which mechanization projects have been started. Many of the projects were not accompanied by profitability calculations. What is more important, most projects grew out of previous projects. By growing out of previous projects I mean that a development which has taken place within a certain project is pursued further in the next. It is rather like saying that if it is beautiful weather today then the chance is great that the same will be the case tomorrow. This means that production-technical development can largely take place as an autonomous process within the engineering department, as long as it stays within the bounds of economic feasibility.'

'But we agreed that technological development was what kept our own production feasible,' Mr Thrasher exclaimed, not without exasperation.

'That feasibility is best guaranteed, in my opinion, when the technical development is matched with simultaneous social development and not treated as being independent: when the design of new production processes is oriented towards the employment of few skilled workers instead of many unskilled workers; when the economy of production is seen as a constraint and not as a goal, and the satisfaction from labour as a goal that can only be achieved by economic means.'

'Quite elegantly put, but rather idealistic. We're not in the business of providing satisfying work, but of producing sophisticated products for an acceptable price,' he said.

'And when that price rises because the production costs rise due to the consequences of dissatisfied labour, according to your ideas, the production techniques do not have to change but solutions must be sought in the area of labour relations and a stronger hold on the activities of the worker. These are two things that have escaped from the toolkit of the manager, and which are probably out of his reach due to changes in the social and political climate.'

'Well in that case labour is digging its own grave and pricing itself out of the market,' Mr Thrasher interjected.

'And dragging you along with them. We can export our production facilities to cheaper countries but a healthy market in the more expensive countries still remains a necessity. Our workers form such a market. That means we must have both a viable development and production department in order to remain a viable market for our own products,'

I was still standing next to the blackboard, chalk in hand, trying to clarify the point I wanted to make by illustrating it. Mr Thrasher must have noticed this too when he said:

'Well, what are you going to show me on the blackboard?'

I laughed self-consciously, realizing that, as usual, he had sidetracked me by pursuing the seeming inevitable developments in the past, and by his enduring conviction that the course of events could not be changed. His subjective freedom to choose was much smaller than the alternatives that were presented. The norms by which alternatives were weighed could not be discussed. I decided not to give up so easily. I drew my two axes on the board and again explained superficially, as I had often done before, how complexity could be described in a two-dimensional manner. And how complexity can be used to compare two different aspects of one organization or two different organizations with regard to one aspect. In this case we took the first alternative to describe the problems individuals are presented with and the capacity for problem solving of those individuals.

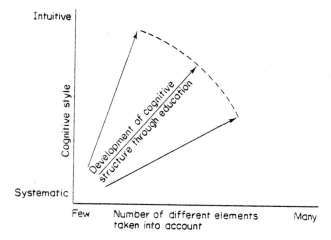

Figure 6.2   The development of the individual's cognitive structure through education

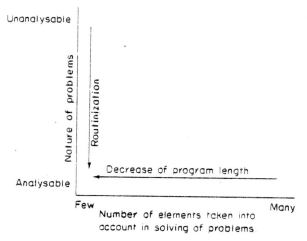

Figure 6.3   Development of the nature of work due to the improvement of the knowledge of products and production processes

'If we can agree that the rise in the level of general education, as illustrated in the previous figure, raises the problem-solving capacity of the individual worker, we can present this as a shift away from the origin. If you can also agree with me that the general tendency is to design production facilities that can do without skilled labour, that is, production facilities that reduce the complexity of the problems that have to be solved by the worker, then we see a growing discrepancy between the ability of the individual and the demands of the production processes for solving problems. Even non-Marxist sociologists and psychologists can agree that such compulsory under-utilization is detrimental to the motivation of the individual to contribute effectively to the common production process.'

184

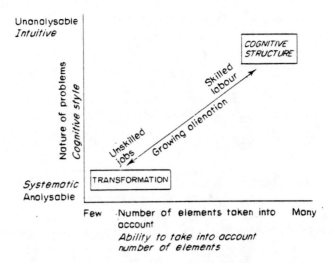

Figure 6.4 Growing dissonance between the ability of the individual worker and the demands set by the organization. Alienation of the worker because of the content of his task

'So?'

'So if we recognize that this growing discrepancy is detrimental to the production process we should try to reduce it. There is very little we can do to the level of education of our employees apart from raising it, so as an alternative we have imported unskilled labour, a form of inverted colonialism. We have come to realize that this last solution is very unattractive. That means that we must choose between two other alternatives.

(a) accept the situation of a growing absenteeism and low quality work as side-effects of alienating work;
(b) formulate a policy that will lead to more interesting work.

The first seens unacceptable to me, so I opt for the second. The process of mechanization and automation itself is already a shift to a more skilled activity. But it is a second order phenomenon.'

'Just for the sake of discussion I am willing to go along with your line of thought.' Mr Thrasher said. 'What intrigues me is how can your switch be explained in an historical perspective?'

'That is already partially explained by the two previous diagrams. In a more practical perspective we can say that the industrial revolution fed on, and fed, the technical development in the nineteenth century. Until that time, only craftsmen produced products of some complexity. When the understanding of the production process was deep enough, when the definition of the product was clear enough and the precision of the production process high enough, it became possible to split up the production into such small tasks that the execution only needed manual or physical dexterity instead of the intelligence or the experience of the worker. All problems of the production process had already been solved it its design. The intelligence and experience was necessary in the design and construction phase of the industrial process, and no longer in the production.

When Henry Ford started producing automobiles on an assembly line, he could fall back on a large pool of uneducated labour, mainly becoming available from agriculture. He created a match between the unskilled labour that was predominant around Detroit and the 'new' understanding of industrial production methods. These methods were made possible by the interchangeability of both parts and production machines. Or more specifically, by the ability to define tolerances and to meet them.'

I expected Mr Thrasher would say something, but as nothing was forthcoming, I went on: 'The same thing happened with our own company. It was started in an agricultural environment because it could tap the uneducated and unskilled labour pool available. It is even said that there was an agreement between management and the local church authorities who were mainly responsible for the education of the population which said that the company would keep them poor if the church saw to it that they remained dumb.'

Mr Thrasher looked out of the window. The rain had subsided and orange light breaking through the clouds accentuated the colours. His fingers tapped the rim of the desk and when I saw his face take on a faraway look I knew for certain that I had lost his attention. As long as I did not present solutions for the problems which he too, knew that existed it would stay difficult to keep his attention. If only I had created openings where he could have sought acceptable solutions.

He turned towards me, and with a bland smile said:

'And so?'

Now it was my turn to give a deep sigh, rush my hands over my face and look out of the window. I went back to my chair.

'There is no simple solution. If there had been you would certainly have found it yourself.'

He looked at me with pursed lips, giving himself a parsimonious though absentminded expression. The gap in our talking accentuated the humming of the factory. The noise level was much lower because it was Friday afternoon. Much of the factory was already closed for the weekend. He turned to me.

'Maybe you are right. Routine jobs are the essence of industrial production—a mode that has not changed much in the last century whereas the social environment has. I remember some articles you sent me on automobile production in Sweden which is based on a hypothesis similar to yours. And in comparison an article about the problems of starting a factory in America in a setting that had up until then not known such a form of work and which remained closed for a number of months due to labour troubles. What I find most troubling is that there seem to be no solutions to this dilemma. Economically we have hardly any leeway for choice,' he said.

'That means that only a small course correction is possible,' I replied. 'This does not exclude a larger change in the long run as long as the chosen course is persisted in. The question we must answer is: are we going to follow the preset course or are we going to use the little leeway we have to find alternatives?'

'I admire your optimism. I fear it is based on a lack of experience.'

This time I was not going to step into his wide-open trap. Experience is always an appropriate escape. He looked at me through the top of his gold-rimmed spectacles with raised eyebrows waiting for my answer. I looked back at him trying to keep my face as empty of expression as I could. His starting position was much stronger than mine so I would have to answer.

'Only optimists set out on explorative journeys. Pessimists stay at home, fight to consolidate their positions, fight against change. I don't mind too much what my optimism is based on. I can agree with you that it cannot be on experience. The only thing I can hope is that it is based on understanding acquired by systematic analysis. And also that this optimism does not preclude finding new solutions to old problems.' I realized that I was speaking rather harshly.

'All right, get on with your optimistic talk of organizational change,' he said and smiled in his fatherly manner.

'Thank you. I'll first summarize the main points of the problem as I have presented it. The general tendency in industrial technology has been and is, to standardize products and production techniques in such a manner that all forms of problem solving become routinized. We replace skilled, and therefore expensive, labour by unskilled labour and machines. This replacement is based on the assumption that unskilled labour is cheap and readily available. However unskilled labour is becoming scarce and expensive. Expensive, not necessarily in the sense of direct payment, but in the sense of absenteeism and poor work. Unavailable in the sense that the general education of our population is rising steadily. The idea that skilled workers can be used to do unskilled work is false. These two developments lead to the growing dissonance between available jobs and available workers. The automation process itself demands highly skilled labour but this is a second order variable which makes it less interesting in the long run.'

'What do you mean by a second order variable?' Mr Thrasher asked.

'I can best illustrate it in the following manner. It may take a group of ten engineers a year to automate a certain task. But that task may be fulfilled by a hundred different workers over a number of years. That means that the engineers have the ability to change skilled labour into unskilled labour at a certain speed, whereas the result is expressed by the total number of jobs lost forever. Expressing this mathematically, we can say that the change in the labour force is the integral of the engineers' capacity to change the production process over time. Or seem from the other side, his capacity can be expressed as the first derivative of the change in the required labour force.'

'You mean as in mechanics, where speed is the first derivative of the distance and the distance is the integral of the speed over a certain time?'

'Exactly.'

'Not a bad comparison. And not unlike the comparison I like to make with investments,' Mr Thrasher said.

'There we are in complete agreement. It is quite usual to view automation projects, i.e. the work of automation engineers, as investments.'

Mr Thrasher looked out of the window again. The light was gone. The vivid details were now lost in the rain that had returned. In the courtyard the starting of cars could be heard. People were going home. Mr Thrasher didn't tap the rim of his desk, but pensively rubbed his index finger with the tips of the fingers and thumb of his other hand.

'What you said before I asked about the second order variable is becoming more clear now. In the classical sense the engineering department is organized in an economic manner. Their way of organization partly defines the things they do, and completely defines how they do it. This, what and how, does not reflect what you would or what we should want them to do.'

I nodded, not wanting to answer in the hope that he would formulate in his own words what I had been trying to explain. He looked down at his desk and collected bits of dust or dirt from the top by pressing his index finger onto them, transporting them carefully to the side and then rubbing his fingers and thumb. He repeated this ritual a number of times before he went on.

'According to your analysis, the mechanization of a certain task demands that the task be completely understood. Only then can all activities be programmed and translated into, let's call it, a mechanical language. This mechanical language demands that the complete task can be split up into small units, into defined operations. This, according to you, is achieved by standardization of parts and the definition of acceptable tolerances.' He was silent again. His face became more lively when he went on: 'You know, in his context, it is interesting to note that in my own experience as a product developer, when we didn't quite understand why something worked in some cases and not in others, this always resulted in narrowing down the tolerances. This in turn always resulted in protests from the engineering department.'

'That still occurs across the courtyard and still elicits the same protests from the engineering department.'

All of a sudden he seemed bored again, as he tried to suppress a yawn. Evidently I had interrupted his line of thought. As he didn't go on, I did.

'If we go on from the hypothesis that the nature of the production equipment that is developed by the engineering department, determines to a large extent the nature of the work that has to be done in the factory, then that department is crucial to the attempted changes in the nature of the work done in the factory. However, because the structure of that department is rigid and strong, we will meet a strong resistance to change when we attempt to influence their own work.' Mr Thrasher looked at me with an incomprehending expression. I would somehow have to regain his interest.

'You just spoke of your own experience in the development department,' I said. 'I expect that you must have had similar problems as you see here?'

'Oh yes, we were always at odds with the engineering department. But our organizations were so much smaller then, than they are now. We could smoothe things out so much easier,' he answered in a flat tone. 'We all knew each other and could always call on each other to get the help we needed. Most of us were busy with the same problems at the same time. Things are quite different now. The development department has nearly 300 employees and the engineering department over 400. Of all those people I only know a few by name. When I want to get something done nowadays, it is difficult for me to find out who can do it. So I always end up asking either Mr Barton or Mr Ripple.' He was silent for a while. 'We knew what was possible and what wasn't. We had tried most of the things ourselves. Now I see people repeat nearly the same kind of experiments we did because they lack our experience.' Again he was silent and slowly rubbed his finger. A disappointed, aggrieved elderly gentleman. 'When I visit the department, my hands often itch to help, to tell them what alternatives to pursue. Immediately I realize that I must not, that the working circumstances are now quite different from those in my own time.'

'I think you have an important point there. Could you take the comparison between then and now a little futher?' I asked.

'It can hardly be compared. We had a department of 4 engineers and physicists and something like 15 assistants. The engineering department was right next door. It was not always clear who did the developing and who the engineering. Many of our experiments were combined. Now the two departments are miles apart. The development department is full of specialists, each an expert in a specific aspect of the problems concerning the technology of our problem.'

'Do you think it is more difficult to achieve good results now than in your time?'

'On the one hand I do, on the other hand I don't. In our time we had to generate all the necessary knowledge ourselves or acquire it from scientific or technical literature. Now we have specialists in all the different fields. From a coordinative point of view it is much more difficult now. It is extremely hard, for an individual, to stay abreast of all the technical and scientific developments. People like Mr Barton still understand the whole field in detail. Because they are at the hierarchical top of the department they hardly get the chance to use their understanding, to contribute substantially to the solution of specific problems.' While talking Mr Thrasher had become more animated again. It was clear that he felt compassion for the dilemma Mr Barton was in. It was a dilemma in which he had previously made a choice. A choice away from the understanding of the scientific and technical background of the products towards the more influential and socially esteemed area of management. A choice which he seemed to regret every now and then — certainly when he was confronted with the highly motivated people from the development department.

'What do you think was the main motivation for the improvement of the products?'

'To be quite honest, the incorporation of our newly gained knowledge. When you acquire knowledge on how something works you naturally try to show that your new solution is better than the previous one. This nearly always led to a two-sided fight. One against higher prices the other for higher quality,' he said.

'Did this bring you into conflict with your sales department?'

'Not really. They always tried to keep the price down. At that time the quality of the product was the main influence on sales. There were only very few features on which our quality was compared with that of our competitors. There was not much competition.'

'Has that changed?'

'Of course it has. The margins within which we can expect improvments are so much smaller. And the number of features that are seen as part of the quality of the product have increased. Furthermore there is little difference between our competitors and us. That implies that if we want to achieve improvements which are recognizable for the customer a lot more work is involved now than in my time.'

'Would that involve greater changes in production machinery?. I asked.

'Of course. As I said earlier. In such circumstances dimensional tolerances became narrower. This demanded a much higher precision of the production apparatus and the material used. These developments in turn demanded a much deeper knowledge of the mechanisms that made such precision possible.'

'That might imply that there should be an even closer link between the engineering department and the development department than there was in your time,' I replied.

'Certainly. They are mutually dependent. They need insight into each other's problems in order to find out what are the most critical points in the whole system of product and production process,' he said.

'You said that due to increased competition the pressure on the price had increased. I could also imagine that the timing of the introduction of new developments also became more important.'

'That's certainly true. As the difference in quality became less evident the emphasis now fell on smaller details of design and quality. From this point of view it is quite understandable that the commerical department tried to pressure us into an early introduction of the in-line tube,' Mr Thrasher said.

'The meeting made that plain. The solution that was accepted was one of a more formal mode of coordination and planning. We still meet regularly with Mr Southend. He keeps on referring to the plans we have made but always has to accept that the deadlines cannot be met because more urgent problems crop up,' I said.

'The sales department, more often than not, has a simplistic view of developing new products,' Mr Thrasher interrupted.

'Why is it so complicated? Why can't we stick to the plans we've made?' I asked.

'At a certain stage in the development, we are up against a bottleneck,' Mr Thrasher said. 'When such a problem has been solved, it quite often becomes evident that new problems are directly related to the solution of the previous problem, either in the product itself or in the production process. All these things take time to sort out.'

'What seems important to me,' I said, 'is that the necessary time to sort out these problems can be sought in either the length of the time span or in the number of people and the amount of equipment and money which are made available. The commercial department is increasingly dependent on the time span. The development department is mainly concerned with the capacity. This last variable proves very difficult to regulate. This makes it difficult to remain with the accepted time limits.'

'You must agree with me that the sales department is right in demanding commitments on the dates of introduction?' Mr Thrasher demanded.

'That is just what I have tried to make clear,' I answered.

As always he was caught in the middle. He agreed with all of the sensible though incompatible demands set by different parties. He was clearly in a role conflict. Due to his own experience as a product developer he was sensitive to the desire for discretion in decisions concerning the planning of the development department. On the other hand he lived in competition with the Vice President of the division, concerned with the commercial aspects of this product line. Whatever decision he took, there would always be a number of parties that would have to be disappointed. For Mr Thrasher, the most likely decision was no decision. The alternative which he sought, though, was an organizational form that would take these decisions out of his hands and bring them into an institutionalized negotiation context. Such a negotiation structure did not fit into his own organizational environment.

Mr Thrasher rubbed his finger and looked out of the window. The lights in the development building had nearly all been turned off. Only the lights in the corridor could be seen through the opaque glass of the partitions between the rooms and the corridor. I got up and went to the blackboard.

'Because I am weak at presenting the problem clearly, I will try to illustrate it as best I can schematically. The original problem was the coordination between the development department and the engineering department. I have tried to make clear that the task structure of both departments influence their ability to communicate. In other words that communication problems are partly a result of the manner in which work is split up over different individuals within departments. We have agreed that the engineering department is thoroughly differentiated and formalized. All the tasks are highly specified. It can be represented as follows.' I drew the picture on the blackboard (see Figure 6.5).

'That's clear. Result of high differentiation is low flexibility,' Mr Thrasher remarked in a rather bored tone.

'If we look at the development department,' I went on, 'the picture is quite different. We see there is less differentiation and that the specificity of tasks is

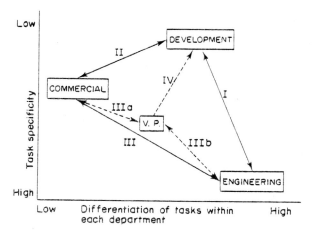

Figure 6.5   Interdepartmental dissonances

much lower. If we insert them in the same diagram, we get the following image.' (See Figure 6.5).

'According to your theory the distance between the two task structures signifies the interdepartmental dissonance which results in communication interference,' Mr Thrasher interrupted.

'Quite right!' I answered. 'Where would you put the commercial department?'

'In the right-hand top corner,' he said.

'Why?'

'Nearly everybody in that department does the same kind of work. The differentiation is mainly along geographical lines. The type of work, the problems they have to solve are about the same. You see, I am getting to understand your vocabulary.'

'That brings the diagram up to the next point.'

'Let's number the other conflicts for the sake of efficiency,' Mr Thrasher added.

'Instead of viewing the work you do, we are going to create a department. We split up your job in different tasks. Where would you place yourself?'

'In between the commercial department and the engineering department,' Mr Thrasher said without hesitating.

'Why?'

'That should be quite clear. I am in conflict with all three departments,' he laughed.

'You have inverted the logic we used. Does it represent the work you do?'

'That is difficult to assess.' He was silent for a while as he stared at the blackboard, leaning over backwards in his chair.

'I might place myself closer to the development department, if I didn't realize that it would be due to the fact that I hold a strong preference for that work.'

'The result of such a position could be an ulcer,' I said.

'I doubt it. In the first place because it doesn't really worry me. In the second place, I come to realize, looking at your diagram, that the three departments are about equidistant. This might imply that it is not very interesting for them to deflect their differences in opinion to me. That may explain why they only come to me when there are grave problems concerning the allocation of resources in all three departments.'

'What do you mean by resources?' I asked naïvely.

'You know damned well that I mean the time of specific members of the departments,' he said testily, narrowing his eyes.

'Of course I do. I only wanted to be sure that we agree on the diagnosis,' I said.

He nodded thoughtfully. 'Agreeing on the diagnosis doesn't help much if we have no cures.'

'If there were easy cures, they would have been used long ago. Let's not look for them but see if we can develop the diagnosis further.'

'All right,' he said and leaned back in his chair. All of a sudden he seemed bored again.

'The perspective up to this point has been interdepartmental. Now we have to return to the departments themselves. We agreed that the engineering department has a highly differentiated task structure. But what about the control structure? At the production end of their process we see that there is a higly differentiated and formal control structure. In the design group we see that the control structure is also formal and differentiated, but that the chief designers somehow fall outside this control structure. They fall within a separate structure together with Mr Ripple. One can't call him a bureaucrat.'

'Oh he can be at times, when it concerns orders that are being executed in the workshop or the machine factory. All of a sudden he can be sickly on details,' Mr Thrasher interjected.

'You mean his behaviour is not consistent?'

'You could put it like that,' Mr Thrasher answered.

'I would like to interpret that in the following manner. In the engineering department we find a mix of two control structures. On the one side the chief designers and the project workshop. In the last group informal control is mainly based on the recognition of professional competence. One could call it a craft attitude. The production group has a highly formal and differentiated structure. This results in an intradepartmental dissonance, or rather two types of dissonance. One between the two types of control structures and one between the control structure of the design group and the task structure of the whole department. The first could be called an intergroup control structural dissonance. It means that considerable energy has to be spent smoothing out internal differences. You yourself have just illustrated this point with your pointing out of Mr Ripple's two types of behaviour when he is either concerned with problems in the design group or within the production side of the department.' (See Figures 6.6 and 6.7).

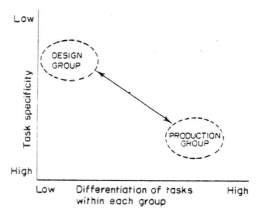

Figure 6.6   Intradepartmental inter-groups dissonances

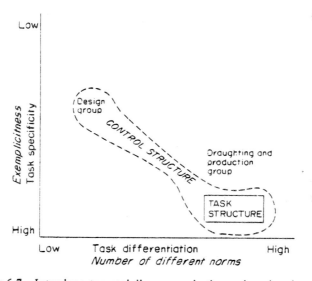

Figure 6.7   Intradepartmental dissonance in the engineering department

'Your illustration implies that the production side of the engineering department is consistent because there is a fit between task and control structure?' Mr Thrasher asked.

'Quite right. There are relatively few problems there as long as the demands from the environment come to them in an orderly manner.'

'I must agree it fits with the picture you sketched at the beginning. How does it fit into the previous picture of the conflicts I am in?' Mr Thrasher demanded.

'Please, not so fast. Let's first go on to sketch the situation in the development department. How would you rate the way in which the department is controlled?' I asked.

194

'The strange thing is that in all these years it hasn't really changed much. The department has grown at a tremendous rate, though. That it could remain the same is mainly due to the fact that people like Mr Barton and some of his colleagues have been there for more than 25 years.' He was silent for a while. 'In your typology I would say that the department has a control structure in the upper left-hand corner. Characterized by a strong personal influence of Mr Barton and the heads of the subdepartments. Because he keeps abreast of the developments in the whole technical field his decisions are acceptable to his subdepartments,' Mr Thrasher said.

'From what you say, I understand that the type of leadership in the engineering and the development department is similar,' I said.

'Of course. It is based mainly on their pioneer experience.'

'If we combine the control and task structures of the development departments a discretion dissonance emerges (see Figure 6.8). In an optimal

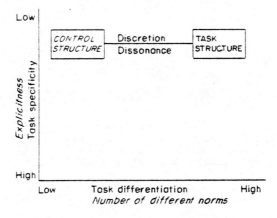

Figure 6.8   Intradepartmental dissonance in the development department

situation the control structure would infringe minimally on the freedom of the specialists as far as he himself can determine the manner in which he is going to solve his problems and what facilities he needs. The necessary coordination between specialist tasks would not be achieved in a centralized manner but rather by an intensive cooperation between specialists on related programs. What do we see in reality? There is a centralized management in the department. Mr Barton personally directs many of the activities and defines individual priorities. This leads to instability in the work load of the individual specialists. At the start of the day they often have little idea of what they are going to work on during the day.'

Mr Thrasher lifted his hands as to stop my monologue. 'There are two points I want to make. The first is that you centre the problem around Mr Barton, which I think is unjust. He is placed in an organizational environment, specifically the factory and the commercial department. This environment demands swift reactions from his department. The second point I want to make is that the original idea of a more formalized planning system was directed at relieving some of the pressure from the management of the development department.' He laid his hands on the rim of the desk and looked rather smug.

'If I gave the impression that it's all Mr Barton's fault, then I have done that unintentionally. I admire him for the coolness with which he reacts to the demands from his environment. I could try to show you that the existing control structure is the natural consequence of an historical process. It is a result of the tremendous growth you mentioned, the technical development of the product towards maturity in its life cycle, and most important of all by the organizational context in which the whole department is embedded. However, it would lead us too far astray from the original topic.'

'Yes. The planning aspect is more to the point,' Mr Thrasher said.

'All right. Let's go back to the nature of the problems that have to be solved in the process of developing our product. These problems are very complex. The knowledge of the phenomena that influence its functioning is stretched to its utmost. Many of the possible solutions we define are achieved by following hunches, and turn out to be dead-end attempts. If we can agree to this view, and also on the opinion that cooperation between a large number of specialists is necessary, then we have a common starting point for our next step.'

'I have no difficulty with that. I know from experience that finding a solution to a problem that has bothered you for a long time often depends on noticing circumstantial information that has hitherto escaped your attention,' Mr Thrasher said.

'Well. If that is true, it should make it nearly impossible to plan the outcome of the different parts of the development program,' I said.

Mr Thrasher laughed derisively. 'You have seen that for yourself. You have tried but haven't succeeded.'

My first meeting with Mr Thrasher sprung to mind. How my former superior had forecast that the problem as presented could not be solved. I remember how I had not heeded his warning and had gone ahead anyway. The demand for a simple solution to a tremendously complex problem had in the beginning thwarted every attempt at even understanding what the problem was. It had taken me a long time to realize that even if I had succeeded in finding a technically feasible solution, it would have been unacceptable because it would influence the relations between the different departments and therefore jeopardize the position of Mr Thrasher. He was married to his own problem.

'What alternatives can we devise in order to insure that the product developers can be as effective as possible?' I asked.

'It's best to leave them alone. See to it that they get the material and equipment they need.'

'If that is so, they must also be left alone by the commercial department and the factory. You must protect them against demands from their environment.

You must allocate time and resources, the assistance of other departments and personnel. Planning such departments means planning their resources and not their results,' I said.

'The one implies the other,' Mr Thrasher answered.

'I'm not going to argue on that. What is certain is that when you plan results but do not plan and actually allocate resources there is no chance of success. It is the latter which has been the case in our planning attempts. The resources were never available as we had planned them.'

Mr Thrasher was silent for a while. He disliked my abrasiveness. He looked at me attentively. He was tired and longed to go home. On the other hand he probably thought that now was the time to round off the conversations we had been having. Then a new phase could be started—either with or without me.

'I remember a note you sent me,' said Mr Thrasher. 'In your opinion we had to make commitments for the future. If that could not be done, if the commitments were not going to be kept, you wrote that it was not worthwhile to try and make a realistic plan. You wrote that you doubted those commitments could be kept in our organization. At the time I found it a harsh judgement. All the more because you gave it without much explanation. The evidence however seems to be on your side.'

There seemed little for me to reply to this. After a while Mr Thrasher went on. 'Can you also explain what you wrote, using your theory?'

'That is part of what I am aiming at. In the diagram (Figure 6.5) we see that the commercial, development, and engineering departments have very different task structures. The consequences are communication problems based on a lack of understanding of 'who does what' in the other departments. On top of that we see that there are differences between task and control structures within the departments, leading to their own inherent dissonances. This leads to the following conclusions.

(1) There is a lack of internal fit within departments.
(2) There is a lack of fit between departments; between
    (a) the task structures;
    (b) the control structures.

Until now the levels of analysis have been relatively clear. The next step is more difficult from an analytical point of view. It concerns subsets of the previous sets.'

'Not so fast please. When looking at the, let's see, intradepartmental relations, those within each department, a solution could be found by matching the control and task structure.'

'But . . .'

'Don't interrupt me!' Mr Thrasher exclaimed.

'—or vice versa,' he went on.

'I don't mean that.'

'Don't interrupt me all the time.'

I was silent. He looked at me angrily as he went on, 'That would not solve the problem, as you have pointed out. The change in one of the structures might aggravate the interdepartmental dissonances between the same structural aspects.' He kept on looking at the blackboard, the tips of his fingers pressed together, wide spread.

'I have never looked at it that way,' he said and looked at me. I didn't dare to say anything after his sharp admonitions. I was glad though, that he understood it so clearly.

'So from your academic point of view it means that if you try to change something on one level you must not only analyse what happens on that level, but also on the levels above and below the one you're looking at.' Again he looked intently at the blackboard and flexed his fingers while keeping the tips touching. It reminded me of the game children play with a toy made from a folded square of paper which opens up in two directions. I wanted to go on with the analysis but didn't dare until he stopped brooding over the diagrams.

'The distinction between the different levels is clarifying. I also sense there must be much more to it than we have seen. However it's hard to vizualise. For instance the relation between the commercial department and the market in which they operate. If we see what happened at the meeting, I think that relation is one of the most influential.' He now turned towards me, and showed that I could go on.

'I think that can be vizualized too. However, I wonder if this is the right moment to do it because we may lose track of the analysis as presented upto this point,' I said.

'All right. Get on with it.'

'We've had the intra- and interdepartmental dissonances. Now we should look at a subset of the previous analytical sets. Such a subset may consist of the heads of the different departments, and yourself. At a certain point in time, you operate as a functional group within the organization. You have to solve certain problems, take decisions and you are a link between your departments and the rest of the management of the company.'

'In the line of the linking-pin idea,' he said.

'You could put it that way.' We were silent for a while.

'And what would you want to signify with the depiction of such a group?' Mr Thrasher asked.

'Maybe you could tell me,' I said.

'All right. Let me see. First we could see what the intra-group structures are like. After that we can see what the dissonances are between our group and the departments or other groups we are related too. The latter would form quite a complicated picture, I imagine,' Mr Thrasher said.

'That's for certain. All the more because these relations are situated on different hierarchical levels,' I said.

'You mean for instance between us and the Board of management and between us and individual departments in our own organization.'

'Yes in the last case the member of your group, who is also the head of that department, is the medium for transmitting the dissonance between your group and his department,' I said.

'You imply that he is put under stress by having to fulfil this double role,' Mr Thrasher said.

'Quite right.'

'What can you say about the ability of an individual to bear the consequences, the stress, of such conflicting demands?' he asked.

'That lies outside the scope of the theory.'

'Why?'

'The theory is concerned only with those characteristics of an individual that concern his direct relations with his environment in the two areas described; his problem-solving capacity and his social behaviour. The resistance to stress is an internal characteristic. Everything which goes on inside the individual falls outside my perspective. I am a stranger in that field.'

'Do you think a same type of analysis could be used there?' he asked.

'I don't know. The difficulty will be the description of the new elementary level. Something I would not dare speculate on.'

'All right. Let's go back to the principle behind the manner of analysis. I think I am beginning to understand it more clearly.' Mr Thrasher got up from his chair and walked to the blackboard.

'One of your original figures concerned what you called, partial inclusion. If we combine that with what you said just now, we see that each member is not only a member of the total organization. What is more important, that partial membership is itself split up into membership of different subgroups; often with quite different characteristics. For instance Mr Ripple is a member of his own department, of the design group within the department, of the management team, etc.'

Mr Thrasher stood in front of the blackboard, chalk held delicately between finger and thumb, hesitating. He looked at me, replaced the chalk on the ledge under the blackboard and returned to his chair.

'I forget how you represented it,' he added.

'In this case it would be very difficult. But I can try.' While drawing on the board I resumed (see Figure 6.9). 'First we have the engineering department. The design group is a subgroup of this department. If we represent Mr Ripple as a cylinder and the departments as discs we get the following picture. The management team is another disc, in which he is also partially included.'

'Not a very clear picture I must say, but I see what you mean. It makes it more complicated, but also makes what happened at the meeting clearer,' Mr Thrasher said.

'Shall we discuss that the next time?' I asked, 'It's getting late.'

'Don't you have time? I'd rather round off our discussions now that I feel I have some grasp on the material.' He didn't wait for an answer but went on immediately. 'To begin with, the main point of interest isn't the context of the decisions but rather their consequences on the manner of working in each department—the task structures. Because these tasks structures vary widely

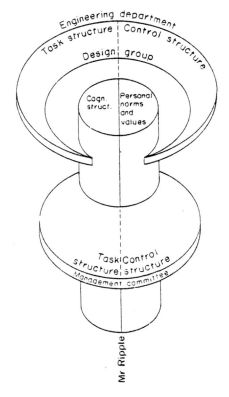

Figure 6.9   The individual as a member of different groups
and therefore as a transmitter of inter-group dissonance

over the different departments, their reaction will be different too. Then, we have the different levels on which all the members of the group at the meeting have to operate. This may set incompatible demands on them. And finally the internal problems of each department, possibly due to your dissonances, influence the amount of freedom the members of the meeting have in accepting compromises.' Mr Thrasher looked quite pleased with himself, and I remained silent.

'What can we do about it?' he asked, smiling.

'To use your own words, find out what freedom you have to implement alterations in the whole network. The alternatives themselves must be found out by first analysing where the strongest or largest dissonances occur. If these become clear, then one can see what can be done about them, by weighing the consequences agains each other. A likely candidate for change seems the engineering group. The main problem you will have to tackle is to show that the loss of efficiency, as defined by the utilization of different capacity groups, is offset by the gain in flexibility of reaction to changes in the environment.'

Mr Thrasher looked at me with a desolate smile as he said: 'Your diagnosis is realistic. The cure is impossible.'

Bibliography

Ashby, W. R., *An Introduction to Cybernetics*, London, Methuen, 1964 edition.

Atkin, R., *Multidimensional Man*, Harmondsworth, Penguin, 1981.

Beer, S., 'Under the twilight arch', *General Systems*, 5, 9–21 (1960).

Bell, G. D., 'Determinants of span of control', *American Journal of Sociology*, 73, 100–9 (1967).

Benguigni, G. and D. Monjaudet, *Etre cadre en France*, Paris, Dunod, 1970.

Blau, P. M., 'Parameters of social structure', *American Sociological Review*, 39, 615–35 (1974).

Blau, P. M. and R. A. Schoenherr, *The Structure of Organizations*, New York, Basic Books, 1971.

Blaug, M., *Economic Theory in Retrospect*, London, Heinemann, 1968.

Blaug, M., *The Methodology of Economics*, Cambridge University Press, 1980.

Blumenthal, S. C., *Management Information Systems*, New Jersey, Prentice-Hall, 1969.

Boulding, K. E., 'Economics as a moral science', *The American Economic Review*, 59(1), 1–12 (1969).

Bruner, J. S., J. J. Goodnow and G. A. Austin, *A Study of Thinking*, New York, John Wiley, 1956.

Burns, T., 'Comparative study of organizations', in V. H. Vroom (ed.), *Methods of Organizational Research*, Pittsburg, The University of Pittsburg Press, 1967.

Burns, T. and G. M. Stalker, *The Management of Innovation*, London, 1961.

Burrell, G. and G. Morgan, *Sociological Paradigms and Organizational Analysis*, London, Heinemann, 1979.

Carnap, R., 'Logical foundation of the unity of science', in *International Encyclopedia of Unified Sciences*, Volume 1, No. 1, Chicago, 1938.

Comstock, D. E. and W. R. Scott, 'Technology and the structure of subunits: distinguishing individual and workgroup effects', *Administrative Science Quarterly*, 22, 177–202 (1977).

Dahrendorf, R., *Class and Class Conflict in Industrial Society*, Stanford, Stanford University Press, 1959.

Dill, W. R., 'Environment as an influence on management autonomy', *Administrative Science Quarterly*, Volume 2, pp.409–43.

Emery, F. E. and E. L. Trist, *Towards a Social Ecology*, London, Plenum, 1975.

Etzioni, A., *Complex Organizations*, New York, Free Press, 1961.

Festinger, L., *A Theory of Cognitive Dissonance*, Evanston, Ill., Row, Peterson (1957).

Flavell, J. H. *The Developmental Psychology of Jean Piaget*, New York, Van Nostrand, 1963.

Freund, J., *The Sociology of Max Weber*, translation from 'Sociologie de Max Weber' by Mary Ilford, Penguin University Books, 1972.

Galbraith, J. K., *The New Industrial State*, Boston, Houghton Mifflin, 1967.

Galbraith, J., *Designing Complex Organizations*, California, Addison-Wesley, 1973.

Georgiou, P., 'The goal paradigm and notes towards a counter paradigm', *Administrative Science Quarterly*, 18(3), 291–310 (1973).

Goffman, E., *The Presentation of the Self in Everyday Life*, New York, Doubleday, 1959.

Goslin, P. A., *Handbook of Socialization Theory and Research*, Chicago, McNally, 1969.

Gouldner, A. W., 'Cosmopolitans and locals: towards analysis of latent social roles,' *Administrative Science Quarterly*, 1, 281–306 (1957); 2, 444–80 (1958).

Grimes, A. J. and S. M. Klein, 'The technological imperative: the relative impact of task unit, modal technology and hierarchy on structure, *Academy of Management Journal*, No. 16, 583–97 (1973).

Gross, N., N. S. Mason and A. W. McEachern, *Explorations in Role Analysis*, New York, John Wiley, 1958.

Hage, J., 'An axiomatic theory of organizations., *Administrative Science Quarterly*, 10(3), 294–326 (1965).

Hall, R. H., 'Intraorganizational structural variation; application of the bureaucratic model', *Administrative Science Quarterly*, 7, 295–308 (1962).

Hall, R. H., *Organizations, Structure and Process*, Englewood Cliffs N. J., Prentice-Hall, 1972.

Harvey, E., 'Technology and the structure of organizations', *American Sociological Review*, 33, 247–59 (1968).

Heady, F., 'Bureaucratic theory and comparative administration', *Administrative Science Quarterly*, 3, 509–25 (1959).

Hickson, D. J., C. R. Hinings, C. A. Lee, R. E. Schneck and J. M. Pennings, 'A strategic contingencies, theory of intraorganizational power', *Administrative Science Quarterly*, Volume 16 (1971), nr. 2, p.216–229.

Hickson, D. H., D. S. Pugh and D. C. Pheysey, 'Operations technology and organization structure: An Empirical Reappraisal', *Administrative Science Quarterly*, 14(3), 378–97, 1969.

Hoffer, E., *The Ordeal of Change*, New York, Harper and Row, 1952.

Hrebiniak, L. G., 'Job technology, supervision and work group structure', *Administrative Science Quarterly*, 19, 395–410 (1974).

Kahn, R. L., D. M. Wolfe, R. P. Quinn, J. D. Snoek and R. A. Rosenthal, *Organizational Stress: Studies in Role Conflict and Ambiguity*, New York, John Wiley, 1964.

Keen, P., *The Implication of Cognitive Style for Individual Decision-Making*, Doctoral Thesis, Harvard University, 1973.

Khandwalla, P. N., *The Design of Organizations*, New York, Harcourt Brace Jovanovich, 1977.

Kimberly, J. R., 'Organizational size and the structuralist perspective: a review, critique and proposal', *Administrative Science Quarterly*, 21, 571–97 (1976).

Knight, F. H., *The Economic Organization*, New York, Aug. M. Kelly Inc., 1933.

Koestler, A., *Darkness at Noon*, London, Penguin, 1956.

Kohlberg, L., 'The cognitive-development approach to socialization', in D. A. Goslin (ed.), *Handbook of Socialization Theory and Research*, Chicago, McNally, 1969.

Koontz, H. and C. O'Donnell, *Principals of Management*, New York, McGraw-Hill, 1968.

Köster, W. and F. Hetzel, *Datenverarbeitung mit System*, Berlin, Luchterhand, 1971.

Lasch, C., *The Culture of Narcissism*, New York, Warner Books, 1979.

Lawrence, P. R., and J. W. Lorsch, 'Differentiation and integration in Complex organizations, *Administrative Science Quarterly* 12, (1967) 1–47.

Lawrence, P. R., and J. W. Lorsch, *Organization and Environment: Managing Differentiation and Integration*, Boston, Graduate School of Business Administration Harvard University, 1967.

Lawrence, P. R., and J. W. Lorsch, Developing organizations: Diagnosis and Action, Reading, Mass: Addison-Wesley 1969.

Lewin, K., *Field Theory in Social Science*, London, Tavistock Publications, 1963.

Linton, R., *Study of Man*, New York, Appleton Century-Crofts, 1936.

Linton, R., *The Cultural Background of Personality*, New York, Appleton-Century-Crofts, 1947.

Lotka, A. J., *Elements of Mathematical Biology*, New York, Dover, 1956.

Machlup, F. *Essays in Economic Semantics*, New York University Press, 1963.

Mansfield, R., 'Bureaucracy and centralization: an examination of organization structure', *Administrative Science Quarterly*, **18**, 477–88 (1973).

March, J. G. and H. A. Simon, *Organizations*, New York, John Wiley, 1958.

Marx, K., *Early Writings*, Edited and translated by T. B. Bottomore, New York, McGraw-Hill, 1964.

Mayo, E., *The Social Problems of an Industrial Civilization*, London, Routledge and Kegan Paul, 1945.

Medawar, P. B., 'Induction and intuition in scientific thought', *New York Review of Books*, **24**(1), 13 (1977).

Merton, R. K., *Social Theory and Social Structure*, (rev. edn.), Glencoe, Ill., Free Press, 1957.

Milgram, S., *Obedience to Authority*, London, Tavistock, 1974.

Mohr, L. B. 'Organizational technology and organizational structures', *Administrative Science Quarterly*, **16**, 444–59 (1971).

Nadel, S. F., *The Theory of Social Structure*, Glencoe Ill., Free Press, 1957.

Nagel, E., *The Structure of Science*, New York, Harcourt Brace and World, 1961.

Naipaul, V. S., 'India: renaissance or continuity', *New York Review of Books*, **23**(21/22), 3–11 (1976).

Neiman, L. J. and J. W. Hughes, 'The problem of the concept of role — a survey of the literature', *Social Forces*, **30**, 141–149 (1951).

Nicolis, G. and I. Prigogine, *Self Organization in Non-Equilibrium Systems*, New York, John Wiley, 1977.

Nyström, H., 'Uncertainty, Information and Organizational Decision-Making: A Cognitive Approach', *Swedish Journal of Economics*, 131–9 (1974).

Parsons, T., *The Social System*, Glencoe Ill., Free Press, 1951.

Perrow, C., 'A framework for the comparative analysis of organizations', *American Sociological Review*, **32**(2), 194–208 (1967).

Pugh, D. S., D. J. Hickson, C. R. Hinings, K. M. Macdonald, C. Turner and T. Lupton, 'A conceptual scheme for organizational analysis', *Adminstrative Science Quarterly*, **8**, 289–315 (1963).

Pugh, D. S., D. J. Hickson, C. R. Hinings and C. Turner, 'Dimensions of organization structure', *Administrative Science Quarterly*, **13**, 65–106 (1968).

Rapport, A. and W. J. Hovarth, 'Thoughts on organization theory', in Walter Buckley (ed.), *Modern Systems Research on the Behavioural Scientist*, Chicago, Aldine, 1968.

Roethlisberger, F. J. and W. J. Dickson, *Management and the Worker*, Cambridge, Harvard University Press, 1939.

Samuelson, P. A., *Foundation of Economic Analysis*, Cambridge, Mass., Harvard University Press, 1947.

Shull, F. A., A. L. Delbecq and L. L. Cummings, *Organizational Decision Making*, New York, McGraw-Hill, 1970.

Simon, H. A., *Models of Man, Social and Rational*, New York, John Wiley, 1957.

Stanfield, G. G., 'Technology and organization structure as theoretical categories', *Administrative Science Quarterly*, **21**(3), 489–93 (1976).

Stinchcombe, A. L., 'Bureaucratic and craft administration of production', *Administrative Science Quarterly*, **4**, 168–87 (1959).

Strasser, S., *Fenomenologie en Empirische Menskunde*, Deventer, Van Loghum Slaterus, 1970.

Thompson, J. D., *Organizations in Action*, New York, McGraw-Hill, 1967.

Thompson, J. D. and F. E. Bates, 'Technology, organization and administration', *Administrative Science Quarterly*, **2**, 323–43 (1957).

Toulmin, S., *The Philosophy of Science*, London, 1953.

Udy, S. H., 'Bureaucracy and rationality in Weber's theory', *American Sociological Review*, **24**, 791–5 (1959).

Van Aken, J. E., *On the Control of Complex Organizations*, Leiden, Martinus Nijhoff, 1978.

Van de Ven, A. H., A. L. Delbecq and R. Koenig Jr., 'Determinants of coordination modes within organizations'. *American Sociological Review*, **41**, 322–38 (1976).

Vickers, G., 'Rationality and intuition', in J. Wecksler (ed.), *On Aesthetics in Science*, Cambridge, MIT Press, 1978.

Weber, M., *The Theory of Social and Economic Organization*, Oxford, Oxford University Press, 1947.

Webster's Third New International Dictionary, Springfield, G. and C. Merriam, 1966, p.1590.

Wecksler (ed.), J., *On Aesthetics in Science*, Cambridge, MIT Press, 1978.

Weick, K., *The Social Psychology of Organizing*, Reading, Mass., Addison-Wesley, 1969.

Willis, D. G., 'The Functional Domain of Complex Systems', in H. von Foerster and G. W. Zopf (eds), *International Tracts in Computer Science and Technology and Their Application*, Volume 9, Pergamon Press, 1962.

Woodward, J., *Management and Technology*, London, H.M.S.O., 1958.

Zangwill, O. L., 'The consequences of brain damage', in L. Hudson (ed.), *The Ecology of Human Intelligence*, London, Penguin, 1970.

Zijderveld, A. C., *De theorie van het symbolisch interactionisme*, Meppel, 1973.

Author Index

Ashby, W. R., 20, 68, 71, 98
Aston group, 31, 37–40, 58
Atkin, R., 78

Bates, F. E., and Thompson, J. D., 38
Bell, G. D., 57
Benguigni, G., and Monjaudet, D., 121
Blau, P. M., 31, 103–4, 106
Blaug, M., 34, 187
Blumenthal, S. C., 153
Boulding, K. E., 18
Bruner, J. S., 92
Burns, T., 16
Burns, T., and Stalker, G. M., 31, 40, 54
Burrell, G., and Morgan, G., 138

Carnap, R., 19
Comstock, D. E., and Scott, W. R., 33

Dahrendorf, R., xv, 138
Dill, W. R., 44

Eddington, A. S., 32
Einstein, A., 31, 95
Emery, F. E., and Trist, E. L., 68
Etzioni, A., 101, 103

Festinger, L., xvii
Flavell, J. H., 93
Freund, J., 95

Galbraith, J., 103
Galbraith, J. K., 77
Georgiou, P., 75, 78
Gofman, E., 64
Gombrich, E., 32
Gouldner, A. W., 117
Grimes, A. J., and Klein, S. M., 57
Gross, N. et al., 112

Hage, J., 23
Hall, R. H., 25, 57
Harvey, E., 31, 54

Heady, F., 39
Hickson, D. H. et al., xvii, 37, 49, 155–160
Hoffer, E., 95
Hrebiniak, L. G., 57

Kahn, R. L. et al., xvi, 97, 104, 118, 129
Keen, P., 91
Kepler, J., 29
Khandwalla, P. N., 52
Kimberly, J. R., 31, 33, 54
Knight, F. H., 102
Koestler, A., 120
Kohlberg, L., 166
Koontz, H., and O'Donnell, C., 16
Köster, W., and Hetzel, F., 155

Lasch, C., 142
Lawrence, P. R., and Lorsch, J. W., 31, 50–52, 59, 166
Lewin, K., 68
Linton, R., 104, 112
Lotka, A. J., 77, 140

Machlup, F., 20
Mansfield, R., 40
March, J. G., and Simon, H. A., 31, 46, 68
Marx, K., 127
Mayo, E., 78
Medawar, P. B., 32
Merton, R. K., 120
Milgram, S., 166
Mohr, L. B., 57

Nadel, S. F., 23
Nagel, E., 19, 32
Naipaul, V. S., 65–66
Neiman, L. J., and Hughes, J. W., 112
Newton, I., 26, 74
Nicolis, G., and Prigogine, I., 20, 77
Nyström, H., 90

Parsons, T., xv, 22, 114
Perrow, C., 45–50, 58, 84, 104, 124
Piaget, J., 93

Prigogine, I., and Nicolis, G., 20, 77
Pugh, D., 38, 40, 58

Rapoport, A., and Hovarth, W. J., 17
Roethlisberger, F. J., and Dickson, W. J.,
 78

Samuelson, P. A., xvi
Shull, F. A. *et al.*, 54, 59, 101
Simon H. A., 31, 41, 43, 46, 49, 68
Stanfield, G. G., 55
Stinchcombe, A. L., 42
Strasser, S., 18

Thompson, J. D., 31, 38, 40–45, 58, 135,
 158

Thompson, V. A., 54
Toulmin, S., 21

Udy, S. H., 39

Van Aken, 166
Van de Ven, 57, 104
Vickers, G., 94

Weber, M., 39, 126
Weick, K., 77
Willis, D. G., 96
Woodward, J., 24, 31, 34–37, 58

Zangwill, O. L., 92
Zijderveld, A. C., 57, 64

Subject Index

alienation, 126, 164
ambiguity, xvi
analysis, 62
analytical orientation, 57, 79
analytical problem solvers, 91
analysability, 84
anascopic analysis, 57, 64
anomie, 120
anthropology of organizations, 112
aspects of organizations, 62–67
authority, 67, 114
authority ambiguity, 118
authority recognition dissonance, 120
authoritarian relationships, 67
automaticity, 38
automation, 146
autonomy dissonance, 125
axiomatic theory, 23

bottom-up analysis, 57, 153
bounded rationality, 4
bureaucracy, 30, 39, 126
bureaucrat, 116
bureaucratization, 78

categorization of production systems, 35
centrality, 156
centralization, 39
coalitions, 58
coercion theory of society, xv
cognitive model, 90
cognitive structure, 79, 88
collaboration, 59
common sense realism, 21, 137
communication, 52
communication ambiguity dissonance, 131
communication coordination dissonance, 131
competition, 141
complexity, 19, 68
compliance, 101, 113
configuration, 39
conflict, xvi, 59

conflict model of society, xv, 137
content of a system, 75
contingency, 156
control, 48
control, technology of, 153
control structure, 79, 117
conventions, 60, 116
convergent thinkers, 92
cooptation, 121
coordination, 43, 49, 52, 76, 106, 123
cosmopolitan, 117
criticism, 33
culture structure, 120
cybernetic models, 84

decision making, 96, 112
determinism, 138
development, technological, 145
differentiation, 50, 53, 76, 113
dimensions, 26
dimensional analysis, 75
dimensions of complexity, 69
discretion, 48
discretion dissonance, 124
dissonance, 73
divergent thinkers, 92
division of labour, 43, 71, 80, 101
domain, 26, 76, 87

element, 62
emergence, doctrine of, 19
empirical indicators, 24
empiricism, 31
environmental variables, 44
evolution, 140–148
extensive dimensions, 72
external effects, 144

feedback, 49
flexibility, 39
flexibility dissonance, 125
formal language, 21
formalization of roles, 39, 157, 159

formalization of theories, 23
functional aspect of an organization, 79
functional coordination, 123

generative mechanism, 21
goal paradigm, 75

harmony model of society, xv, 57
Heisenberg effect, 18
hierarchy, 102
homogeneity of tests, 105
horizontal specialization, 101, 107
human relations school, 30

iconic models, 22
implementation, 153
incentive theory, 78
inclusiveness, 19, 62
industrialization, 142
information transmission costs, 152
inputs, 81
instrumental action, 41, 158
insubordination, 67
integration, 51, 53, 106, 132
integration theory of society, xv
intensive dimensions, 72
intensive technology, 41
interdepartmental conflicts, 57
interdepartmental dissonances, 131
interdependence of work flows, 38
interlevel dissonance, 115
interrelatedness of problems, 70
inter-sender conflicts, 97
intra-organizational conflicts, 57
intra-sender conflicts, 97, 119
intuitive problem solvers, 90
irrationality, 77

katoscopic analysis, 57
knowledge technology, 34

leadership, 122
linearization, 96
local, 116
long linked technology, 42

management theory, 16
market system, 140
materials technology, 38
measurement theory, 23–25
mechanics, Newtonian, 74
mechanistic structure, 39, 54
mechanization, 146
mediating technology, 41

nature of man, 32
natural order, 21
nepotism, 121
normative ambiguity dissonance, 125
normative complexity, 115
normative theories, 167
norms and values, 79

obedience to authority, 166
office, 104
order, 61
organic structure, 40, 54
organization, 60
organization development, 29
organization, theory of, 17
organization theory, 17
organized complexity, 17
operations technology, 37
outputs, 84
overload dissonances, 99

person-role conflict, 92
personnel selection, 121
pervasiveness, 159
planning, 107
plausibility of explanations, 24
pooled interdependence, 43
positive theories, 167
power, 48, 155–63
pragmatic aspects of theories, 21
presuppositions, theoretical, 24
price theory, 139
process theories, xv
production control, 86
program overload dissonance, 109

quantitative dissonances, 73, 99

rational organization models, 78
rationalism, 31
raw materials, 47, 80
received view, 70
reciprocal interdependence, 43
reduction of complexity, 96
reduction of uncertainty, 90
relation dissonance, 73
relative complexity, 74
responsibility ambiguity, 120
responsibility recognition dissonance, 120
role, 104, 112
routinization, 103, 105, 146

schizophrenia, 118

scientific management, 30
segregation, 107
self-organization, 20
semantic aspects of theories, 22
sequential interdependence, 43
skill, 86
social groups, 63
sociostructure, 111
sociotechnical systems, 30
specialization, 39, 76, 105
specificity, 103
specificity of evaluation, 38
standardization, 39
statistical thermodynamics, 71
strata, 62
structural dissonances, 99
structural rigidity, 142
structure, 43, 45, 54
structure of a system, 75
structure, theory, xv
substitutability, 156
system, 62
systematic thinkers, 91

task ambiguity dissonance, 110
task structure, 79, 88, 101

Tavistock Institute, 30
technical complexity, 36
technical rationality, 41
technoeconomic uncertainty, 53
technological change, 143
technological imperative, 40, 99, 129
technology, 41, 45, 54, 79, 86
technology of organizing, 138
thermodynamics, 17, 71
top down analysis, 57, 150
transformation, 81
typologies, 16

uncertainty, 157
uncertainty gap, 90
underutilization·dissonance, 98

variability of problems, 70
variational dissonance, 73
vertical specialization, 101, 107
voluntarism, 138

workflow immediacy, 156
workflow integration, 38
workflow rigidity, 38